LEARNING BY DESIGN

*Mary Kalantzis
and
Bill Cope*

LEARNING BY DESIGN

Mary Kalantzis
and
Bill Cope

COMMON GROUND PUBLISHING 2016

First published in 2005 in Melbourne, Australia
by Common Ground Publishing LLC

Second edition published in 2016 in Champaign, IL
by Common Ground Publishing LLC
as part of The Learner books

Copyright © Mary Kalantzis and Bill Cope 2016

All rights reserved. Apart from fair dealing for the purposes of study, research, criticism or review as permitted under the applicable copyright legislation, no part of this book may be reproduced by any process without written permission from the publisher.

Library of Congress Cataloging-in-Publication Data

Kalantzis, Mary.
 Learning by design / Mary Kalantzis and Bill Cope.
 pages cm
 "First published in 2005 in Melbourne, Australia by Common Ground Publishing LLC as part of The Learner book series."
 Includes bibliographical references.
 ISBN 978-1-61229-468-1 (pbk : alk. paper) -- ISBN 978-1-61229-469-8 (pdf)
 1. Education--Experimental methods. 2. Educational innovations. I. Cope, Bill. II. Title.

LB1027.3K35 2014
371.39--dc23

2014005668

Table of Contents

Introduction — ix

Part I: Learning in Theory

Chapter 1
New Learning — 1

Chapter 2
The Knowledge Society — 11

Chapter 3
The Conditions of Learning — 30

Chapter 4
Curriculum — 43

Chapter 5
Pedagogy — 57

Chapter 6
Measuring Learning — 76

Chapter 7
The Learning by Design Framework — 85

Chapter 8
Creating Common Educational Knowledge — 122

Part II: Learning in Practice

Chapter 9
Learning by Design: A Marriage of Theory and Practice   141
    Peter Burrows

Chapter 10
The Emergence of Pedagogical Mentors: The Project-consultants   158
    Peter Burrows

Chapter 11
The Role of the Teacher as Theory-enactor and Author-publisher   177
    Peter Burrows

Chapter 12
Professional Learning and Enacting Theory: Or Trying to be a
Lifelong/Lifewide Teacher-Learner while Hanging on to Your Sanity   195
    Anne Cloonan

Chapter 13
Innovation in Queensland Education: Multiliteracies in Action   209
    Mary Neville

Chapter 14
Effective Teaching and Learning: Pedagogy and Multiliteracies   236
    Rita van Haren

Chapter 15
Approaching Learning by Design as an Agenda for Malaysian
Schools   260
    Ambigapathy Pandian and Shanthi Balraj

References   287

Introduction

THE LEARNING BY DESIGN APPROACH

This book tells the story of an experiment in classroom and curriculum transformation, and the professional learning of the teachers who participated in the experiment. That experiment involved the practical application of the learning theory outlined in this book to everyday classroom practice. We have called this approach, *Learning by Design*. The need for a new approach to learning arises from a complex range of factors—among them, the changes in society and the economy; the potential for new forms of communication made possible by emerging technologies; and rising expectations amongst learners that education will maximise their potential for personal fulfilment, civic participation and access to work.

The *Learning by Design* team of researchers and teachers came together in order to create and reflect upon new and dynamic emerging learning environments. Commencing in 2003, they embarked on a series of research and development activities in Australia and Malaysia exploring the potentials of new pedagogical approaches, assisted by digital technologies, to transform today's learning environments and create learning for the future—learning environments which could be more relevant to a changing world, more effective in meeting community expectations and which manage educational resources more efficiently. One of the key challenges was to create learning environments which engaged the sensibilities of learners who are increasingly immersed in digital and global lifestyles—from the entertainment sources they choose to the way they work and learn.

The second part of this book tells the story of what happened for the hundred or so teachers who participated by taking up the Learning by Design approach in its pilot phase—in Victoria, Australian Capital Territory and Queensland, Australia, and in Penang, Malaysia. The Learning by Design approach involves teachers in professional learning experiences which introduced them to an explicit theory of learning and provided them with tools for designing, sharing and reflecting on classroom choices and learner experiences. As a part of this process, the participating teachers developed, trialled and published 'Learning Elements' or learning designs (a cross between a lesson/program plan and a curriculum resource). The effect of this work was to push a number of frontiers in professional practice: to extend teachers' pedagogical repertoires, thereby adding to the level of engagement and the range of forms of engagement with learners; to turn teachers and learners into knowledge creators rather than knowledge absorbers; and to use digital content creation and publishing tools to add a new level of professional transparency and accessibility to teachers' work. This work is comprehensively documented on the web (www.L-by-D.com)

The first part of the book discusses the background to the *Learning by Design* approach and the theory underlying it. It is by no means the case, however, that the theory came before the practice. The theory is based in part on a myriad of intellectual influences, as well as earlier research and development activities into curriculum and learning including the Social Literacy Project (Kalantzis & Cope, 1989), the 'genre' approach to literacy (Cope & Kalantzis, 1993b), the 'Multiliteracies' project (Cope & Kalantzis, 2000b; New London Group, 1996), the 'New Learning' charter (Kalantzis & Cope, 2001a), and our research into the emerging forms and impacts of digitisation (C-2-C Project, 2001-2003; Cope & Kalantzis, 2004b; Kalantzis & Cope, 2004a). Although these were some of the ideas and influences that have been brought to the *Learning by Design* approach, it is in reality the result of several years of dialogue, of working closely with teachers to develop new practices which are ambitiously pushing the frontiers of learning, but which we can also be confident will work, which engage learners and produce powerful learning outcomes. The conversation continues, as the ideas associated with *Learning by Design* continue to develop and more practitioners test and refine them in new settings, bringing fresh perspectives to the research and development cycle.

The *Learning by Design* approach is also an attempt to imagine and test innovative tools and learning environments in which the blackboard, textbook, exercise book and test are augmented and at times replaced by digital technologies. In the case of Learning *by* Design, this is not simply a case of 'digital makeover' of legacy teaching practices; it is a process of imagining how learning may be different and more effective. And for this transformation to occur, the role of the teacher may well change dramatically. It seems most likely, for instance, that the teacher of the near future is going to need new tools, tools that allow them to be creative designers of learning experiences in collaboration with their professional peers, outside experts and the broader school community. Indeed, some of the design of learning content will be with the learners themselves as their work is published by the teacher for access by other students. They will need tools which are easy to use and accessible, which are conceptually rigorous yet flexible and become the basis for transparency and accountability that moves these new professionals beyond reliance on textbooks and mandated syllabuses. Imagining and creating these new tools has now became a co-requisite of educational reform.

In this spirit the 'Learning Element', used by the participating teachers/researchers, takes the form of a Microsoft Word template which can be printed out as a physical resource, or saved as a digital 'learning object' into any standards-compliant Learning Management System or elearning software system (Common Ground, 2003-2005b; Cope & Kalantzis, 2004b). Learning Elements can be collaboratively created and shared through the online publishing system, CGPublisher (Common Ground, 2003-2005a). The *Learning by Design* approach, in the cases described in this book, has trialled CGPublisher as its publishing platform (The *Learning by Design* Website, 2004-2005).

The critical point of the *Learning by Design* approach, however, is not the technologies. The technologies present a wide range of potentials. Indeed, the first phase of so-called 'elearning' environments replicate and often even accentuate all that was inadequate about the traditional classroom—transmission of received knowledge, individualised learner communication, question and answer routines, narrowly focused tests and uneven access to learning resources (Cope & Kalantzis, 2001, 2003). Some of the first phase elearning environments even represent a reduction in the quality of traditional classroom. Despite their aura of newness, they are just as irrelevant to the needs of the knowledge society as the traditional classroom. The significance of the new technologies is that, as media, they allow for very different ways of engaging, relating and communicating.

In fact, it is the role of the teacher that is critical, and the pedagogy they use, and in this sense the new technologies can play an important supporting role to the teacher as learning designer and learning manager.

Recent research shows that the professional capacity of the teacher is one of the most critical factors in the learning experience of children at school and of even greater influence at times than other variables such as socio-economic background or the curriculum (Darling-Hammond, 2001; Hatie, 2003; Rowe, 2003). This is the reason why we have chosen to focus on pedagogy in the *Learning by Design* approach as a crucial aspect of teacher professionalism.

Amongst Australian education systems, for instance, pedagogy— or the dynamics of teaching and learning—has been widely recognised in recent years as a crucial contributor to effective education. It has been directly linked in policy documents to the goal of achieving positive educational outcomes for all learners. The New South Wales Public Education Inquiry notes that the key to school reform and improvement is 'setting up enabling and generative conditions, and providing intellectual and material resources for a focus on pedagogy {and} facilitating teacher development, ownership and problem-solving around issues of pedagogy' (Public Education Inquiry NSW, 2002).

One prominent and regularly emphasised pedagogical challenge is the rapidly changing social, cultural, economic and technological conditions that exist in contemporary society. A recent paper from the Victorian Department of Education notes that 'around the world, curriculum provision models are being challenged by the need to be more relevant for twenty-first century learning' (Victorian Government, 2003). With a similar emphasis on the need for curriculum reform to meet changing social, cultural and employment conditions of the twenty-first century, Education Queensland's 2010 document discusses the importance of 'developing pedagogy for the post industrial environment' . A number of departmental initiatives in recent years in Queensland have heeded the 'call to pedagogy and curriculum reform', perhaps the most influential amongst which has been the 'New Basics' and 'Productive Pedagogies' initiatives in Queensland (Luke & Freebody, 2000; Queensland Government, 2003). These initiatives recognise that learning needs to be more general. Rather than being simply the three Rs and the inculcation of a standard set of facts and figures, initiatives such as the 'new basics' instead focus on creating a kind of person— one who is a socially productive citizen and knowledgeable in a deeper sense of the word.

Similarly, the Nelson review of the Australian teaching profession (Australian Government, 2003) notes the need to develop in schools 'a culture of innovation', and stipulates that this begins with teachers and the pedagogical processes they employ to encourage learning. The report speaks of the need for 'teachers {to} adopt creative approaches, take calculated risks within agreed frameworks, reflect constantly on their teaching and on student outcomes, reach out to share community resources, work together to achieve the best outcomes for students, and embrace technology that enhances their work and students' learning (Australian Government, 2003). The Australian Council of Deans of Education in their New Learning: A Charter for Australian Education also underline the kinds of innovative pedagogy required by the demands of classroom diversity, globalisation, new technologies, workplace transformation and a panoply of other forces (Kalantzis & Cope, 2001a).

The other country in which a pilot of the *Learning by Design* approach was established, Malaysia, is also in the midst of a series of pedagogical transformations. The most dramatic is the staged transition of the language of instruction of all teaching of Science and Mathematics to English. Alongside this

Introduction   *xiii*

is the introduction of new technologies into the learning environment and an expectation that new learning environments will engage students more actively than was possible in the traditional classroom dominated by the teacher didact. Clearly, in its pivotal role of reflecting and shaping the microdynamics of teaching and learning, pedagogy is crucial to all these changes.

Responding to this context, the *Learning by Design* approach is based on four key ideas:

1. Tremendous changes are occurring in the domains of work, citizenship and personal identity. For example, the new information and communications technologies and globalisation have brought much more **diversity** to people's lives and they way they work and relate to each other. Classrooms are thus filled with learners whose informal learning resources and life experiences are extremely varied. How do we recognise these diverse experiences and build on them to create the best learning outcomes for our students?
2. Learning experiences transform people. They result in the learner being able to know or do something they did not know or could not do before. Memorising and repeating information that has been directly transmitted by the teacher does not necessarily mean that anything was been learned beyond the skills of memorising and repeating. The *Learning by Design* tools are based on a philosophy of teaching and learning that values a variety of active ways of knowing. Teaching that harnesses diversity and leads to learner transformation involves a number of **knowledge processes** that need to be made explicit and part of a teacher's pedagogical repertoire. Assessment and evaluation attempt to record the knowledge that has been learnt and the capacities that students have acquired.
3. For all subjects, students need to have the skills associated with literacy—reading, writing, speaking and listening. More broadly conceived as 'communications', there is much more to literacy today than there was in the past. The changes that have occurred in the world however mean that literacy itself is no longer singular and standard. It is now multiple, in two ways: different *social languages* (dialects, professional or technical languages etc.); and the *multimodality* of contemporary communications environments, particulary digitally-mediated enviroments (overlaying the linguistic, visual, audio, gestural and spatial modes of meaning). This change in literacy today is called

Multiliteracies. All subject areas require that learners understand these multiple modes of meaning—in maths, science, history, literature and so on.

4. A fourth important idea in the *Learning by Design* approach is the need to reconsider traditional classroom organisation and learning resources. The sources of learning and the places where learning occurs have rapidly expanded. Much learning happens outside of classrooms, for example—engaging with new technology, playing games, travel and so on. Teachers and learners are integrating a wider range of sources of learning and forming **knowledge producing communities**. The *Learning by Design* tools provide a way for educators to reflect on their choices, document their learning programs, map curriculum, share effective practice and write up learning community goals. They also allow students to build, share, collaborate upon and publish portfolios of the work they have created digitally. The result will be greater transparency and accountability amongst those who share responsibility for education. The traditionally closed door of the classroom, and its primarily oral and thus intrinsically ephemeral discourse patterns, is thrown open, and learning interactions recorded in such a way that they become publicly visible to peers, to the educational organisation, to parents and communities.

Readers may wish to read this book straight-through in the traditional way, from theory (Part 1) to practice (Part 2); or they may prefer to begin with the real-world examples of *Learning by Design* explored in chapters 9–15. Certainly the intertwined nature of theory and practice is central to the *Learning by Design* approach; and the experiences documented in Part 2 show the researchers engaging with the theory as they apply it in school settings. Reflective practice is at the heart of this approach and some readers may wish to introduce themselves to the theory via the practice—hence commencing with Part 2.

Part I

Learning in Theory

CHAPTER 1

New Learning

This chapter considers the ways in which the emerging 'knowledge society' requires a radically new approach to learning. Globalisation and new technologies, amongst other social forces, are impacting enormously on people's lives. These social forces are affecting the conditions of work, civics and personal identity.

These changes require that learning and education prepares people to engage meaningfully in the world in new ways. These are profound changes. They mean that schools need to change and need to reconceptualise what learning is—not simply in terms of curriculum content, but also to interrogate more deeply conceptions of literacy, knowledge and even the purposes of learning.

A revolution is occurring in education. This revolution is being fuelled in part by the new information and communication technologies. Fundamentally, however, the change is in the human relations of learning. This book tells the story of an experiment in changing the relations of learning—the *Learning by Design* approach.

But change what? The reference point for the changes we will describe in this book is the traditional classroom. In its original form, this classroom was essentially a communications technology, a room large enough for a teacher to talk to twenty, thirty, even forty learners at once. Its classical oral communications modes were the teacher exposition, question and answer involving one learner at a time and whole-class recitation in unison. For most of the time an individual learner had to sit in silence. The primary written communications medium in this classroom was the textbook (closely following the state-directed syllabus). The learner produced their work (a piece of writing, a test) for an audience of one—the assessing teacher. The main official trace of the student's work was a recorded score. The teacher was pivotal in the predominant communication patterns of the traditional classroom, orchestrating classroom talk, directing students to the textbook and marking their work or their tests. Lateral peer-topeer communication was practically unmanageable and when it did occur, it was mostly 'off task'.

This classroom was the medium for the transmission of disciplinary knowledge, inculcating a rudimentary 'basics', divided for convenience into 'subjects' or 'disciplines'. At the heart of these disciplines were the 'three Rs': reading, writing and arithmetic. The substance of these basics tells a lot about what was assumed to be the nature of knowledge. School knowledge was a kind of shopping list of things-to-be-known—through drilling the 'times tables', memorising spelling lists, learning the parts of speech and using correct grammar. There were problems with this kind of curriculum, and these were not with numeracy and literacy per se, but with the underlying orientation to knowledge. Wasn't there more to being a good communicator and mathematically capable? Wasn't there more to knowledge than the black and white rigidity of right and wrong answers (and if you were in any doubt about this, the test answers would set you straight). And what kinds of persons would be formed by a schooling in which knowledge was about being told things by authority figures and passively accepting that their answers were always correct? If the underlying lesson of the old basics was about the nature of knowledge, then it was a lesson which was appropriate for a society which expected its workers to take orders unquestioningly at work and its wives to take orders at home, or to fight loyally in the wars of the nation-state. Much of the time, however, the traditional classroom was a place of passivity, boredom and failure. And even this made a certain kind of sense, as poor results at school served as a moral lesson in a society where most jobs were drearily unskilled, not requiring much beyond work discipline and the capacity to put up with boredom. If that's where you ended up, it must be your own fault for not doing better at school.

This type of education, in other words, worked perfectly well for a society in which learners were destined to belong to traditional workplaces which required deference to authority and whose skills requirements were minimal, predictable and stable. It was well suited to the creation of homogeneous and submissive citizenries in the service of the old nation-state. It was appropriate to the development of compliant personalities. There was even a logic of sorts in having a large number of learners 'fail' at school; it was a way of rationalising lack of opportunity for a large part of the society.

This world has now gone, or at least it is going, or at least it has gone in the more affluent parts of the developed world. This kind of schooling is becoming less and less relevant to the needs of learners— any learners, in any part of the world.

Table 1.1: The Changing Social Order

	Early Industrial Society	**Developed Industrial Society**	**Knowledge Society**
Work	Value in fixed capital, not the skills of workers, who are mostly unskilled. Minimal, predictable, stable work expectations. A premium placed on discipline, reliably taking orders.	New technologies, the humanisation of work; higher levels of skill and communicative and interpersonal capacities required in the workplace.	Value in human skills and relationships, intangible Organizational knowledge and service values. Complex and changing expectations require flexibility, creativity, innovation, initiative.
Civics	Citizens expected to be passive and loyal to leaders. An homogenous citizenry, or one at the very least where people are expected to become the same. Uncritical loyalty to leaders expected.	Blurring of the boundaries between public and private realms, developing democracy, migration, globalisation.	An active, aware, multicultural citizenry. Many levels of civic participation and responsibility (community organisations, corporate ethics, varied local, national, regional, global levels of governance).
Personal Life	Ideally compliant personalities, accepting of established structures and values, respectful of authority figures, taking orders. The nuclear family as the model, and the gender relations that go with it.	Identity and diversity become more important issues. Transformations in family life away from the model of the nuclear family, multichannel media, diverse communities, more engaged personalities.	Multiple family types, multilayered identities, tolerance, ethics, responsibility, resilience.

A series of related social changes are occurring, encapsulated in part by the idea of an emerging 'knowledge society'. In the economy, value is increasingly located in the intangibles of human capacity, organisational flexibility, business processes, customer relationships, brand identity, technological know-how, product aesthetics and service values. This represents a shift away from the old grounding of value primarily in fixed capital and basic skills. This is not to say that knowledge was unimportant before; it is simply to argue that knowledge now takes a uniquely central place. In the domain of citizenship, the dynamics of belonging and governance now occur at multiple and overlapping levels—from community organisations and workplaces, to self-regulating professions, to communities of common knowledge and shared taste, to the increasingly federated layers of local, regional, national and supranational government. In the domain of personality, identity differences are becoming ever-more accentuated, and the keys to stable personality are responsibility, resilience and tolerance. These changes we will discuss in more detail in Chapter 2.

These are profound changes; they mean that schools need to change. And indeed schools have been changing for some decades. The inspiration for these changes is even older than that, and the original spokespeople for the 'modern' school include such foundational thinkers in the field of education as Maria Montessori (Montessori, 1964 (1912)) and John Dewey (Dewey, 1966 (1916)).

Their impact was enormous. Gradually, over the course of the twentieth century, schools changed—particularly in the kindergarten and elementary or primary years: the classroom with the teacher at the front was replaced by learners facing each other around grouped desks; the teacher-didact was replaced by activity stations along the lines of Montessori's designs; and a change in focus from knowledge content (syllabuses as lists of contents to be followed term by term, and textbooks that follow the syllabus, and tests that determine whether learners have absorbed the facts and theories presented to them) to learning how to learn. Some things, however, have changed less—the architecture of schools, and the role of examinations in assessment and credentialing.

As we will argue in this book, the rate of social and technological transformation today is such that the pace of change in schools is likely to pick up still further. Schools of the near future are likely to drift even more radically away from their roots in early industrial society. And this is because they will be doing things which traditional learning environments were incapable of doing. The new learning environments will:

- foster a culture of innovation based on calculated risk;
- require learners to think and act as collaborative team players;
- reward problem posing as much as they do creative solutions;
- respect profoundly different personalities and develop resilience;
- create active citizens who are autonomous and contribute as much as they benefit from the supports of governance;
- form persons who are securely grounded in the local community yet, at the same time, outward-looking and globally concerned;

- encourage thinking which draws upon multiple sources of knowledge, noting variable perspectives, knowledge orientations and approaches to problems;
- cultivate a capacity for lifelong and lifewide learning;
- develop the ability to communicate using the new multimodal information and communications media, and to critically interpret their messages. Indeed, these are some of an emerging 'new basics'. These basics are essential for the knowledge society. To meet learners' needs, educators will need to address these new basics, remaking themselves and the designs of the environments in which they engage with learners. To do this they will require new tools which support new ways of working.

Take the three 'R's, for instance. The fancier contemporary words for these old basics are literacy and numeracy. Of course, mathematics, reading and writing are today as important as ever, perhaps even more important. However, literacy and numeracy can either stand as substitute words for the old basics, or they can mean something new, something appropriate to the new learning. When they are merely substitute words for the old basics, they are mostly no more than statements of nostalgic regret for a world which is disappearing, or else they reflect our incapacity as adults to imagine anything different from, or better than, our own experiences as children at school. 'Let's get back to the basics', people say, and the operative words are 'get back'.

When we use the term 'new basics' we are indicating a very different approach to knowledge. Mathematics is not a set of correct answers but a method of reasoning, a way of figuring out a certain kind of system and structure in the world. Nor is literacy a matter of correct useage (the word and sentence-bound rules of spelling and grammar). Rather, it is a way of communicating. Indeed, the new communications environment demands much more than the old rules of literacy. Although spelling remains important, it is now something for spell-checking programs or the predictive text of mobile phones, and email or SMS messages do not have to be grammatical in a formal sense (although they have new and quirky conventions which no school will teach—abbreviations, friendly informalities and cryptic 'in' expressions). Spelling drills are made redundant either because the machine will do the job, or because the machine becomes an ad hoc teacher of spelling—you find out and learn the spelling of words as you need use them.

Many texts, moreover, involve complex relationships between visuals, space and text: the tens of thousands of words in a supermarket; the written text around the screen on the news, sports or business program on the television; the text of an ATM; websites built on visual icons and active hypertext links; the subtle relationships of images and text in glossy magazines. Texts are now designed in a highly visual sense, and meaning is carried as much visually as it is by words and sentences. This means that the old basics which teach adverbial clauses of time or the cases around the verb 'to be', may either be abandoned as less than germane to today's communications needs, or at least to be supplemented by learning about the visual design of texts (such as fonts, point sizes, heading weights and dotpoint lists—the stuff today of word processing, desktop publishing and PowerPoint presentations which use concepts and requires skills that in the past were mostly confined to the acrane craft of typesetting). It also means that the old subject division between language and art is not as relevant as it once was.

Nor is literacy any longer only about learning so called 'proper useage'. Rather, it is also about the myriad of different uses in different contexts: this particular email (personal, to a friend), as against that (applying for a job); this particular kind of desktop publishing presentation (a newsletter for your sports group), as against that (a page of advertising); and different uses of English as a global language (in different English speaking countries, by non-native speakers, by different subcultural groups). The capabilities of literacy involve not only knowledge of grammatical conventions but also effective communication in diverse settings, and using tools of text design which may include word processing, desktop publishing and image manipulation.

More than new contents like these, however, the new basics are also about new kinds of learning. Literacy, for instance, is not only about rules and their correct application. It is about being faced with an unfamiliar kind of text and search for clues about its meaning without immediately feeling alienated and excluded from it. It is also about understanding how this text works in order to participate in its meanings (its own particular 'rules'), and about working out the particular context and purposes of the text (for herein you will find more clues to its meaning to the communicator and to you). Finally, literacy is about actively communicating in an unfamiliar context and learning from your successes and mistakes.

Even more profoundly, education always creates 'kinds of persons'. What is the moral economy of a spelling drill? The old basics formed people who had learnt rules and could be relied on to obey them; people who would take answers to the world rather than regard the world as many problems-to-be-solved; and people who carried 'correct' things in private spaces of their heads rather than flexible and collaborative learners.

In the same spirit, the new basics set out to shape new 'kinds of persons', persons better adapted to the kind of world we live in now and the world of the near future. The new learning will be:

- *General in its focus,* rather than specialised on the particular needs-of-the-day. Today's relevance is tomorrow's anachronism. Besides, to be truly relevant in an immediate sense, there are simply too many areas to cover. This produces the phenomenon of the 'crowded curriculum' in which formal education institutions are now simply expected to cover too much ground. Or, it produces the 'shopping mall curriculum' in which students are provided too much choice and each choice is too particular. The paradox of this moment of particularity, change and diversity in all areas of knowledge and human experience is that formal education needs to become more centred, and more focused on a few core areas of learning. Each of these core areas must be studied at a higher level of generality than the traditional subject areas, must be relevant to a broad range of students with quite different life destinations, and must be applicable in very different contexts. The specifics are more likely to be learnt in professional training programs, from help menus, from whatever experiences life turns up—in informal learning settings, in other words. Even professional courses (in vocational education and higher education) are going to need to increase the level of generality at which they operate to stay relevant to a more rapidly changing technological, business and community context.
- *About creating a kind of person,* with kinds of dispositions and orientations to the world, and not just persons who are in command of a body of knowledge. These persons will be able to navigate change and diversity, learn-as-they-go, solve problems, collaborate and be flexible and creative.
- *Interdisciplinary in its nature,* breaking down the old subject or academic discipline boundaries. In fact, the number of subjects or core learning areas may be reducible to as few as five or even three (say, humanities, technology, society/economy). These will involve deeper engagement with knowledge in all its complexity and ambiguity.

Herein lies an enormous challenge, and an enormous opportunity for education. What education does—building the knowledge capital of a society as well as the sensibilities to navigate ambiguity and complexity—is now fundamental. Traditional classrooms and traditional bureaucratic education systems, cannot provide society what it now requires. The agenda of the new learning is to meet the needs of the knowledge society in a globalised world.

This is to paint a picture of change in very broad, historical brushstrokes. However, history is not a succession of neatly defined periods. Today, you will find sites which reflect all three of these paradigms for learning; and within one of these sites you will find moments and incidents which reflect one approach, and others another. You will find this variation from country to country, from school system to school system, from school to school, from classroom to classroom, and even from one moment to the next within the life of one classroom.

In the contemporary developed world, the logic of the twentieth century modern school predominates. The purpose of this book is to set an agenda for what we call the 'new learning'—to imagine what a new phase of education would be like, and in fact, what it is already like in the most innovative educational practices of today. This, we believe, is not simply an act of imagination—a wilful utopianism. Given the changes occurring today (globalisation, community diversity, technologies, work, new kinds of persons with different sensibilities), the new learning we are speaking of will become a necessity. Unless, that is, schools are to slip into a crisis of irrelevance. We'll know when such a crisis arrives, because it will translate into employers' complaints about graduates, into discipline problems at school, into a general community angst that schools are not teaching learners what they need for the contemporary world. On these indicators, in many places, the crisis has already arrived.

Table 1.2: Changing Education

The Institutionalised Mass Schooling of Early Industrial Society	The Twentieth Century Modern School	*Learning by Design*: A Vision for New Learning
The classroom: desks in rows, a blackboard at the front, bare walls, or at most some lettering charts or a map.	Learners work around groups of desks, different functional or resource areas around the classroom, children's work decorates the walls.	No need for classes to be colocated: students work in groups, or individual students work collaboratively using networked computers—at home, in small collaborative work areas, in the school's information resource centre, at community located project sites.
My classroom, my work: Private spaces for teachers and learners, in the case of teachers examined only by inspectors and in the case of learners examined only by teachers.	A space that increasingly brings in and engages outsiders: aides, parents, community members.	A fully transparent place, of community collaborations, online publication of teacher created programs and resources, student portfolios etc.
Classroom discourse: teacher-dominated: recitation, question and answer.	More student dialogue, hampered by traditional classroom architecture.	Extensive lateral student to-Student communications, teacher as learning designer and learning manager.
Presented facts and theories (in the textbook, by the teacher); student repetition.	A focus on experiential learning.	A balance of knowledge processes: experiential, conceptual, analytical and applied.
Memorisation, repetition, learning by rote, 'correct' answers. The teacher as didact.	'Inquiry' learning, child centred education, student opinions and points of view encouraged. The teacher as learning facilitator.	Balanced learning, involving a variety of activity types or knowledge processes. The teacher as designer and manager of learning.
Content knowledge for a stable society.	Learning as a process (learning how to learn) for a changing society.	Intellectual depth through a balance of process and content knowledge.

Students as receivers and absorbers of knowledge, as determined by syllabus, textbook and test.	The syllabus is less rigid about content, textbooks are less central, tests become more sophisticated.	Contextual learning, learning in communities of practice, learning how to participate in learning communities.
Sameness: all students on the same page, every learner doing the same work and moving ahead at the same pace.	Limited acknowledgement of student differences, but constrained by classroom architecture and timetable demands; individualised learning; some self-paced learning.	Differences: cultures, interests, abilities catered for through flexible physical and learning architectures; multilearner environments, group paced learning.
Incentives of reward (mainly marks and grades) and punishment.	Traditional rewards remain, albeit in the form of more sophisticated assessment regimes; some traditional punishments abandoned or made Illegal.	A premium placed on student engagement; incentives designed into the learning experience— the range of learner activities or 'knowledge processes', the collaborations in the learning community; assessment by peers, of publication of portfolios to be shared with peers, parents and the community.
Written text privileged.	More images, diagrams and other forms of visual representation, but written text on the printed or handwritten page still predominates.	Multimodality in learner meaning making, reflecting the complexities and richness of the new media.

CHAPTER 2

The Knowledge Society

This chapter considers the series of related social changes that are encapsulated by such terms as the knowledge society, the new economy, the high-tech economy, the twenty-first century economy, a culture of lifelong learning—all common expressions denoting fundamental structural and societal changes. Such terms reflect the fact that value in organisations, communities and nations can no longer be meaningfully measured by their fixed and financial assets alone, but by the skills and knowledge of their people.

The consequences for education are enormous. Lifelong and lifewide learning will be the reality for most, and the majority of workers will be knowledge workers in the broad sense. In fact, teaching itself will perhaps be recognised as the central profession of the knowledge economy. The ramifications of the knowledge society also extend beyond the economy into into the domains of identity and citizenship. Education is key in developing persons who have a strong sense of identity in an increasingly shifting, fragmented world. It is critical that education creates a kind of person who can successfully navigate our transformed and transforming society.

SHIFTING CONDITIONS

'Knowledge economy', 'knowledge worker' and 'knowledge management' are three phrases that are frequently used to describe what is new about contemporary work and productive life (Stewart, 1998). Perhaps these terms are used too easily, too glibly even. However, the term 'knowledge' does point to three key aspects of today's organisations, and today's economy:

> *Technological*: The knowledge economy is heavily dependant on technologies which assist the flow of information—within enterprises, between enterprises and between enterprises and consumers (Castells, 2000, 2001). Herein lies the primary basis for productivity improvement and competitive advantage. Moreover, these are technologies more infused with human meaning than ever before, their human interfaces

11

drenched with textuality, visual symbology and representational and cultural force .

Commercial: In the knowledge economy, the capital value of an enterprise's asset base and the market value of its tradeable products is increasingly located in intangibles—brand, reputation, business systems, customer base, intellectual property, human skills and the capacity of the organisation to capture, systematise, preserve and apply knowledge.

Cultural: Human needs have been transformed to the point where, in the marketplace, consumers focus on representations as much as they do on physical entities—design, aesthetics, concepts, brand associations and service sensibilities (Cope & Kalantzis, 2002).

In some important respects, this analysis of the near future simply develops and extends lines of thought that are decades old, found in the early predictions of the coming of a post-industrial or information society (Bell, 1973; Masuda, 1980) and those who try to account for a new 'reflexive' cognitive, aesthetic and community sensibilities in late modernity (Lash, 1994).

These are large generalisations. What, in practical terms do they mean for the domains of work, citizenship and the identity of persons? Creating good workers, actively contributing citizens and persons of stable and resilient identity are three of the fundamental objectives of education.

NEW WORK

Workers of the future will require skills and sensibilities that are significantly different from those of the past. If the predominant image of the old economy was the factory and the smokestack, the image of the new economy is the worker sitting in front of a computer screen. Information and communications technologies dominate the so-called 'knowledge economy'.

Actually, despite the hype, we don't just live on knowledge, as if the economy has suddenly abandoned making things for trading in information and symbols. We cannot live on symbols alone. But symbols are nevertheless everywhere. They are at the heart of new technologies, and especially the technologies of digital convergence— communications, automated manufacturing, e-commerce, the media. Even in the manufacturing sector where people still energetically make things, they often make them today with the assistance of screen-based technologies, and these are linguistically, visually and symbolically driven. The production line is still there, but now robots are screwing on the bolts. These technologies, moreover, are constantly shifting.

The new technologies are software rather than hardware intensive, as well as flexible and open to multiple uses. Software replacements are made far more frequently than was the case for plant replacement in the old economy. This means that technical knowledge has a shorter and shorter shelf-life. Up-skilling needs to occur continuously. Indeed, contrary to the old economy process of deskilling (in which a complex work process was broken into narrower tasks requiring less skilled workers—the logic of the classical production line), workers in all sectors of the economy today need to be multiskilled, to be more flexible, more able to undertake a range of tasks, and able to shift from one task to another as needs be. The key to organisational effectiveness and enhanced productivity, even the value of an organisation, is no longer grounded in the value of its fixed assets and plant, or at least not in that alone, but in the skills and knowledge of its workforce. Indeed, technology is now very much a relationship between tools and the knowledge of these tools in people's heads. Wealth increasingly has a human-skills, rather than a fixed-capital basis.

And how do organisations in the new economy work? How do they go about their business? The hierarchy has been flattened somewhat and there is less middle management. People work in teams and increasingly workers are expected to participate in the process of management. Self-managing teams are formed, in which the 'team leader' is no more than the first amongst equals. 'Responsibility', 'empowerment', 'commitment' and 'motivation' are the qualities of a good team member. And, to achieve this, the vertical lines of communication that characterised the old command management are replaced by horizontal communication with peers—in team meetings, maintaining quality standards, problem-solving, and generally performing the function of self-management as well as doing the actual task. Meanwhile, the business focus of the organisation also broadens beyond the old bottom line. One version of this broadening is the 'triple bottom line' where, as well as concentrating on money, the organisation also focuses on people and the environment.

Now workplaces have cultures. Workers are supposed to buy into the vision and mission of the organisation, to take on corporate culture, to be the corporate person. Culture, in fact, has become a powerful new management technique, the glue that holds the new organisation together, replacing the glue of highly structured system and order which held together the old workplace. It's all about winning employee commitment by setting up systems of belonging, and a framework of corporate believability in which the organisation hopes to win the faith of the employees (Cope & Kalantzis, 1997b).

At the same time, the nature of 'the job' changes. Gone is the stable career path, based on seniority. Jobs don't last so long; people swap employer, or even industry more regularly. Careers will head off on unheard-of tangents, and one's credentials come to be made up of accumulations of experience which might previously have been regarded as bizarre. What a worker takes with them from one job to the next is a 'portfolio' of experiences, and the more varied and broadly focused this portfolio, the more rounded and valuable they will appear to a new employer.

These are all knowledge things, relationship things, things of human rather than fixed capital. Most importantly, they are all things that are made by learning. Learning has become pivotal to the whole economy. For the learning which is now required, the old education simply won't do. The new economy requires new persons: persons who can work flexibly with changing technologies; persons who can work effectively in the new relationship-focused commercial environment; and people who are able to work within an open organisational culture and across diverse cultural settings.

The purpose of education is not just to serve the needs of the economy by creating useful workers. The economic rationale behind much of today's talk of educational change is itself too narrow. To speak in boldly simple terms, making useful workers is only one of the three fundamental roles of education. The other roles are to create fully participating citizens, and to shape persons at home in their identity. To be useful and successful in today's work, individuals need to be able to participate, to be good 'corporate citizens'. The also to be a certain kind of person, comfortable with their identity and able to give something of themselves in their work.

The knowledge economy does not denote simply a rise in technology industries or increasing computer useage, important though these developments are. Rather, the phrase is best used to identify a society transformed in the broadest sense by new relationships to knowledge. And to speak of knowledge workers is not just to refer to a particular niche of workers, but to a typical worker in the new economy. Neat separations will increasingly be more difficult to impose; all workers will need to learn throughout and across their lives; and education will be the key to both individual prosperity and national growth and security. Preparing tomorrow's knowledge worker is perhaps the key task for contemporary educators and societies, and their success in this task will be reflected in the performance of economies and the welfare of nations.

Of all the management theorists, Drucker has one of the longest views, in part for the simple reason that he has remained a cogent commentator on organisational change into a ripe old age (P. Drucker, 1998, 2001). In his 1993 book, *Post-capitalist Society,* he reflects on the change in the following terms:

> When I first began to study management, during and immediately after World War II, a manager was defined as 'someone who is responsible for the work of subordinates'. A manager, in other words, was a 'boss', and management was rank and power. ... But by the early 1950s, the definition had already changed to 'a manager is responsible for the performance of people'. Now we know that this also is too narrow a definition. The right definition is 'a manager is responsible for the application and performance of knowledge' (P. F. Drucker, 1993).

As for the knowledge that is now the central value at the heart of organisations and contemporary management cultures, there is nothing clear or empirically stable about it. In fact, the organisation was now a place of instability and contest.

> The organisation of the post-capitalist society of organisations is a destabiliser. Because its function is to put knowledge to work—on tools, processes and products; on work; on knowledge itself—it must be organised for constant change ... . It must be organised for the systematic abandonment of the established, the customary, the familiar, the comfortable, whether products, services and processes, human and social relationships, skills or organisations themselves. ... {E}very organisation of today has to build into its very structure the management of change. It has to build in organised abandonment of everything it does (P. F. Drucker, 1993).

If the educational basics of the traditional classroom produced well-disciplined but compliant persons who relied on the stability of the facts and theories they had been taught, the new learning will need to shape a different kind of person, a person with the skills and capacities of adaptability, flexibility, initiative and innovation required by the new workplace.

NEW CITIZENSHIP

In almost every respect, citizenship—the condition of civic participation—is in a state of profound flux. Citizenship can no longer be interpreted as the act of voting, of choosing government. For example, the relevance and power of the nation-state has progressively been shrinking. With economic globalisation and deregulation, the state is less able to influence economic conditions. In fact, the state is itself getting smaller and smaller—with the privatisation of traditional publicly-owned industries (airlines, telecommunications, banks), as well as with large cutbacks to the welfare state's safety net. As the old nation-state declines in strength and relevance, there are many more realms of participation, of self-governing citizenship in a much broader sense: in local communities, in workplaces, in cultural groups (Kalantzis, 2000).

With this decline of the old civic, power and cultural influence are also in some respects being spread around more—to locally diverse communities, as well as to transnational forms of government such as the European Union, and to global webs of global influence (business, trade, the media). People increasingly find that they are multiple citizens, sharing the responsibilities of governance in many different ways in different parts of their lives. This process occurs in self-regulating professions, or sporting associations, or in ethnic diasporas in which you can vote in elections for places where you do not live as well as the place where you do live, or in Indigenous groups which will sooner or later enjoy a unique kind of sovereignty in their native lands. As a consequence, nations are arguably becoming less relevant as a focal point for cultural identity.

As citizens, we now simultaneously belong to many more kinds community at the local, the regional and the global level. Singular citizenship in which a person is exclusively a citizen of the nation state, and the electoral process is the sum total of their participation, is being replaced by multiple citizenship, in which there are many, overlapping forms of self government, many levels of self-government in a larger sense, and many places where you belong. In each case, participation is much more than a matter of voting. Indeed, the way you participate in each of these places, and the way you belong, is distinctively and different, special to that place.

This is the likely shape of a truly multicultural future, a kind of 'civic pluralism' in which, quite contrary to the logic of sameness which drove the old citizenship, the key to civic harmony is respecting and valuing diversity. In fact, the most fundamental right of all is the right to be different, the right to be true to yourself. Even the meaning of entitlement and fairness changes—to have equivalent access does not mean you will be provided with the same services; and you don't have to be the same to be equal. Government supports groups providing services for themselves (such as community support groups or community-based non-government schools), in which they are given a considerable degree of autonomy in creating what works best for them—be that schools, or aged care, or the arts, or media.

If the educational basics of the old citizenship were education systems which set out to forge national strength by creating cultural homogeneity, the new learning is going to have to shape a new person, with a very different set of skills of participation, as well as a very different values orientation. It will, in short, be a very different kind of learning.

NEW IDENTITIES

Just as remarkable as the changes in work and the changes in civics, are the changes which are occurring in the very nature of our persons—changes influenced by the shifting conditions of technology, commerce and culture.

To take the technology revolution first, this not only changes the way we work and the way we participate as citizens. It even changes our persons. From the old world of broadcasting to the new world of 'narrowcasting', consider what has happened to one medium, television. Instead of the pressures to conformity, pressures to shape your person in the image of the mass media when everybody watched the old 'national networks', we now have cable television—fifty channels at first and hundreds to come. The channels cater, not to the 'general public', but to ever-more finely defined communities: the services in different languages, the particular sporting interests, the genres of movie. Not to mention video and DVD extending choice by genre and by language to tens of thousands of titles. Soon on-demand TV will be streamed though the Internet. And to take the Internet itself, the millions of sites reflect any interest or style you want to name, nurturing a myriad of ever-more finely differentiated communities. Then there's the phenomenon of 'pointcasting' and web syndication, where the user customises the information feed they want—requesting information to be streamed to them only about a particular sporting team, a particular business sector, a particular country of origin. As a part of this process, the viewer becomes a user; transmission is replaced by user-selectivity. And instead of being passive receptors of mass culture, we become active creators of information and sensibilities which precisely suit the nuances of who we are and the image in which we want to fashion ourselves.

In fact, digital convergence turns the whole media relationship around the other way—the digital image of a new-born baby which can be broadcast to the world through the family's personal website, or the digital movie which you can edit on your computer, burn on a CD or broadcast from your home page. There is simply more scope to be yourself in this technology environment, and to be yourself in a way which is different—the huge variations in the look and feel of weblog sites is a case in point. The technology convergence comes with cultural divergence, and who knows which is the greater influence in the development of the other? The only thing which is clear is that technology is one of the keys to these new kinds of self expression and community building. It is part of a process of creating new persons—persons of self-made identity instead of received identity, and diverse identities rather than a singular national identity. In this context, senses of belonging will arise from a common commitment to openness and inclusivity.

In the area of domestic life, family forms and gender identities are in the middle of a long and sometimes painful process of transformation. Women are increasingly found in the workforce, and the traditional domestic division of labour, as well as the identity-frameworks supporting it, have fallen into a state of uneasy uncertainty. For emerging adult identities, if we are to take suicide and certain areas of education performance as just two measures amongst many, the changes in nature of masculine identity and roles have thrown up as many difficulties as the changes in feminine. At the same time, a plethora of family alternatives is emerging, each based on their own domestic economy, their own mixes of unpaid homework and paid external work—extended 'ethnic' families, nuclear families, single parent families, indigenous groups in which family coincides with community, singles, gay couples.

Not only do these present different practical life alternatives; they also present different identity alternatives, lifestyles whose designs are such that they can only be lived by radically different 'kinds of person'. At the same time, the neat separation between the two economies, domestic and public, becomes blurred, not just in terms of the gender locations as men and women now have to perform in both places, but also in terms of the old institutional separations. So, we witness the emergence of the 'family friendly' working conditions which encourage the lifestyle choices of 'new men' and 'new women', and the possibility of working at home or telecommuting in which family and work are not physically separated.

These changes suggest social chaos, fragmentation and uncertainty. They feel like an emotional roller-coaster in which we are often ill-prepared to deal with the changes going in our lives, the diversity so close to us, the personal choices now available to us, and a world of identity and lifestyle alternatives in which, it seems, there are no clear models of normality. Yet how can these changes enhance rather than undermine our sense of ourselves, our humanity?

Table 2.1: Changing Educational Conditions

	The Command (Early Industrial) Society	The Receptive (Developed Industrial) Society	The Reflexive (Knowledge) Society
Work	Value in fixed capital: plant and infrastructure. Hierarchical command structures. Raw 'labour power'. The unmediated financial 'bottom line'.	Growing importance of 'human capital': technical knowledge and skills. Move to teamwork and flattened hierarchy. Workplaces have a single culture to which workers have to 'clone'. The career worker. New methods to achieve the traditional 'bottom line'.	Critical role of information and communication technologies. Value in intangibles. Collaborative work groups. Dynamic, inclusive and internally diverse organisational cultures. The portfolio worker. Three or four 'bottom lines'.
Citizenship	The act of voting (if you are lucky). The strong paternal state (welfare state, communism, fascism). Cultural homogeneity: processes of exclusion or assimilation.	The diminishing state (deregulation, privatisation, welfare cutbacks). Fragmenting citizenship. Tokenistic multiculturalism.	Multiple citizenship: workplaces, professions, community organisations, ethnic diasporas, transnational communities, different levels of government. The sensibilities of civic pluralism: resilience, open-ness, tolerance, a global outlook.
Indentities	Mass media creates a mass culture. Consumers: generic commodities. Fixed gender roles. Singular identities.	Relatively few media channels, concentrated in the hands of a few. Growth of 'consumerism'. Unsettling changes in gender roles. Uneasily juxtaposed multicultural identities.	Proliferation of media; lowering of barriers to access to the means of cultural creation and communication. Consumers form a myriad of niche markets each with its own eye to product design, branding, service relationships. Complex and varied gender roles and sexual personas. Multilayered identities.

Despite the seeming descent into social fragmentation, we end up more connected than ever. Today we live in more and more narrowly defined communities, but also in many more of them—workplace, ethnic, sporting, sexual-preference, religious, hobby-interest—and the sum-total extent of these many communities for any one person is often enormous. In each of these communities, you are a different kind of person, interacting in a different kind of way. Your own identity becomes multilayered; your personality multiple (Cope & Kalantzis, 1998; Kalantzis, Cope, Noble, & Poynting, 1991).

And how can our new persons be better persons, rather than debilitated by these changes? The answers lie in shifting the focus from the personal to the interpersonal. The personal is about shaping oneself in the image of others, recognising oneself in one's similarity with other models of gender or national identity, and making oneself into one person. The interpersonal is about negotiating differences, and in a world of growing difference this is about strategies for finding common ground, collaborating with strangers and the morality of compromise. You don't have to agree with a person, or even like them, to get on with them as co-workers or customers, or in neighbourhoods. In fact, who they are, what they can do and who they know may even be useful. Diversity may well be highly productive. Prejudice, arrogant self-certainty and intolerance are now socially destructive parts of the old personality, confident in their own normality. With new freedoms, in which the freedom to be yourself is central, come new social responsibilities—to respect and if possible work productively with people whose personal choices and aspirations are different.

These changing conditions of personal identity also present enormous challenges to schools. How do they respond meaningfully, let alone assume the important role of actively shaping stable, productive and happy persons.

CHANGING SUBJECTIVITIES, NEW LEARNING

As discussed earlier in this chapter, the wide-ranging social changes that are encapsulated in the term 'knowledge society', reverberate on a variety of levels. Whether it be in the realms of civics, work or everday cultural life, we are in the midst of enormous change. To remain apt, education must reflect these changes. Maybe even, there are times and places where educators can lead change.

Take civics. For better or for worse, the key phenomenon in the realm of civics is that the nation-state is shrinking. Whatever the root causes—small government conservatism, globalisation, or the new dynamics of a post cold-war world—the realities of this change are everywhere to be felt.

The society of self-regulating community—civil society—is becoming a more significant locus of action and decision. The Internet is governed, not by any state, but through the community of experts and interested parties that is the World Wide Web Consortium. Diasporic communities are governed, not by home governments, but by highly distributed community organisations whose points of connection are common cultural principles. In education, we are witnessing the rise of community and private schooling and the self-managing public school. And the need for teaching to become an increasingly self-regulated profession. As the state contracts, there is no alternative to creating governance structures within the communities of practice of civil society.

With the shrinking of the state, a certain kind of society disappears, too. Compare the relationship of state and civil society today with the command societies of the twentieth century—the communism of Lenin and Mao, the fascism of Hitler and interwar Japan, and the paternalistic regimentation of the west's welfare state. When a greater capacity to decide and act is devolved to civil society, a higher level of participation and reflexivity is required of citizens.

So deep is this change that it extends even to the nature of personality or identity. The society of the strong state established relationships of command and compliance at every level, not just in the state itself but in workplaces (the bosses and supervisors whose orders were to be obeyed), in homes (the heads of households who made decisions and disciplined), in schools (the orders of headmasters and teachers, mandated curricular content and tests of definitively correct answers).

Take that archetypical command personality, Howard Roark, modern architect and towering individual in Ayn Rand's pro-capitalist novel, *The Fountainhead*. At the vanguard of unadorned modernism, he stands alone against the world, unwilling to compromise his designs, and for his singularity of purpose, he triumphs. In almost the same moment, anti-capitalist Mexican artist Diego Rivera was painting the heroes of modernity on the murals of the Rockefeller Centre in New York. Overlooking the mighty works of modern man— the cities, the bridges, the the industrial landscapes whose horizons are punctured by smokestacks—stand the heroic engineer, the heroic architect, the heroic intellectual, the heroic political leader, the heroic gang-supervisor, and his Rockefeller patrons also hoped, the heroic capitalist. Rivera was removed from the job when it became obvious amongst the faces of the heroes was a likeness of Lenin. Notwithstanding twentieth century sensitivities to their ideological differences, Roark's and the Lenin's were equally command personalities, and in that sense substitutable in the tableau of modernism. Both left and right, in their time, lionised command personalities.

For every command personality, there had to be a multitude of unquestioning functionaries, and upon their compliance, the system depended. The ideal citizen of the strong state was compliant; the ideal worker of the capitalist or communist industrial enterprise was compliant; the ideal learner in the classroom of disciplined knowledge was compliant.

Today, the command personality is an anachronism. At work, for instance, crude command structures are replaced by a more sophisticated cultural co-option—the co-option of team work, vision and mission and corporate culture, in which everyone is supposed to personify the enterprise, to think and will and act the enterprise. Roark's aesthetic insistence has become an archaism—he would let his business fail before compromising on the rigorous modernism of his designs. 'Any colour you like, so long as it's black', said that other heroic command personality, Henry Ford. Today, there can be no entrepreneurial heroism because the customer is always right and products and services need to be customised to mesh with the multiple subjectivities of niche markets—the big SUVs, the smart sports cars, the spacious family cars, the micro cars for crowded cities, cars of any hue and trim—so many permutations, in fact, that sometimes an individual order has to be placed before a vehicle is manufactured. Fordist mass production is displaced by today's mass customisation.

In our lives as cultural beings as well, there has been a profound shift in the intersubjective balance of power. Take something so fundamental as narrative. In everyday family and community life, the narratives of gaming have become a bigger business than Hollywood. From the most impressionable of ages, children of the Nintendo, PlayStation and X-Box generation have become inured to the idea that they can be characters in narratives, capable of determining or and at the very least influencing the story's end. They are content with being no less than actors rather than audiences, players rather than spectators, agents rather than voyeurs, users rather than readers of narrative. Not content with programmed radio, they build their own play lists on their iPods. Not content with programmed television, they read the narratives of DVD and Internet streamed video at varying depth (the movie, the documentary about the making of the movie) and dip into 'chapters' at will. Not content with the singular vision of sports telecasting of mass television, they choose their own angles, replays and statistical analyses on interactive digital TV. Meanwhile, the auto-creative potentials of the digital media and the 'semantic web' have only just been opened with phenomena such as blogging. These potentials create new economies of cultural scale, geographies of distribution and balances of cultural power. The costs of owning the means of production of widely communicable meaning have been hugely reduced, and, with this, the small and the different has become as viable as the large and the generic.

Whether it be in the domains of governance, work or cultural life, the command society is giving way to the society of reflexivity. Or so we might say in moments of strategic optimism. In moments of pessimism we might experience these same phenomena as fragmentation, ego-centrism, randomness, ambiguity and anarchy. And when this pessimism turns to fear, we might want to return to earlier, simpler command structures—in nations, workplaces, households and schools.

Pessimists and optimists alike can agree that we are in the midst of a transformation that is creating new forms of subjectivity and new kinds of personality. These transformations can be viewed both from within a systems perspective and beyond it. From a systems point of view, these are the kinds of governance structures, the kinds of organisation and the kinds of people required today, for the most conservative, small government and pro-enterprise points of view. We hear these points of view expressed in the public rhetoric of innovation and creativity, the knowledge economy, and individual autonomy and responsibility. Notwithstanding the high-sounding rhetoric, left to run their course, these transformations may only legitimate and even exacerbate systemic inequities—iniquities, indeed.

History, however, is more open-ended than that. Inevitably, human systems are so complex that they allow possibilities outside the scope anticipated by their progenitors and apologists. For every moment when the ideologues of small government succeed in shrinking the state, there is another moment in which people learn the civilities of self-government in their various communities of practice; for every moment when command structures in workplaces are replaced by collaborationist structures, there is another moment in which people acquire the collaborative competencies of socially-directed work; for every moment when compliant personalities are replaced by the egocentrism of individualism, there is another moment in which new relationships of codependence and mutual reliance are created and the bonds of sociability are extended and deepened. Whatever the domain, there is a shift in the balance of power and in the moral economy of agency which favours egalitarianism and liberty. And this despite and beyond prevailing systems and structures of power. From this something genuinely new could emerge.

Whether one's agenda is to support today's systems of governance, work and culture or to create new and more equitable ones, subjectivity and agency loom larger than they did in the era of the command society. Yet, all-too-often our institutions and practices of schooling reflect epistemological and personality frames of the command society, such as the communication patterns of classroom discourse, the information architectures of curriculum or the rigid expectations of 'right' and 'wrong' answers in testing regimes.

We educators have been struggling to develop a new dynamics of agency for a century now, starting with the progressivisms of John Dewey and Maria Montessori. One of the solutions to the problem of agency in learning has been a 'constructivism' derived from a twentieth century psychological canon in which Piaget's theories dominate. In the context of a command society, however, their emphasis was upon the level and extent of receptivity at a particular age or at a particular cognitive stage. The raw materials of 'intelligence' were biologised, and variations were accounted for in terms of individualised 'capability' and the increments of what was supposed to be innate, universal development. Today, the cognitive sciences do a similar psychological job. Their agenda is to account for the mechanisms of receptivity more than mechanisms in which learned knowledge is genuinely made by conscious agency.

If, however, one follows and extends a line of thought begun by Vygotsky, other possibilities for pedagogy emerge. If knowledge is more a social than a individual psychological construct, if learning is the stuff of active appropriation of the world in a social context, if educability amounts to more than equation of external transmission with individual receptivity, what then are the bases of a theory of pedagogy?

Building on Vygotsky, we propose an epistemologically rather than psychologically grounded theory of learning. By 'epistemological', we mean what we *do* to know. As humans, we might be driven by the mystery of human consciousness, but the critical question is what we do with its drives. The *Learning by Design* approach posits the following 'acts of knowing': we experience (by immersion, making tacit connections in familiar or new contexts); we conceptualise (by abstracting, naming things and developing explicit generalisations); we analyse (inferring and interpreting cause, effect and human interest); we apply (by making an intervention in the world of useable things and meanings, be that intervention predictable and appropriate, or innovative). In every one of these acts of knowing, we learn the world by doing something the world.

The command society could never trust learners to be agents of knowing. Instead, they were the receptors of knowledge—although even this was a conceit of power, as now we understand the perennial role of the reader, the listener or the viewer. We thought they were receptors because this illusion also drove our politics, our workplaces, our public culture and our pedagogy. In hindsight there was resistance as often as there was compliance, even if that resistance was branded subversion, or laziness, or failure at school.

Today, we can remain under no such illusion. The increasingly critical self-governing structures of civil society, the tricks and tropes of the self-managing work team, the user-driven narratives of popular culture, make any such illusions impossible. The children of Nintendo will simply walk up the wall if the pedagogy served up to them by institutionalised schooling does not engage every fibre of their subjectivity. The workplace of the near future will simply be uncompetitive if their workers do not contribute their all, from their creative potential to their ability to maintain relationships of supple reflexivity across the myriad of niched customers and affiliates. The cultures of the near future will ossify if they fail to leave space for the 'readers' to follow their own proclivities and shape their own cultural ends.

The minute one allows so much scope for agency, one finds oneself facing layers upon layer of difference. One discovers actually existing agencies in the massively plural, and not the fabrications and falsifications the command society with its one people one state nationalism, of the regime of mass production and mass consumption, and of the pretensions to cultural homogeneity of the society of mass media and mass culture. The differences are material (class, locale), corporeal (race, gender, sexuality, dis/ability) and circumstantial (culture, life experience, interest, affinity). We can acknowledge these differences, perform neat demographic metrics and, in the name of diversity, build programs to suit group by group. Or we may think we can, at least until we encounter a deeper difference which, in the interstices of these demographics, or even solidly in the middle of each demographic, which defies neat categorisation and prediction. These differences are manifest in the profoundly variable dispositions and sensibilities one encounters from person to person. This is the stuff of the lifeworld, not individualised personality. Such difference is accountable in terms of the infinitely variable and therefore always uniquely complex range of socio-cultural influences that come to bear on any one individual. The more we take agency for real, the more multifarious its manifestations become.

And to face all these agencies one classroom! The solution of the command society was one teacher talking at the middle of the class, one textbook telling one narrative one chapter at a time, one test which told of one way of knowing. The result was assimilation to the middle way, or failure.

Constructivism blandly suggests we bring agency into this picture. It's as if we can give all learners the same dose of agency, commensurate with their stage the template of human developmentalism. But it's not just agency in the abstract that we have to harness. The complexity is such that the simple nostrums of constructivism serve us poorly indeed.

If it is to be at all relevant, the classroom of the reflexive society must allow alternative starting points for learning (what the learner perceives to be worth learning, what engages the particularities of their identity). It must allow for alternative forms of engagement (the varied experiences that need to be brought to bear on the learning, the different conceptual bents of learners, the different analytical perspectives the learner may have on the nature of cause, effect and human interest, and the different settings in which they may apply or enact their knowledge). It must allow for different learning styles (preferences, for instance, for particular emphases in knowledge making and patterns of engagement—experiential, conceptual, analytical or applied). It must allow for different modalities in meaning making, embracing alternative expressive potentials for different learners. And it must allow for alternative pathways and destination points in learning.

There are perils as well as enormous possibilities in a time of intensifying subjectivity and difference. More than reactive, new learning must be creative, itself a force for change rather than merely reflective of change. And the transformations wrought by new learning must simultaneously be systemic, rhetorical and in the everyday practices of teaching and learning.

EDUCATION: WHERE TO NEXT?

The change in the social conditions of learning have thrown down an enormous challenge to educators. One response is to try to do everything but to succeed at nothing—the 'crowded curriculum' or the 'shopping mall' curriculum. Another is the 'anything goes' approach, in which inequality ends up being rationalised as diversity. And still another response is to butt out—education can't deal with issues of identity and personality because they've simply become too big and too hard; it should just stick to its core business. None of these responses is adequate. So, what is to be done?

Education today has a much larger role to play in creating socially productive persons. As a consequence of these changes, a 'new basics' is emerging for education. The old basics of the three Rs must be reconceptualised, in order to reflect contemporary changes to learning. New learning will be *general in its focus,* rather than specialised on the particular needs-of-the-day. It will be about *creating a kind of person*, with kinds of dispositions and orientations to the world, rather than simply commanding a body of knowledge.

These persons will be able to navigate change and diversity, learn-asthey-go, solve problems, collaborate, and be flexible and creative. Finally, new learning will be increasingly *interdisciplinary*, requiring deeper engagement with knowledge in all its complexity and ambiguity. The new basics are about promoting capability sets, reflexive and autonomous learning, collaboration, communication, and broadly knowledgeable persons.

For one thing, technology will become central to all learning, a proposition that is arguably more complex than it first appears. Technologies of digitisation have the potential to transform learning relationships for the better, but this potential does not automatically follow from their use in learning contexts; it needs to be actively harnessed.

Learning today must also be both lifelong and lifewide. The learning of our recent past was something which happened primarily in school and formal institutional settings. The lessons learnt as a young person in these settings were sufficient to prepare you for life. Lifelong learning means that education is no longer located at a discrete time on your life, your one chance to learn, a time when you learn things that are sufficient for life. Specific skills and knowledge learnt today may be obsolete in twenty years time or even five years time, and we will increasingly need to retrain and relearn throughout life. Formal educational institutions will not become less important in this new learning environment, but their role will change dramatically. No longer will they be so self-contained, so neatly separated as an institution.

Future schooling, in other words, will involve new locations, new relationships and new accountability measures. Work must be done not only on improving the 'basics'—reducing staff/student ratios and improving school infrastructure. It must also extend to reconceptualising the school as a place of community building and sociability.

The new lifelong and lifewide frame of reference for learning also changes what formal educational institutions should be teaching. The old learning focused on fixed content knowledge: undeniable facts and theories-to-be-applied, vocational skills and technical information, and these were supposed to last for life. Applied today, this kind of education becomes instantly redundant. In fact, it fosters a rigid way of thinking which will be counterproductive for the workers, citizens and persons of the near future.

The new learning is less about delivering a body of knowledge and skills that will be good for life and more about forming a kind of person. This person will be aware of what they don't know, capable of working out what they need to know and be capable of creating their own knowledge, either autonomously or in collaboration with others.

And, despite the increasing pressure to specialise, the focus of all education should be on underlying and transferable capacities, not only the specifics of an area of specialisation. In fact, in formal education settings there is an increasing need to move towards more general and more comprehensive education, around technology (science, mathematics, applied sciences), commerce (working together sociably), and the humanities (cultural understandings, capacities for intercultural interaction and boundary-crossing).

When it comes to lifelong and lifewide learning, it's not enough to be learning in new settings, such as work-integrated learning, nor to be blurring the boundaries which once separated formal institutionalised education from the rest of life. The transformation also needs to be in the very way knowledge itself is constructed, the content of curriculum, even the purposes of learning. Even within the old institutions of learning, the focus must be on preparing students for lifewide learning, and developing the capacity to learn in other settings.

How do we address the enormous challenges these changes have thrown down for education? It is one thing to talk up education, even to spend more money on it. Yet it is quite another to work out what the 'knowledge society' and 'new economy' is, what the money should be spent on, and even whether an economic focus is sufficient for education. The only thing which is clear, is that spending money on old-style education or narrowly focused skills-for-work education is a mistake, perhaps even a waste of time and money.

Political rhetoric on the growing importance of education is evident on a global scale. Research also indicates that the education sector is growing in most nations; that the expansion of higher education, in particular, has become a key global issue; and that even traditional industries such as manufacturing and agriculture are becoming more knowledge-intensive. These are global trends, despite their greater visibility in advanced industrialised nations.

More fundamentally even than the economic arguments, education is also one of the main ways to deliver on the promise of democracy. Learning promises individuals greater social mobility: more access to material resources through better paid employment; a greater capacity to participate actively in the processes of government; and the personal dexterity that comes with knowing the world. It promises communities improved employment prospects, increased self-determination and extended access to the wider world. The key challenge, however, is to ensure that education fulfils its democratic mission, through quality teaching, a transformative curriculum, and dedicated programs which address inequality. Targeting groups disadvantaged and 'at risk' must be done, not on the basis of moral arguments alone, but also on the basis of the economic and social dangers of allowing individuals and groups to be excluded.

The issue, however, is not merely one of quantity, of simply providing more education for more people. While many nations persevere with education structures founded in the nineteenth century or earlier, the new economy demands different and creative approaches to learning. Schools, at least in their traditional form, may not dominate the educational landscape of the twenty-first century. Neat segregations of the past will crumble; disciplines will merge; givens will give. A radical restructuring of learning is required to prepare students, workers, and citizens of the twenty-first century.

New learning is not a fad. Indeed, nations which resist educational change are arguably imperilling the success and prosperity of their citizens in the long term. Whatever the merits of globalisation, its influence is inexorable and undeniable. Already, globalisation has substantially altered the dominant conditions of work, citizenship and identity. Learning must adapt accordingly. Successful education in the twenty-first century will promote active citizens—secure in their identities, and with a broad range of skills and sensibilities. Above all, successful education will mean embracing the principles of new learning.

CHAPTER 3

The Conditions of Learning

The key questions for this volume, and the *Learning by Design* approach, are what makes for success and failure in learning? And how do we best design the learning experiences that constitute pedagogy, curriculum and education?

Rather than focusing on the native differences between the capabilities of individual learners—theories of pedagogy which emphasise the psychological or the 'innate'—the *Learning by Design* approach instead focuses on the socio-cultural differences between learners. In this chapter, we argue that Belonging and Transformation are fundamental conditions of effective learning. Belonging occurs where formal learning engages with the learner's experiential world (lifeworld). Successful engagement must recognise difference and actively take account of the diverse identities of learners. Transformation occurs when a learner's engagement is such that it broadens their horizons of knowledge and capability. The *Learning by Design* approach seeks to identify the kinds of educational environments in which these conditions of learning are met.

LEARNING, AND LEARNING 'BY DESIGN'

The starting point for our theory of learning is that people learn naturally—they learn from living, growing and having experiences. This is called informal learning (everyday learning). Schooling is about designing experiences for people to learn. This is called formal learning (learning by design). The best of formal learning accounts for and integrates informal learning into its patterns and routines.

Humans are born with an innate capacity to learn, and over the span of a lifetime learning never stops. Learning simply happens as people engage with each other, interact with the natural world and move about in the world they have built. Indeed, one of the things that makes us distinctively human is our enormous capacity to learn. It is in our nature to learn, education or no education, curriculum or no curriculum, pedagogy or no pedagogy.

Education is the conscious nurturing of learning in a community which has been designed primarily for that purpose. Within education, curriculum is a consciously designed framework for learning a body of knowledge, be that a discipline or a coherent set of social competencies or capacities. And within curriculum, pedagogy is the conscious application of knowledge processes to the task of learning.

The relationship between learning and education can be clarified by the distinction that is often made between formal and informal learning. We will propose this dichotomy for the moment, although we will want to soften the edges of its sharp dualism a little later in the argument. The distinction, however, might be framed in the following way:

Table 3.1: Informal versus Formal Learning

FORMAL LEARNING	INFORMAL LEARNING
• Deliberate: conscious, systematic and explicit. • Efficient: structured and goal oriented. • Exophoric: for and about the 'outside world'. • Analytical: abstracting, generalising, supra-contextual, transferable.	• Amorphous: haphazard and tacit. • Unorganised: incidental, accidental, roundabout. • Endogenous: embedded in the lifeworld, and so much so that it is often all-but invisible. • Organic: contextual, situational.

Given the growing depth of contextual diversity (communities of practice, personal and cultural identities) and given the quickening pace of technological and social change, the balance of relevant learning is shifting into the informal domain. For instance, the technologies of today's workplaces have changed to rapidly in recent years that few of the skills required for their use could have been learnt in formal educational settings.

This immediately produces a crisis of relevance for the formal domain, for the profession of educators, in fact. Jim Gee, one of the international research team on 'Multiliteracies' project, asks the provocative question of why learners who hate school (from all socioeconomic backgrounds) will spend 50-100 hours playing what is in fact a highly intellectually demanding a video game? He analyses the dynamics of a number of games, from the more benign 'civilisation' simulations to the most aggressive of 'first person shooter' games. Common to all, he concludes, is an understanding of the nature of learning more sophisticated than most formal education settings. This entails: learning which is highly active; learning that recruits, challenges and morphs identity; learning in which navigation paths are made by the player to the extent that the learner becomes an insider and producer, not just 'consumer'; learning which is multimodal, requiring the simultaneous or alternative manipulation of image, text, number, icon, artefact, space and sound; learning which is intrinsically critical as the player looks for deception around every corner or even attempts to outwit the game by breaking its rules; learning which is staged, where mastery by levels involves a cycle of introducing challenging new skills followed by practice which makes these automatic and reflexive; learning which encourages risk in an environment of safety where real-world consequences are eliminated or reduced; and learning which encourages the development of metaknowledge because you get better at the game as you come to appreciate its design principles. Conventional classrooms, Gee concludes, are often not particularly good at any of these very effective pedagogical moves (Gee, 2003). Nevertheless, the general capacities engendered by the games are eminently transferable to the world of the new media and technologies (websites, computer program, a general facility with electronic technologies), and much more so than the kind of literacy and numeracy still taught in schools.

Video games are the stuff of sophisticated learning, to be sure, and this is learning quintessentially in the informal domain. More and more of our skills, capacities and knowledge are being acquired from informal learning settings such as this—interpersonal and cultural as well as technical knowledge.

Indeed, today we are facing a practical crisis in the domain of formal learning. More is being learnt in the domain of informal learning, and learners seem to be finding that domain more relevant and more engaging. We are reaching the realisation that much is wanting in traditional, formal education. Take, for instance the tricks and tropes of the discourse of formal learning, such as answering the question the way the teacher wants by guessing what's in their head, or techniques for answering multiple choice questions, or 'being good at exams'. These habitually open opportunities for some kinds of people and close them for others (Bernstein, 1971), and which neglect the range of human 'intelligences' (Gardner, 2002) which can fruitfully be brought to bear on a learning situation. Or the kinds of limited instrumental rationality and naive positivism that surround the texts and disciplinary discourses of traditional schooled knowledge. And take, too, the epistemological ground of book learning and institutionalised education in the opening moments of modernity (Cope & Kalantzis, 2004b; Eisenstein, 1979; Ong, 1958, 1982) as a counterpoint to the potentials of digital text (Cope & Kalantzis, 2004b).

The formal/informal dichotomy is indeed a useful one, capturing as it does these critical aspects of the epochal shift that we have been arguing is underway in education. It is a dichotomy, however, whose edges need to be softened. Rather than considering formal learning to be separate from and outside of informal learning, we would like to propose a slightly different configuration which sees formal and informal learning more as overlapping than as separate or even opposed domains.

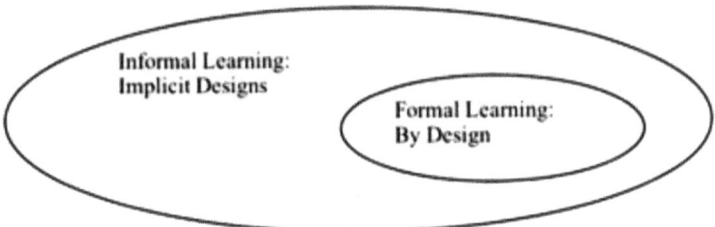

In what we have called the 'new learning', formal learning needs to be consciously contextualised in its informal setting. In practical terms, this means that as well as introducing the facts and theories of traditional learning (the conceptualising bias of traditional pedagogy), formal learning needs to engage with the learner's experiential world, and apply what is learnt in that world. The domains of formal and informal learning need to be brought together more effectively in order to create the more powerful and effective learning required in our contemporary world.

However, as much as we might wish to contextualise formal learning in the broader setting of informal learning, and even integrate the two so they complement each other, there is, an important distinction which needs to be maintained between the two. Informal learning occurs without conscious pedagogical design. Formal learning is learning by design. In the knowledge society, the role of formal learning is likely to become more significant, even if its sites and methodologies now stretch well beyond the walls of the conventional classroom—workplace training, elearning, mentoring programs and the like.

The key defining feature of formal learning is the nature of its 'design'. There is a nice ambiguity in the word 'design', one that we have dwelt upon before in the 'Multiliteracies' research (Cope & Kalantzis, 2000b; Kalantzis & Cope, 2001b; New London Group, 1996). Design can denote morphology or the sense of invisible inner structures or inherent relationships of cause and effect. There is no imperative that such designs have been consciously fabricated. Do the makers of the video games have a clearly understood and articulated theory of pedagogy when they make them? They may, but they need not, and they probably don't. The world of everyday learning is the world of this kind of design. But designed it nevertheless is, if only from the point of view of the salutary *ex post facto* question 'how did this learning occur'?

However, there's another important sense of the word 'design', and that is the act of fabrication, both mental and physical. Learning 'by design' denotes the agency, premeditation that is characteristic of education. These designs are the stuff of the characteristically self-conscious pedagogical moves, teaching frameworks and organisational forms of education as we currently understand it. They are also the stuff of curriculum artefacts—written lesson and program plans, textbooks, tests, school buildings, elearning systems and the like.

In everyday parlance, we call the domain of formal learning 'education'. To be sure, education is built on the very ordinary (and extraordinary) fact of learning that is at the core of our natures. In its most powerfully effective moments, it builds upon and integrates itself with the learners' experiences in the domain of informal learning. Education, however, is different from everyday, informal learning insofar as it is deliberate—learning is addressed in a relatively conscious, systematic and explicit way. It sets out to be efficient—as the end is learning, the processes of engagement are designed to meet that end via as direct a route as possible. And its reference point is primarily exophoric—although it is absolutely in the world, in an important sense education is not of the world. Education is not an end in itself. It is for use in the 'outside world' and refers to the 'outside world', positioning itself as externally representative and reflective of the world.

In each of these respects, everyday learning is different from education. Everyday learning happens in ways that are relatively unconscious, haphazard and tacit. It happens in ways that are often circuitous, incidental, fortuitous or even accidental. Everyday learning is deeply embedded within the world. The distinguishing feature of education (and curriculum and pedagogy) is that learning happens by design.

LEARNER DIVERSITY

In the *Learning by Design* approach we take native intelligence as a given. We are not so interested in differences in native capacity between one individual and the next because it is impossible, almost by definition, to do anything much about our natures. Socio-cultural differences, by contrast, are things we can address. Besides, inherent differences between our native capacities are hard to unscramble from cultural differences. Our task as educators, then, is to do what we can with those parts of the jumble of social and natural influences where we can have some impact..

So what are the cultural conditions of learning? For the moment we will speak of learning in general, whether it is embedded in everyday life or whether it is learning by design. The form and extent of learning is determined by the conditions in which it occurs. And some conditions are more favourable than others.

Two conditions, particularly, impact on learning: first, whether a person's identity, subjectivity or sense of themselves has been engaged; and second, whether the engagement is such that it can broaden their horizons of knowledge and capability. By 'engagement', we mean connect with, interest, enthuse, even influence. Unlike innate capacity, these conditions are things we can do something about. When learning happens by design, we can, in other words, create conditions which improve the chances of engagement. And creating the optimal conditions for active engagement enhances pedagogical, curriculum and educational outcomes.

BELONGING

> Learning Condition 1: BELONGING—A learner will not learn unless they 'belong' in that learning.

In order to learn, the learner has to feel that the learning is for them. They have to feel they belong in the content; they have to feel they belong in the community or learning setting; they have to feel at home with that kind of learning or way of getting to know the world. In other words, the learner's subjectivity and identity must be engaged.

Learners have to be motivated by what they are learning. They need to be involved as interested parties. They have to feel as if that learning is for them. The learning has to include them. And if they are learning in a formal educational setting such as a school, they also have to feel a sense of belonging in that social and institutional context. The more a learner 'belongs' in all these senses, the more they are likely to learn.

Belonging to learning is founded on three things: the learning ways, the learning content and the learning community. From the learner's point of view, the 'learning ways' question is: 'Do I feel comfortable with this way of knowing the world? (Or, do I feel at home with this style of thinking or way of acting? Do I feel it can work for me? Do I know it can help me know or do more?) The learning content question is: 'Do I already know enough about an area of content to want to know more?'. ('Do I already know so much about something that I naturally want to know more'. Or 'Do has my appetite been sufficiently whetted by what little I already know to want to know more?') And the learning community question is: 'Do I feel at home in this learning environment? (Or 'Do I feel sufficiently motivated to take on the learning tasks required by this environment as my own and feel safe enough in this space to be able to risk moving into new domains of knowledge and action?')

The learner's subjectivity, however, is always particular, and it is this particularity which must be engaged. Here, the concept of 'difference' is helpful because it highlights some dimensions of learner particularity.

Our natures may be taken as a departure point for understanding our differences. Sex, race and (dis)ability supply a biological or corporeal starting point for understanding the basis of our differences. But this is only the beginning. Difference is also self-identified and socially ascribed. This is when the cultural accretions to our natures, and our social relations of difference, become so very manifest and critical. Dimensions of difference include: ethnicity/race (and indigenous, immigrant, minority and colonising positions), gender (and sexual orientation), socio-economic group, locale (global and regional) and (dis)ability.

By contrast with the descriptive semantics of difference, 'diversity' is the stuff of normative agendas, where difference becomes the basis of a program of action. Difference the insistent reality becomes diversity the agent of change. We live with the fact difference. We do diversity. Many a historical and contemporary response to difference, however, is hardly worthy of the name 'diversity'—racism, discrimination and systematic inequity. As a normative agenda and social program, diversity also stands in contradistinction to systems of exclusion, separation or assimilation.

However, difference can sometimes be a less than helpful concept and diversity programs counterproductive, and particularly so when stereotypical generalisations are made on the basis of gross demographics—about Chinese learning styles, boys' communication styles or the conditions of socio-economic disadvantage, for instance.

The gross demographics of difference, of course, do capture powerful realities—the dimensions of gender, age, ethnicity/race, locale, socio-economic group and (dis)ability. They stare you in the face, as does the difference these demographic realities so predicably seem to make when it comes to educational and social outcomes. But they are not in themselves factors which affect learning. We will call these gross demographics 'Difference 1'.

Behind the gross demographics lie human attributes that are the underlying substance of these differences—experiences, interests, orientations to the world, values, dispositions, sensibilities, communication styles, interpersonal styles, thinking styles and the like. This is the raw material of identity, the stuff of the 'lifeworld' (Cope & Kalantzis, 2000a; Husserl, 1970). This we will call these underlying attributes 'Difference 2'.

The lifeworld of Difference 2 is the everyday lived experience that learners bring to a learning setting. It is the person they have become through the influence of their family, their local community, their friends, their peers and the particular slices of popular or domestic culture with which they identify. It is a place where the learner's everyday understandings and actions seem to work, and so much so that their active participation is almost instinctive—something that requires not too much conscious or reflective thought. The lifeworld is what has shaped them. It is what has made them who they are. It is what they like and unreflectively dislike. It is who they are.

The underlying attributes of lifeworld difference form the basis of identity and subjectivity. These attributes are the fundamental bases of a learner's sense of belonging in an everyday or formal learning setting, and their levels of engagement.

From the point of view of these underlying differences, the gross demographics of Difference 1 are as often deeply deceptive as they are immediately helpful. Measure any one underlying attribute of lifeworld difference and you will find greater internal difference within a demographically defined group than the average difference between groups. Look at the differences between girls and boys within a particular ethnically defined group, or within different age groupings. It is not long before the internal differences between members of that group are so great as to indicate that the ethnic descriptor is far too simple a variable. Or take gender differences. Once again, ethnic and age variations mean that gender dynamics may be played out in entirely different ways.

Difference 1 is a powerfully revealing 'first take' on learner differences. Difference 2, however, is where the realities of difference truly lie. And on the measure of Difference 2, the extent of internal difference within any group defined in terms of Difference 1 attributes, will be greater than the measure of average difference between Difference 1 groups.

Table 3.2: Lenses on Difference

Difference 1: Gross Demographics	Difference 2: Underlying Lifeworld Attributes
• Gender • Age • Ethnicity/Race • Locale • Socio-economic group • (Dis)ability	• Experience • Interests and orientations • Values • Dispositions and sensibilities • Communication and interpersonal styles • Thinking styles ... and the like.

There's also the question of which differences are individual and which are shared across groups. The identity of any individual is always multilayered. Even when we consider it from the point of view of Difference 1, every individual embodies a unique mix of gender, age, ethnicity/race, locale, socio-economic, (dis)ability dimensions, and within any one of these dimensions, quite specific and often complex and multiple configurations emerge (the Italian-Australian with one Jewish grandparent, who speaks limited Italian with two grandparents, to take an ethnicity example). An individual partially shares gross demographics and underlying attributes with a wide and overlapping range of groups, but the particular mix of group attributes is invariably unique—and that's what makes the person an individual (Cope & Kalantzis, 1997b).

Unless learning engages with the specifics of individual and group identities, it will not be productive. The dilemma for teaching is that, no matter how much filtering is done by the Difference 1 variables of age, locality, subject choice or ability level, groups of learners invariably remain different. Education, then, needs to start with a recognition of difference. The challenge, then, is how do we engage all learners in classrooms of difference? In other words, how do we do diversity?

For behind the demographics are real people, who have always-already learned and whose range of learning possibilities are both boundless and circumscribed by what they have learned already and what they have become through that learning. Here we encounter the raw material difference—human experiences, dispositions, sensibilities, epistemologies and world views. These are always far more varied and complex than the immediate sight of the demographics would suggest. Learning succeeds or fails to the extent that it engages the varied subjectivities of learners. Engagement produces opportunity, equity and participation. Failure to engage produces failure, disadvantage and inequality.

THE DYNAMICS OF DIFFERENCE

- We are creatures of subjectivity, identity and motivation—intuitive, instinctive and deeply felt.
- The 'lifeworld' is the ground of our existence, the already-learned and continuously-being-learnt experience of everyday life.
- The lifeworld is deeply permeated by difference; in fact, we live in a myriad of diverging and interacting lifeworlds.
- The individual is uniquely formed at the intersection of many group identities; they are a unique concatenation of many group identities, and live in and through multiple or multilayered identities.

In all its difference, the lifeworld is the first site of learning, not only in the chronological sense (babies and young children) but in the extended sense that it is always prior to, or the foundation of, any education in the formal sense, or learning by design. It is from the start and always remains a place of deep learning, albeit in primarily amorphous, unorganised and endogenous ways. The lifeworld is the ground of all learning, including the secondary processes of learning by design.

And as learning occurs through engagement, engagement must be with learners in their lifeworld reality, and that reality is marked by extraordinary difference.

TRANSFORMATION

> Learning Condition 2: TRANSFORMATION—Learning takes the learner into new places, and along the this journey, acts as an agent of personal and cultural transformation.

Learning is not simply about recognising and affirming difference. There's much more to effective education-for-diversity than that. A conservative multicultural approach goes no further than recognising and affirming cultural difference. This is the preservationist or museum approach to diversity: recognise difference, then patronise it.

Recognising difference is not enough. Staying where you are is not learning. Learning is a journey away from the learner's comfort zone, away from the narrowness and limitations of the lifeworld. As much as learning needs to affirm identity and create a sense of belonging, it is also a process of travelling away from the familiar, everyday world of experience. This journey is one of personal and cultural transformation.

The learning journey takes two paths, along two axes. Both of these journeys are away from who you are, and sometimes in unsettling ways.

The first is a depth axis, or learning what's not immediately or intuitively obvious from the perspective of everyday lived experience. This may challenge everyday assumptions—that the earth is flat, for instance, or that certain unreflectively held values such as racism or sexism are socially sustainable.

The second is a breadth axis, in which you travel to unfamiliar places in the mind and perhaps also in reality. This is a kind of cross-cultural journey, and deeply so because it involves a genuine crossover. The place to which you travel becomes part of you, part of your repertoire of life experience, and in fact another aspect of your identity. These journeys can be understood as narratives of sorts.

They are life narratives of self-transformation and growth. But they are only that when the learner is safely and securely in the centre of the story. Retrospectively, the learning story runs like this: who the learner was, where they went, the things they encountered, and what, as a consequence of their learning, they have (knowingly) become. In this story, learning is the key thread in what turns out to be a kind of cultural journey.

If the lifeworld is the place of belonging, the place from which learners depart, the new world of knowledge might be called the 'transcendental'—a place above and beyond the commonsense assumptions of the lifeworld (Cope & Kalantzis, 2000a; Husserl, 1970).

The learning journey from the lifeworld to the transcendental takes the learner into realms that are necessarily unfamiliar but never too unsettling in their unfamiliarity. Education will not result in learning if the landscape is unseeable, unthinkable, incomprehensible, unintelligible, unachievable. Learners must travel into cultural territories which take them outside of their comfort zones, but not so far in any one stage of the journey that the journey takes the learner into places that are so strange as to be alienating. The journey will involve risk, but the risk will only be productive if the learning environment feels safe, if it is a place where the learner feels they still belong even if only as a traveller. The learner needs scaffolds— learning prompts or support—which reassure them as they face of the risks of alienation and failure in the realm of the unfamiliar. Vygotsky calls this the 'zone of proximal development' (L. Vygotsky, 1962; L. S. Vygotsky, 1978).

Ideal learning settings scaffold or provide support as learners move into a zone of partial but as yet incomplete intelligibility. With all the motivation in the world to learn Chinese, there's no point for a beginner to start in the third year of the program, or for an aspiring mathematician to try to learn calculus before arithmetic. This brings us back to Learning Condition 1, the need to engage with identity. Learning Condition 2 now tells us that this engagement has to be achievable as well as aspirational. It also brings us back to the necessity to engage with the complex particularity of different learners, emphasising the need to take a journey into strange places which genuinely adds something new to that particularity. For every student in every learning setting, the comfort zone of proximal development is going to be different. Herein lies the key dilemma of the whole educational project.

Those who succeed best in a particular learning setting will do so because that setting is just right for people like them. The level of risk in moving into a new area of learning is one they are comfortable to take. Those who do not succeed so well, do so when the distance between who they are and what they are learning is too great, when they don't feel they belong in the content or the setting and when the risks of failure outweigh the benefits of engagement.

All too often, however, learning seems to gel for some kinds of students (such as the 'mainstream' learner, attune to dominant educational values) and not for other kinds. The challenge for educators—learning designers—is how to make learning gel for all students.

And why do we need to learn? What is the role of formal, institutionalised learning? Why is the educational project so important to us? Why do we bother with learning by design when the lifeworld is already so profoundly a site of learning? The answers to these questions are as much practical as they are idealistic. It is because learning can transport you into new lifeworlds. Learning provides access to material resources in the form of better paid employment; it affords an enhanced capacity to participate in civic life; it promises personal growth. Upon education rests one of the key promises of modern societies. The world is tragically unequal, and for practical purposes most people regard this inequality as inevitable. Education, however, assures us of equity. Inequality is not unjust because education affords all people equivalent chances.

There is no equity in education unless the two learning conditions are met. Learning has to engage with students' identities, and these identities must be recognised as different. It must take people into unfamiliar places, and these places have to be unfamiliar in just the right measure. That measure can only be based on precisely who the learner is—all the lifeworld attributes combine to define who they are as an individual. Success is achieved when the measure of distance is appropriate to the learner. Failure occurs when the measure of distance is inappropriate to the learner. If the distance between the lifeworld and the learning is too great, the educational effort will be misdirected, compromised or ineffectual. And if there is no distance between the lifeworld and what it to be learnt, learning will be diminished or illusionary. The distance between the lifeworld and what is to be learnt must be productive.

Education that Works

Belonging is a generalised condition of learning, whether learning is endogenous to the everyday lifeworld, or whether it is by conscious design. In the case of the former, belonging usually comes easily; in the case of learning by design, belonging needs to be a conscious endeavour. Spaces of formal learning are strangely not of the world, and for some learners, they prove just too strange.

Transformation, on the other hand, is not the exclusive preserve of education. It may occur in the lifeworld, when for instance surroundings radically change. Migration is an case in point, as are other willed or unwilled, traumatic or relief-giving changes in lifeworld circumstances. Transformational learning in these cases is incidental to circumstantial change.

Education, however, uniquely makes transformation a deliberate project. Transformative learning is the primary purpose of education, or learning by design.

Conditions of Learning

Condition 1: BELONGING—effective learning engages the learner's identity. It builds on the learner's knowledge, experiences, interests and motivation. In any learning community, there is a broad range of difference, and this is because the everyday lifeworlds from which students come are always varied.

Condition 2: TRANSFORMATION—effective learning takes the learner on a journey into new and unfamiliar terrains. However, for learning to occur, the journey into the unfamiliar needs to stay with a zone of intelligibility and safety. At each step, it needs travel just the right distance from the learner's lifeworld starting point.

CHAPTER 4

Curriculum

Our primary focal points in this volume are the processes of curriculum and pedagogy in institutions of formal learning. Pedagogy is learning by design at the level of coherent and complete units of learning. Curriculum pieces together the units of learning to create bodies of knowledge, disciplines of thinking and domains of practice and action. Curriculum and pedagogy are the subjects of this and the following chapter.

In this chapter, three approaches to curriculum are explored: traditionalist, progressivist and transformative. Whilst sharing elements of the first two types, transformative curriculum can be distinguished in its consciously addressing difference amongst learners, using 'texts' from the learners' own lifeworlds and allowing for a variety of ways of knowing. These knowledge processes are considered in further detail in Chapter 5.

APPROACHES TO CURRICULUM

Curriculum is the overall logistics of learning delivery: content (what's to be learnt), media (the resources being used) and teaching processes (the dynamics of teacher-student interaction).

Various forms of curriculum deal with the differences amongst learners in varied ways—and difference there always is, whether the curriculum chooses to recognise it or not. Following are three models—traditional, progressivist and transformative, seemingly representing a historical progression in the development of modern theories and practices of curriculum. In fact, there are some old ideas in the newer models, and all three models are very much alive and well in the schools of today (Kalantzis & Cope, 1993).

Traditional Curriculum

Traditional curriculum reflects both an era (which came to dominance with the emergence of the industrial or command society and mass, institutionalised education), and an approach to teaching and learning which endures today in some countries, education systems, classrooms or even moments of teaching within a contemporary classroom.

Table 4.2: Traditional Curriculum

	Features	Advantages	Disadvantages
Content	• Factual modes of knowing, memory work, learning by rote. • Theoretical modes of knowing: internalising and Applying abstractions that purport to have universal scientific validity in the natural or social worlds. • Canonical and high cultural knowledge: great literature, great art. • National or forms of language and culture: 'standard' national languages, the histories and identity narratives of the 'mainstream' or dominant group.	• Clarity: right or wrong answers on facts, correct or incorrect application of rules of theories. • Testable. • One-size-fitsall curriculum. • Creation of a common culture (everybody knows the same official language, national story, literary canon, basic scientific truths).	• Abstract, decontextualised knowledge. • Simplistic concept of knowledge: received theories taken as truth, facts taken to be final. • Empirical correctness: are the 'facts' always as clear-cut as their representors purport them to be? Are there ever such straightforwardly right and wrong answers? • Theoretical correctness: what's the use of rules when you haven't internalised their rationale?
Media	• Centralised syllabus specifies detailed content and sequence. • Textbooks follow what's been prescribed in the syllabus. • Standardised, system-wide testing measures individual 'performance' against content and discipline knowledge.	• Simplicity, uniformity. • Easy on teachers, who can follow the syllabus, tell students to work through the textbook and teach to the test. • Consistency from one classroom, school or system to another.	• Devalues teacher professionalism. • Generic: not tailored to local conditions or individual learner needs. • Linear and lockstep: progression lesson by lesson, topic by topic, chapter by chapter. • Fails students whose interests, identities and lifeworld experiences don't 'fit' with the subject matter, tenor and

			assumed ideal learning styles of the curriculum.
Teaching processes	• Didactic pedagogy. • Transmission of Curriculum content knowledge to learner. • The teacher is the initiator and centre of classroom discourse. • Classroom talk pitched at the middle of the class.	• Predictability: students can see where the curriculum is going. • Transparency: Communities can see exactly what's going on in the curriculum, and this is likely to fit comfortably with conventional notions of what learning entails.	• Intellectual rigidity. • The learner is assumed to be an empty vessel, and this creates passive, compliant learners. • Learner expression is restricted to a private audience of one: teacher assessable work.

The equity effect of traditional curriculum is selective inclusion. It works for those whose identities happen to fit with the tenor of the curriculum—those from families who are imbued with the values of institutionalised learning, those who enjoy the very narrow range of thinking capacities measured by traditional tests, those whose identity-narrative seems to be most affirmed by the curriculum content, those most comfortable and capable of picking up the cues in classroom discourse and those who have the time and are provided the encouragement to do homework and to read at home.

This kind of curriculum, in other words, works naturally for a particular 'kind of person' who brings particular type of lifeworld experience to the classroom. The rest are excluded, although the assessment system attempts to blame the learner rather than the curriculum. 'Success' is the learner's personal reward. 'Failure' is the learner's own fault.

In traditional curriculum, the patterns of success and failure between various groups are highly predictable. Lifeworld variations contribute significantly to that predictability.

Take literacy learning, for example. The traditional literacy curriculum naturally favours those learners who come from homes full of books, where people do a lot of reading, and where the power of written texts is self-evident. It favours an attention to detail, such as correct spelling. It rewards speakers of 'standard', 'grammatically correct' forms of the dominant language—they succeed instinctively at school language, and on the everyday basis in their lifeworld experience. It favours those who enjoy and are good at the logical games of traditional language textbooks (such as cloze, matching exercises and comprehension exercises) and who are good at tests— where what is being measured is not literacy itself so much as the capacity and inclination to play a certain style of mind game. It favours those who can engage in the peculiar dialogic form of classroom discourse (Cazden, 2001). It favours, in other words, certain kinds of people defined by the way they engage with language in their lifeworlds (Gee, 1997).

Progressivist Curriculum

Progressivist curriculum is somewhat more attune to difference and diversity, and more inclusive than traditional curriculum. But at a certain point and all-too often, it allows the project of equity to fall by the wayside.

Table 4.3: Progressivist Curriculum

	Features	Advantages	Disadvantages
Content	• Primacy of experiential modes of knowing. • 'Constructivist' pedagogy: learners build their own knowledge and understandings. • Knowledge is built on awareness of the self as a knowledge maker. • Curriculum often draws content drawn from local community life, relevant to student experience.	• Engages students as active learners. • Metacognition and selfawareness sharpens knowing and learning. • Attempts to recognise and Honour differences in Background amongst learners. All cultures relative and equal.	• Ambiguities and inconsistencies arise in defining the content and scope of learning. • Anything goes? What is the truth? Or, at the very least, what is more and less valid knowledge drawn from experience? • Not necessarily critical: immersion in experience can still involve subtly assumed answers and correct ways of seeing and interpreting the world. • Sometimes slips into the patronising, conservationist view of cultural differences: the recognition is no more than superficial.

Media	• Broad systems guidelines on learning outcomes. • School-based curriculum development. • Range of resources upon which to draw: library, Internet, community, student experience. • Teacher assessment of learner development, based on professional judgment.	• Teacher engagement: valuing teacher judgement and professionalism. • Possibility of creating learning experiences relevant to local conditions. • Possibility of creating learning experiences relevant to individual learner needs and interests.	• A lot of work; in fact, an impossible amount if it's to be relevant to individual students. • Lack of focus: the 'shopping mall curriculum' becomes the crowded curriculum. • Resources: the 'photocopier curriculum' which often means falling back on traditional textbook content. • Reinventing the wheel: locally produced learning materials almost invariably never see the light of day beyond a particular teacher in a particular classroom. • Spaghetti and polka diversity: patronising and tokenistic recognition of differences in gross demographics. • Lack of transparency and predictability for learners and communities.
Teaching processes	• Focus on curriculum processes rather than curriculum content. • Learnercentred pedagogy.	• Addressing individual learner needs. • Recognising differences in student backgrounds, needs and interests. • Inspiring and building upon learner motivation.	• Not necessarily transformative: students not being sufficiently challenged; going nowhere significantly beyond where they already are. • Subtle or hidden monocultural assumptions about

			ideal ways of learning and what constitutes a constructive contribution

The equity effect of progressivist curriculum, by and large, is selective assimilation. There may well be a superficial honouring of different lifeworlds, perhaps by employing a 'spaghetti and polka' approach which highlights differences, for instance in the form of folkloric colour (Cope & Kalantzis, 1998). Notwithstanding the multicultural days and the special curriculum units on 'other cultures', the literacy and numeracy 'basics' stay as they always were. As does the pattern of academic results. If as a learner you are willing and able take that particular journey, if you can internalise the underlying motivations that will make the core disciplinary curriculum work for you—if you are willing and able to become one of these 'kinds of person'—you may be included into the culture of the curriculum and your results will reflect this. You can come in, and make yourself over in the image of the curriculum, so long as the fundamental framework of seeing, valuing and knowing implicit in that curriculum remains singular and undisturbed. Of course, not to dismiss this kind of progressivism out of hand, the superficial honouring of lifeworld difference may have been just enough to make you feel sufficiently at home to even to embark on this journey. And the result of assimilation may be access, which is undoubtedly a better outcome than exclusion.

What's the nature of the curriculum journey into progressivism? To what will you be assimilating? What kind of person will you become if you manage to make the journey? Underlying 'constructivist' pedagogy, for instance, is a set of deep cultural assumptions. Constructivism assumes a learning style that embodies a particular kind of subjectivity. The self-aware individual is the reference point of all knowledge making and the knowledge that emerges is of their personal making—a matter of perspective, a product of problem solving, circumstantial and subjectively framed rather than universally given and self-evidently true.

Using a constructivist pedagogy, try teaching the Koran in the way devout Muslims believe it should, or elementary particle physics in a such a way that your experience validates the theory. In both these cases, constructivism is destined to fail you. Try using a constructivist pedagogy to teach communities whose entry point into knowledge is not personal opinion and problem solving, but rather lifeworld settings in which teachers and texts are regarded as authoritative. Again, constructivism is destined to fail you. Some kinds of learners may feel more comfortable with facts, theories and the clarity of authoritative texts and received knowledge, at the very least as a starting point before they introduce their own opinion or attempt to solve problems.

After progressivism's invitation to engage—seemingly with such open arms—this is the subtlest of exclusions. The curriculum has invited you in, but only on its own terms. Ostensibly, this is an classroom of open engagement, but if the rules of engagement don't click, you won't do well here. To succeed you need to get with the epistemological strength of the lifeworlds closest to the culture of curriculum, to think in a particular way, act in a particular way, communicate in a particular way and ultimately know in a particular way. The key to success, in fact, is to leave your old lifeworld self at the door.

Take literacy learning again. 'Constructivist' approaches to learning, of which 'whole language' and 'process writing' are well-established examples, foster active learning based on engagement with texts. The emphasis is on immersion in experience. Do a lot of reading and writing and do it regularly, then in much the same way that a baby learns oral language, you will learn to read and write. Despite extending this powerful invitation to learners to engage, the reality often does not match the rhetoric. Process writing, for instance, is based on some culturally specific assumptions about communication which gives primacy to individual expressive voice, an orientation to meaning-making which in turn can be tracked back to the conventional Western notion of the author. This is good for children who are used to talking about themselves, who come from child-centred domestic settings and from lifeworlds in which the voice of the opinionated self is granted primacy. It is not so good for children whose lifeworlds prioritise family, community and the authority of elders. Similarly, progressivist reading pedagogy seems to work best for those who intuitively understand the logic and power of literacy, for middle class children from print-immersed households who unreflectively 'know' the literacy game. It misses the mark when attempting to engage outsiders to the culture of literacy. Ironically, in some respects outsiders to the mainstream literacy game may find the traditional formal literacy curriculum preferable because it is explicit about rules—what a particular unfamiliar but powerful form of language does, and the generic devices it uses to achieve its ends (Cope & Kalantzis, 1993b; Delpit, 1988).

Transformative Curriculum

Transformative curriculum attempts to cater more consciously, directly and systematically to difference amongst learners. Is rationale is simple: to improve equity outcomes, and in so doing work to ensure that one of society's most basic promises is not downright false. Its approach is to avoid dismissing out of hand either traditional or progressivist curriculum. Rather it attempts to supplement these powerful and enduring curriculum forms, building on their strengths and ameliorating their weaknesses.

Table 4.4: Transformative Curriculum

	Features	Advantages	Disadvantages
Content	• Appropriate mix of knowledge processes: experiencing, conceptualising, analysing, applying. • 'Transformative' pedagogy: starts with learner lifeworld experience, but takes the learner to new and unfamiliar places and in so doing realises personal and cultural transformation; a 're-constructivist' pedagogy. • A focus on core concepts and powerful ways of thinking, along with a respect for the empirical world. • …but this always from the starting point of learner subjectivity; transformation must affirm the journey and its lifeworld starting point.	• Engages with learner subjectivity. • A focus on learner sensibilities, capabilities, competence. • Encourages multiple ways of seeing, knowing and thinking. • Transcendental: deepening the knowledge brought from the lifeworld by taking journeys of knowing along the depth axis (noncommonsense underlying realities in everyday life) and breadth axis (unfamiliar places, cultures, circumstances, universes). • Pedagogical familiarity: recruits aspects of both traditional and progressivist pedagogy; supplements rather than negates current teaching practices.	• The challenge of getting the mix right for particular learners in particular learning settings. • The challenge of pushing learners out of their comfort zones—risk must be in just the right measure, and remain with a zone of safety. • Requires high levels of interpersonal intelligence on the part of teachers, and will succeed or fail on that. • The challenge of working from learner subjectivity whilst maintaining academic discipline, intellectual rigour and meeting broader educational goals.
Media	• Educational knowledge management: teacher documentation of learning processes. • A layered systems approach, with teacher curriculum	• Teachers and learners as the source of curriculum content. • Changing the source of knowledge and the basis of	• Won't work without pedagogical scaffolds and top-down commitment from educational systems commitment. • New skills: documenting

	developers at the core, and broader structures of departments, schools, regions and systems assuming the role of a quality filter: commissioning, advising, editing refereeing and showcasing roles. • Publication level 1: banks of locally created, tried and tested learning materials for teacher and learner access within a learning community. • Publication level 2: building a bank of learning materials that can be shared between schools, across an education system and to the wider world.	authoritativeness. • Capturing and sharing the phenomenal amount of excellent curriculum content that is created at the level of the learning institution, by individual teachers and groups of teachers in team taught subjects and programs. • Not reinventing the wheel—showcasing excellent practices and making those experiences widely accessible. • Student-oriented material provides flexibility and choice for learners; creating the possibility of autonomous learning and collaborative learning with peers, as well as scaffolded learning involving the teacher.	curriculum is not the same as doing curriculum. • More work than just teaching a lesson, but in the longer run less work as teachers select and adapt other teachers' work rather then reinvent the wheel. • At least minimal computer access required, Internet connectivity and electronic publishing tools.

Teaching Processes	• Balanced focus on curriculum process and curriculum content. • Collaborative learning: learner-learner, learner-teacher; good learners are good teachers and vice versa; coconstruction of knowledge. • Changing the audience: student meanings shared across a learning community. • Transparency and accountability in access to curriculum content and student work.	• Peer-to-peer learning: learners work collaboratively and publish their work, and this in turn also becomes a part of the curriculum content. • Non-linear learning and a range of navigation paths: students can work through units of work according to their own interest, at their own pace, and focusing on those learning processes within those units of work which best suit their needs and interests. • Accessibility: learning at any time and in any place.	• A dramatic change in classroom ecology. • The student as 'citizen': moving out of protection of the four walls of the classroom; duty of care more challenging. • Quality is harder to ensure and outcomes harder to define, particularly in terms of traditional discipline standards. • Measurement challenges: what constitutes effective learning? • Accountability to parents, school governance structures and the broader community becomes more complex.

The intended equity effect of transformative curriculum is to achieve comparable learning outcomes without prejudice to difference. Indeed, successful negotiation of difference is a fundamental basis for equity. You don't have to be the same to be equal. And lifeworld difference should not make a difference to outcomes.

The effect of traditional curriculum is selective inclusion. The effect of progressivist curriculum is selective assimilation. The intended effect of transformative curriculum is pluralism—a community of productive diversity. Diversity agendas are to be found in all three curriculum forms, sometimes articulated and sometimes not, sometimes promised but sometimes making false promises. Diversity agendas, however, are always there, and at the very least can be discovered in inarticulate action and unmentionable discriminatory effect.

Transformative curriculum embodies a systematic diversity agenda whose intended outcome is equity. It starts with the premise that the lifeworld experiences learners bring to the educational setting are inherently and profoundly different from each other. To learn effectively, any learner has to have a sense of belonging in that curriculum—belonging by participating in ways of knowing which are valued, belonging in the content of the curriculum and belonging in the social environment of the school. At the level of social environment, an educational setting needs to be welcoming and inclusive. At the level of curriculum content, one of the key learning resources needs to be the learner's own knowledge and capabilities. And at the epistemological level, the curriculum needs to be able to recognise and build upon a variety of ways of knowing, however these might be conceptualised, in terms of 'learning styles' or 'multiple intelligences'(Gardner, 2002), for instance.

Furthermore, learning-as-transformation—the journey into new and unfamiliar places that transforms the learner—need not favour a single lifeworld destination. Transformative curriculum is not a matter of 'development', in which you leave your old, less developed self behind. For outsiders, this is a typical trajectory both in traditional and progressivist curricula, by medium of which successful learners find that, in order to succeed, they have to leave lifeworlds which have less of a grip on power in order to move into lifeworlds that do. Rather, it is a matter of recognition of the resilience and vibrancy of marginalised as well as dominant lifeworlds, and setting out to extend one's repertoire without having to deny one's identity or forsake one's roots. This not so much a process of development by means of which the learner travels in one, pre-ordained direction. Rather, it conceives learning as a process of expanding horizons, by which means learners extend their range of knowing and being, but not necessarily in order to leave their old selves behind or to reject original lifeworlds.

Curriculum in Practice

What might transformative curriculum mean in practice? Take literacy learning once again. Here we will use the example of the Multiliteracies pedagogy (Cope & Kalantzis, 2000b; Kalantzis & Cope, 2001b; New London Group, 1996), slightly reframing its terminology to be consistent with the framework of *Learning by Design* introduced later in this volume. Belonging to the content of curriculum involves experiential learning processes which bring into the classroom the texts of learner lifeworld experience. This might be the multimodal texts of popular music, the Internet, television or adolescent magazines. Invariably these texts will reflect highly particularised subcultures, genre, fad or fetish to which a student or a group of students is attached—heavy metal as compared to hip hop, or girls' as compared to boys' magazines. These texts may be strangers to the traditional English curriculum, but at the very least they are familiar to students, and manifestly 'real' to them. They are the texts of lifeworld engagement.

Alternatively or alongside this, and still deploying experiential processes, a teacher might immerse students in new texts that have at least partial purchase on their experiences and interests. This takes learners on a cultural journey away from their lifeworlds, but will only work when the distance, one step at a time, is not so great as to lose them—adolescent romance in girls magazines, for instance, leading into the Romeo and Juliet movie, and some time later to Shakespeare's text.

Conceptual learning processes take learners away from the lifeworld in another way, by unpacking the design features of the texts, otherwise simply experienced in relatively unreflective ways. By the process of abstraction, a concept ('table', generalisable as form and function) takes you one step away from the concrete experience (this table). And a theory, which strings together a number of concepts, creates potentially generalisable knowledge beyond the experential particularities of cause and effect. Critical analytical learning processes lead learners to ask what texts are for and whose purposes they serve. What is the agenda behind a text, action or phenomenon? The answer to this question may not be immediately visible at a first, experiential glance. And transformative or applied learning processes invite learners to create a text of their own, an expression in part of their lifeworld experience but also displaying evidence of a learning journey which has extended their literacy repertoire—writing lyrics for a song in their favourite genre, writing a romance based on their own interpretation of adolescence, or imaginatively transferring what they know and have learnt into a new domain by creating a new and hybrid text. Their actual destinations may be different, but the distance they have travelled will be palpable.

In a sense, this is no more than the ordinary stuff of good teaching. But this ordinary stuff is magically extraordinary when, for any student, the two conditions of learning are met. First, the learner has, notwithstanding the uniqueness of their identity, belonged in the curriculum. They have been part the curriculum, and the curriculum has been part of them. Second, the learning has taken them into a new and unfamiliar place, changed their view of the world, and changed them in some incremental way into a person whose horizons have been broadened. Productive learning is both purposeful and transformative.

Table 4.5: Educational Designs: Past:Present, Future

	Traditional	Progressivist	Transformative
Pedagogy	• Content focus. • Facts, nonnegotiable truths. • Learning by rote. • Teacher dominated classrooms; authoritarian. • Generic, universalistic: differences ignored.	• Process focus. • Inquiry and experiential learning; 'natural' and 'authentic' learning. • Studentcentred classrooms: teachers as facilitators. • Difference recognised, if often in superficial and tokenistic ways.	• Teaching and learning as dialogue. • Pedagogical variations: experiencing, conceptualising, analysing, applying. • Different pedagogical emphases and different sequences for different learners and areas of knowledge. • Honouring lifeworld differences: diversity strategies of belonging and transformation. • Singular ends: equity.
Curriculum	• Centralised syllabus, textbooks. • Traditional disciplines. • Standardised tests, quantifiable results.	• School-based curriculum. • Locally relevant and needs-based curriculum. • Contextrelevant, teacherjudged assessment. • Crowded curriculum.	• 'New basics': knowledge, capacities, sensibilities. • Open-ness to a broad range of content. • Authoritativeness in knowledge and learning. • Assessment of comparabilities. • Measurement for pedagogical and curriculum ends: to open out possibilities rather than seal fates.

			• Educational 'knowledge management': documenting and showcasing exemplary teaching and learning.
Education	• Hierarchical, bureaucratic.	• Devolved. • Developing a 'corporate' culture at the local level	• Subsidiarity and federalism. • Productive diversity. • Civic engagement.

This is a practical vision for transformative curriculum, and the experimental task of the *Learning by Design* approach. What, then are the pedagogical processes that lie at the heart of a transformative curriculum?

CHAPTER 5

Pedagogy

Within education, curriculum defines an area of knowledge, such as a discipline area or a domain of practical competence. Within curriculum, pedagogy addresses the microdynamics of learning or knowledge processes. The four knowledge processes of the *Learning by Design* framework are: experiencing, conceptualising, analysing and applying. The *Learning by Design* approach to pedagogy aims to make teachers more mindful and conscious of what pedagogical processes they are employing, both to ensure it fits the learning goal and to be inclusive of diverse learners who come to know things in different ways. The framework seeks to make pedagogy *explicit* and to create teachers with who are expert in a wide-variety of pedagogical repertoires. Bringing pedagogical assumptions to the fore also assists in the design of successful learning, as it serves as a prompt for teachers to consider incorporating more than one knowledge process.

THE STUFF OF KNOWLEDGE

The theory of pedagogy outlined in this chapter has three sources. The first is the earlier curriculum design, research and development in which we have been involved, including the Social Literacy Project (Kalantzis & Cope, 1989), the 'genre' approach to literacy (Cope & Kalantzis, 1993a) and the Multiliteracies Project (Cope & Kalantzis, 2000b; New London Group, 1996). The second is the theoretical side of the *Learning by Design* approach, in which we attempted to develop a pedagogical schema which would not be unfamiliar to eductors because it mapped against, and was to a substantial degree a derivative of, widely known pedagogies.

The third source for the pedagogy outlined in this chapter is the experience of working with teachers as part of the *Learning by Design* approach. Here, our concern was to establish a connection between teachers' professional discourse and our understanding of current research knowledge and theoretical approaches to pedagogy. This chapter includes some illustrations of our 'crosswalk' approach to mapping the *Learning by Design* pedagogical schema against well-known pedagogical theories such as Bloom or Kolb. Theories of pedagogy are often grounded in the cognitive or psychological stuff of our natures—stuff which we need to take into account, for sure, but which (by nature) we can't do that much about.

To complement these theories, we are proposing an epistemologically grounded theory of pedagogy. Its focus is microdynamics of knowing, or how knowing happens. It is also a theory of pedagogy that it is culturally grounded, in the types of people we have become through knowing. Culture is the sum total of what we have learnt from the context in which we have become knowing people. Culture is what is left by learning, either from the accretions to our natures which have been the result of the everyday learning that is an integral part of lifeworld experience, or the residues left after engagement with formal education. Culture is a product of human invention and socialisation. Knowing and culture are things we can do more about than our natures, although of course we would not want to defy our natures too glibly.

Knowing is the process of connecting the stuff of the mind to the stuff of the world. Knowing is a form of action and to know in this active sense is to learn. Learning is a relationship between the knower and the knowable, in which the learner discovers that the knowable can in fact be known and is perhaps worth knowing.

As people are different and act differently, so too they have come to know in different ways and they know different things. As for ways of knowing, it might be by experiencing (deep understandings, intuitions or judgments based on extended immersion in a particular situation), or by conceptualising (knowing the underlying concepts and theories of a particular discipline, system or vocation), or by analysing (linking cause with effect, interests with behaviours, purposes with outcomes), or by applying (doing something again or anew). These are some of the ways in which knowing is done, and some people are more inclined to learn in one way than in another. As for the different things people know, these are the facts, the values, the interests and the sensibilities that they have learnt in their peculiar world.

Effective pedagogy employs ways of knowing that are capable of drawing the knower closer to the knowable. It also uses learning contents which have purchase on learner lifeworld and educational experience. These may be at times familiar or strange, but never so strange as to be unknowable or alienating in a counterproductive way. Effective pedagogy carefully calibrates the distance between the learner's known lifeworld and the transformational possibilities of the to-be-known. It is the process of engaging with the stuff of the world which affirms (belonging) and extends (transformation) the learner's framework for knowing.

So, pedagogy is a knowledge process. But what is knowledge? If knowledge is the connection between the stuff of the mind and the stuff of the world, we could view this connection narrowly or broadly, depending on the lens we choose to use to view (and thus define) knowledge.

Here is a definition of knowledge as seen through a narrowly focused lens: Knowledge is data, the raw material of everyday experience, the empirical world, the world as directly apperceived by our senses, the tangible world of hard-to-deny facts.

And here is knowledge seen through a slightly wider lens: Knowledge is information; it is data plus the synthesising mental processes that have been applied to that data as it has been aggregated, sorted, categorised and verified. We have information when the stuff of the world has been strung together into stories, reports, counts, illustrations, files and the like.

Yet there's a broader sense in which we are immersed in data and information, to be sure, but in which knowledge is more than just mental processes; it is the product of our actions and our propensity as humans to mean. In this broad sense, knowledge is acting and meaning, as well as thinking.

Acting: Knowing is founded on 'real things', including actual-life experiences (being in the thick of things) and practical applications (having to get things done). In this practically grounded world, thinking is an integral part of the action. And even when somewhat removed from the thick of things and the practical business of getting things done (let's consider the theory of the atom or develop a critique of culture), the thinking is itself form of action—something you do in a place and that takes time and effort. It is a peculiarly human and distinctively cultural act to take the data and information of the world and apply to it the cognitive processes of abstraction (making generalisations which encompass numerous particulars), inference (drawing conclusions), interpretation (drawing together what's significant information from a mass of information), critique (assessing the validity and truth claims) and transfer (applying conclusions drawn in one situation to other possible situations).

Meaning: We transform the world, and ourselves, by making meaning in the world. Meaning is the process of signifying, representing or intending. Meaning may be a way of seeing (selecting focal points of interest by naming them in contradistinction to other points). Or it may be a matter of purpose (meaning to ...), action (meaning through ...) or disposition (meaning by ...).

Knowing is the business of engagement with the stuff of the world. It is more than thinking, although there is no engagement without thinking.

Pedagogy as Knowing in Action

There are four fundamental ways of knowing, four processes of acting and meaning: experiencing, conceptualising, analysing and applying. In these sites of acting and meaning, epistemology (theories of knowledge) meets pedagogy (theories of learning). Each of these four knowledge processes is more or less equivalent to one of the curriculum orientations in the Multiliteracies pedagogy (Cope & Kalantzis, 2000b; Kalantzis & Cope, 2001b):

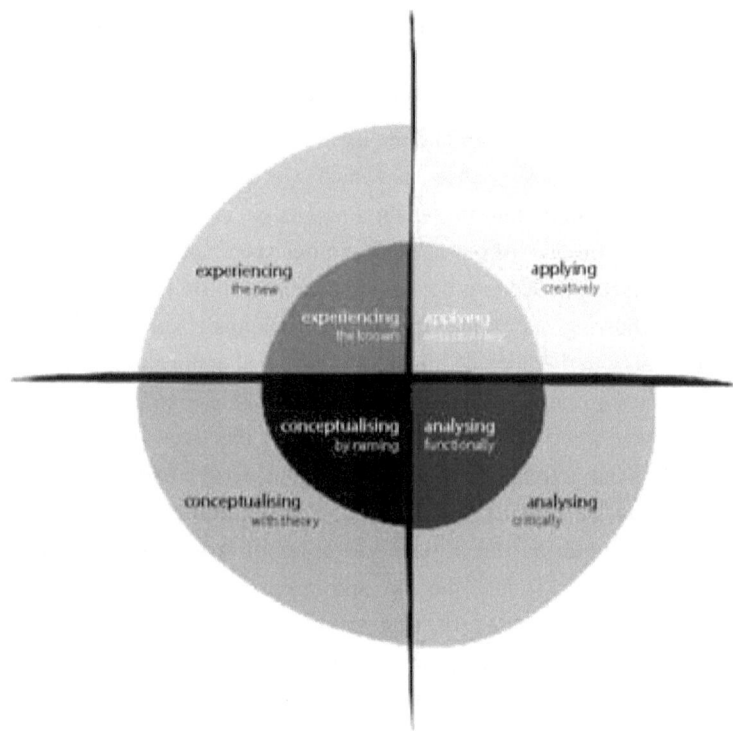

Table 5.1: *Learning by Design* and Multiliteracies Equivalences

Learning by Design: Knowledge Processes	Multiliteracies Curriculum Orientations
Experiencing	Situated Practice
Conceptualising	Overt Instruction
Analysing	Critical Framing
Applying	Transformed Practice

The four knowledge processes of the *Learning by Design* Framework can be briefly defined as follows:

Experiencing
... *The Known:* personal knowledge, evidence from learners' everyday lives.
... *The New:* immersion in new information and experiences.

Conceptualising
... *By Naming:* defining and applying concepts.
... *With Theory:* by putting the concepts together that make discipline knowledge.

Analysing
... *Functionally:* cause and effect, what things are for.
... *Critically:* people's purposes, motives, intentions, points of view.

Applying
... *Appropriately:* 'correct' application of knowledge in a typical situation.
... *Creatively:* innovative application of knowledge, or transfer to a different situation.

When learning is by design, to borrow a musical metaphor, these processes of knowing become 'movements'. There is no necessary order to these movements, nor need there be four in any one moment or sequence of learning activities. However, the concept of movement is intended to indicate an intrinsic dynamism. This dynamism manifests itself in several ways. First, unlike everyday learning in the lifeworld, these are active and explicit moves—conscious at the very least, and also more or less planned and systematic. They are orchestrated. Second, they are not static and clearly defined. Each has a textual dynamic designed into it. One movement leads into another. Pedagogy is composed, arranged, conducted and performed as a whole text. Third, each movement also has an internal dynamic. It has its own opening, body and close. This internal dynamic it seems almost has a life of its own, creating a powerful sense that it has come from somewhere and must be leading somewhere. And that somewhere is often another knowledge process or movement. In fact, each movement begs the other's perspective, particularly as it reaches its close. This is the point of transition from one movement to another, and each of the many possible transitions (from conceptualising to experiencing, or applying to conceptualising, or analysing to applying, for instance) is quite unique.

A particular pedagogical cycle may go through any number of knowledge processes or movements, and any number and varieties of transition from one movement to another, whilst nevertheless sticking to the same theme. To stay with our musical metaphor, each movement is a variation on a theme. Transitions might come rapidly or slowly, and so movements might be frequent or be a long time coming. Movements are, in other words, scalable, from short movements and frequent transitions within classroom discourse to slower movements and less frequent transitions within a longer learning experience that lasts days or weeks or months. Movements and transitions can also be regular or irregular, differing in tempo and varying in modulation.

There is, however, a basic 'unit of capacity' or granularity to a pedagogical process, and that is the theme the variations have been designed to explore. There is a point at which a piece of knowledge is too small a fragment to be called pedagogy, a design for learning: a fraction of a movement, for instance, or a movement that is left isolated and unfulfilled. Such fragments might be used for learning, but they are not learning designs. They could only be characterised as fact, data, input or information.

There is, on the other hand, a point at which a sequence of knowledge movements has attained a certain kind of completeness rather like a whole musical work. Even if only momentary, the relative completeness of a combination of pedagogical movements or a learning design, deserves the name 'pedagogy'. We will call this fundamental unit of capacity a 'Learning Element'. Speaking in conventional pedagogical terms, this basic unit might be the chapter of a textbook, or a sequence of lessons in a lesson plan.

To speak in textual terms now, pedagogy is a genre, a whole text which has characteristic structure and whose dynamic can be defined and described by tracing its sequence of movements. A distinctive beginning, is followed by a middle, is drawn to a conclusion with an end, and by then the range of useful variations on a particular theme will have been explored.

In these senses, then, dynamic and always shifting knowledge processes are at the heart of the learning activities documented in a Learning Element. To elaborate on these knowledge processes, now, they might be characterised as follows as different kinds of action:

Experiencing

... is a knowledge process involving learning through immersion in the real, everyday stuff of the world: personal experience, concrete engagement and

Pedagogy 63

exposure to evidence, facts and data. This is one of the primary emphases of progressivist curriculum.

Experiencing occurs as an unexceptional matter of course in the lifeworld—and the learning that is its consequence tends to be unconscious, haphazard, tacit, incidental and deeply endogenous to the lifeworld. By comparison, the experiencing that is part of pedagogy (learning by design) in its nature tends to be far more conscious, systematic, explicit, structured and exophoric. It assumes a stance in which the experiencing refers to a place outside of the educational setting—by means of textual, visual or audio representation, by simulation or by excursion, for instance.

There are two, quite distinct ways of experiencing:

Experiencing the Known

... is a process which draws on learner lifeworld experience: building upon the learning resource of prior knowledge, community background, personal interests, individual motivation, the everyday and the familiar.

Experiencing the New

... is a process of in which the learner is immersed in an unfamiliar domain of experience, either real (places, communities, situations) or virtual (texts, images, data and other represented meanings). The 'new' is defined from the learner's perspective: what is unfamiliar to them, given their lifeworld origins. To make sense adequate to productive learning, however, the new at least has to have some elements of familiarity; it has to make at last half sense; it must make intuitive overall sense. For learning to occur, it also needs to be scaffolded; there must be means for the parts that are unfamiliar to be made intelligible—with the assistance of peers, teachers, textual cross-references or help menus, for instance. The result is a journey away from the lifeworld along the breadth axis of expanding knowledge, taking a cross-cultural journey of one sort or another.

Conceptualising

... is a knowledge process involving the development of abstract, generalising concepts and theoretical synthesis of these concepts. It involves moving away from lifeworld experience along a depth axis of expanding knowledge—examining underlying structures, causes and relationships, many of which may be counter-intuitive and challenge commonsense assumptions. This is one of the primary emphases of traditional curriculum: teaching abstract concept definitions, rules and disciplinary knowledge frameworks.

Conceptualising occurs in two ways:

Conceptualising by Naming

... is a process involving the development of abstract, generalising terms. A concept not only names the particular; it also abstracts something general from that particular so that other particulars can be given the same name despite visible and situational dissimilarities. In child development, Vygotsky describes the development of concepts in psycholinguistic terms (Cope & Kalantzis, 1993a; L. S. Vygotsky, 1978). Sophisticated adult thinking equally involves naming concepts (Luria, 1976).

Conceptualising with Theory

... is a process by means of which concept names are linked into a language of generalisation. Theorising involves explicit, overt, systematic, analytic and conscious understanding, and uncovers implicit or underlying realities which may not be immediately obvious from the perspective of lifeworld experience. Theorising is typically the basis of paradigmatic schemas and mental models which form the underlying, synthesising discourse of academic discipline areas.

Analysing

... is a knowledge process involving the examination of constituent and functional elements of something, and an interpretation of the underlying rationale for a particular piece of knowledge, action, object or represented meaning. This may include identifying its purposes, interpreting the perspectives and intentions of those whose interests it serves, and situating these in context.

Analysing takes two forms:

Analysing Functionally

... is a process of involving the examination of the function of a piece of knowledge, action, object or represented meaning. What does it do? How does it do it? What is its structure, function, connections and context? What are its causes and what are its effects?

Analysing Critically

... is a process of interrogating human intentions and interests. For any piece of knowledge, action, object or represented meaning we can ask the questions: Whose point of view or perspective does it represent? Who does it affect? Whose interests does it serve? What are its social and environmental consequences? This is the characteristic primary orientation of critique or critical pedagogies.

Applying

... is a knowledge process involving active intervention in the human and natural world, learning by applying experiential, conceptual or critical knowledge—acting in the world on the basis of knowing something of the world, and learning something new from the experience of acting. This is the typical emphasis of the tradition of applied or competency-based learning.

Applying occurs in unexceptional ways in the everyday realm of the lifeworld. We are always doing things and learning by doing them. As was the case with experiencing, we learn by application in the lifeworld in ways which are more or less unconscious or incidental to the process of application, in ways which, in other words, are endogenous to that lifeworld. Application in pedagogy is always a process of more or less consciously taking knowledge out from an educational setting and making it work there. In this sense, it is still exophoric. Applying is about as real as education gets, albeit not as endemically real as the unconscious applications that are of the lifeworld itself.

Applying can occur in two ways:

Applying Appropriately

... is a process by means of which knowledge is acted upon or realised in a predictable or typical way in a specific context. Such action could be taken to match normal expectations in a particular situation, for instance: objects are used in the way they are supposed to be, or meanings are represented in a way which conforms to the generic conventions of a semiotic setting. Never does this involve exact replication or precise reproduction. It always involves some measure of transformation, reinventing or revoicing the world in a way which, ever-so-subtly perhaps, has never occurred before.

Applying Creatively

... is a process which takes knowledge and capabilities from one setting and adapts them to quite a different setting—a place far from the one from which that knowledge or capabilities originated, and perhaps a setting unfamiliar to the learner. It involves taking something out of its familiar context and making it work—differently perhaps—somewhere else. This kind of transformation may result in imaginative originality, creative divergence and hybrid recombinations and juxtapositions which generate novel meanings and situations.

The focus here is on ways of knowing (epistemology) and knowing as meaning and action, rather than upon inherent mental capacities (cognition, psyche)—although of course, there can be no knowing without thinking and psychological processes. Cognition and psychology are the raw materials of learning. At the heart of learning, however, are knowledge processes and these entail meaning and acting.

Or, more precisely, ways of meaning and acting in the plural. There are multiple ways knowing. We have identified four: experiencing, conceptualising, analysing and applying. The particular mix of these four will reflect differences amongst and between:

Cultures: Some cultures, subcultures, institutions, situations or communities of practice may be driven more by one way of knowing than others—they may tend towards relatively unreflective, passive immersion of participants in experience (such as tourism); or relatively disengaged conceptual work (such as some moments in science and theology); or relatively critical interrogation of purposes and interests (such as politics); or highly active but uncritical advocacy (such as salesmanship or propaganda).

Learners: Different individuals may feel more comfortable with, or inclined to use, one learning style in preference to another: learning by immersion in experience; learning by getting a big picture conceptual overview; learning by figuring out what something is for; learning whilst getting done the practical things that have to be done. These need not be the sum total of a learner's knowledge processes, but they may be their preferred starting point.

Knowledge Domains: Some content or discipline domains lend themselves more readily to one way of knowing over others: experiencing in the case of learning to read; conceptualising in the case of chemistry; analysing in the case of social studies; applying in the case of learning a sport or a trade. Although these may well be the predominant emphases of a knowledge domain, they will rarely be the sum total of learning.

Pedagogies: Some forms of instructional design and teaching tend to emphasise certain knowledge processes in preference to others. Western knowledge systems vacillate between objectivism (grounding in the 'facts' of external experience, the 'findings' of theory and the rights and wrongs of appropriate application) and subjectivism (grounding in the 'perspectives' of personal experience, the relativity of interests, and the creativity inherent in the process of applying what one knows). Broadly speaking, objectivism is a bias in what we have called traditional curriculum and subjectivism a bias of progressivist curriculum.

In other words, there have been fashions in pedagogy which have at times favoured some knowledge processes over others; there are disciplines which relied on some more heavily than others; and the preferences of learners and teachers have also played a role. Teachers thus need to be self aware and expert in of the range of knowledge processes that produce learner transformation and ongoing performance. They need to have a wide repertoire and know when to plan, scaffold, and deploy which knowledge process and for which goal.

In the first instance, however, we would not presume to pass judgment upon cultures, learners, knowledge domains or pedagogies. Each seems to suit its own. It is nevertheless important that teachers and learners are knowing participants in their knowing. They should they be as clear about their ways of knowing as they are about what they are knowing. Not only should they becoming more knowing through the process of learning; they should also becoming more knowingly knowing—developing alongside knowledge a parallel metaknowledge.

And when they are clear about the ways of their knowing, they may consciously choose to broaden their repertoire of ways of knowing (or choose not to, but at least are choosing consciously). Transformative curriculum is not in itself defined by the choice to broaden the repertoire of ways of knowing, although when that choice is made, it is evidence of transformative curriculum at work. Rather, it is the business of knowingly making the choice amongst the range of possible knowledge processes.

The knowledge processes represent a kind of conceptual schema, and by means of this schema, the flavour of a particular pedagogy can be identified, and then perhaps also justified. The schema is a way of identifying the epistemological underpinning of a particular piece of learning. Translating this into curriculum, this schema can be embodied as a template or scaffold for designing, documenting and publishing learning content—not in single, prescribed way, but in any way that suits a culture, a group of learners, a knowledge domain or a pedagogical orientation.

The direct relationship between teacher understanding of 'pedagogical knowledge' and the performance of the learner has now been widely accepted (Darling-Hammond, 1998, 2001). In earlier research and development work, we have worked on the issue of 'concept development' in social science (Anderson

& Krathwohl, 2001; Bruner, 1977; Kolb, 1984) etc); and also with the question of an 'explicit metalanguage' in literacy in the work on genre theory (Halliday, 1994; Kress, 1990; J. R. Martin, 1992). In each case, in collaboration with a wide community of practice, we have been able to demonstrate that an explicit focus on what we are now calling 'knowledge processes', enhances the performance of teachers and learners. In each of these projects, as well as the Multiliteracies project, our aim has been to educating the educator whilst also attending to their immediate needs in the classroom.

DESIGNS IN THE PLURAL: SOME CROSSWALKS

The *Learning by Design* approach is not attempting to prescribe a pedagogical formula, and least of all a rigidly defined framework for documenting learning. Rather, its aim is to clarify the shape and form of pedagogy, its various knowledge processes and movements from one knowledge process to another, whatever that pedagogy may be.

To this end, a number of 'crosswalks' have been created, linking the *Learning by Design* concepts with some well known pedagogical schemas and some of the project's antecedent research and development endeavours.

Bloom's Taxonomy

First published in 1956, a revised and updated edition of Bloom's taxonomy was published in 2001 (Anderson & Krathwohl, 2001). The taxonomy focuses specifically on the cognitive objectives of learning.

Table No. 5.2: Bloom's Taxonomy

Learning by Design	**Bloom's Taxonomy**
KNOWLEDGE PROCESSES	EDUCATIONAL OBJECTIVES
	KNOWLEDGE DIMENSION What learners know.
Experiencing	Factual Knowledge The basic elements students must know to be acquainted with a discipline or solve problems in it. - Knowledge of terminology. - Knowledge of specific details and elements.
Conceptualising	Conceptual Knowledge The interrelationships among the basic elements within a larger structure that enable them to function together. - Knowledge of classifications and categories. - Knowledge of principles and generalisations. - Knowledge of theories, models and structures.

Applying	*Procedural Knowledge*
	How to do something, methods of inquiry, and criteria for using skills, algorithms, techniques, and methods.
	- Knowledge of subject-specific skills and algorithms.
	- Knowledge of subject-specific techniques and methods.
	- Knowledge of criteria for determining when to use appropriate procedures.
Analysing	*Metacognitive Knowledge*
	Knowledge of cognition in general as well as awareness and knowledge of one's own cognition.
	- Strategic knowledge.
	- Knowledge about cognitive tasks, including appropriate contextual and conditional knowledge.
	- Self-knowledge.
	COGNITIVE PROCESS DIMENSION
	How learners think.
Experiencing	*Remember*
	Retrieve relevant knowledge from long-term memory.
	- Recognising. (also identifying)
	- Recalling. (also retrieving)
Conceptualising	*Understand*
	Construct meaning from instructional messages, including oral, written and graphic communication.
	- Interpreting. (also clarifying, paraphrasing, representing, translating)
	- Exemplifying. (also illustrating, instantiating)
	- Classifying. (also categorising, subsuming)
	- Summarising. (also abstracting, generalising)
	- Inferring. (also concluding, extrapolating, interpolating, predicting)
	- Comparing. (also contrasting, mapping, matching)
	- Explaining. (also constructing models)
Applying	*Apply*
	Carry out or use a procedure in a given situation.
	- Executing. (also carrying out)
	- Implementing. (also using)
Analysing	*Analyse*
	Break material into constituent parts and determine how parts relate to one another and to an overall structure or purpose.
	- Differentiating. (also discriminating, distinguishing, focusing, selecting)
	- Organising. (also finding coherence, integrating, outlining, parsing, structuring)
	- Attributing. (also deconstructing)
	Evaluate
	Make judgments based on criteria and standards.
	- Checking. (also co-ordinating, detecting, monitoring, testing)
	- Critiquing. (also judging)

Applying	Create Put elements together to form a coherent or functional whole; reorganise elements into a new pattern or structure. - Generating. (also hypothesising) - Planning. (also designing) - Producing. (also constructing)

Kolb's Model of Experiential Learning

First published in 1984, Kolb's approach offers a link between theory and practice, between abstract generalization and the concrete instance, between the affective and cognitive domains (Kolb, 1984). His ideas took learning out of the traditional classroom and into the workplace and community as well.

Table No. 5.3: Kolb's Model

Learning by Design	Kolb
Experiencing	*Concrete Experience* Grasping by apprehension - divergent
Conceptualising	*Abstract Conceptualisation* Grasping by comprehension - assimilation
Analysing	*Reflective Observation* Transformation via intention - convergence
Applying	*Active Experimentation* Transformation by extension - accommodation

Multiliteracies

The Multiliteracies pedagogy was designed as part of broader approach to literacy which recognises diversity of language use and the increasingly multimodality of contemporary communications (Cope & Kalantzis, 1997a, 2000b; Kalantzis & Cope, 1999, 2001b; New London Group, 1996).

Table No. 5.4: Multiliteracies

Learning by Design	Multiliteracies Pedagogy
Experiencing	*Situated Practice* Immersion in experience and the utilisation of available discourses, including those from the students' varied lifeworlds.
Conceptualising	*Overt Instruction* Systematic, analytic and conscious understanding. The introduction of an explicit language to describe the design of meaning.

Analysing	*Critical Framing* Interpreting the social and cultural context of particular designs of meaning; standing back from meanings and viewing them critically in relation to their purposes and cultural context.
Applying	*Transformed Practice* Transfer in meaning-making practice which puts the transformed meaning to work in other contexts or cultural sites.

Social Literacy

The Social Literacy pedagogy was designed for Kalantzis and Cope's Social Literacy social education curriculum materials project (Cope & Kalantzis, 1993b; Kalantzis & Cope, 1989).

Table No. 5.5: Social Literacy

Learning by Design	*Social Literacy*
LEARNING FRAMEWORK	MACRO SEQUENCE The overall conceptual flow of the curriculum units.
LEARNING ELEMENT	MICRO SEQUENCE A lesson or sequence of lessons.
Knowledge Objectives	*Focus Question* A problem to approach through concept generalisation.
Experiencing	*Consider/Input* - Input, stimulus, problem situation. - Questions which lead students to formulate a generalisation - e.g. facts, perspectives/points of view, documents, images. - Model text, text deemed authoritative, problematic text, perspectives juxtaposed, - Strange but intelligible material; familiar yet grounded in students' lifeworld experiences.
Analysing	*Analysis* - From analytical processes (drawing out the content of and meaning of inputs)—what? and how?; - To critical processes (problems/issues raised, opinions, generalisations—why? what for? how wells? - Analytical e.g. (primary): Look at, label, copy, read, put together, sort, research, find out, explain, group, record, draw, write, map, list. - Analytical e.g. (secondary): Describe, identify, write, list, match, draw, name, study, outline, state, record, select, explain, estimate, examine, summarise, compute, research, show, breakdown, give examples, compile, analyse, interview. - Critical e.g. (primary): Ask yourself, talk about, ask questions, debate, compare, guess, choose, decide, work out, locate, change, correct, look around. - Critical e.g. (secondary): Experiment, infer, interpret, generalise, select, differentiate, question, discriminate, distinguish, reject, assess, relate, decide, separate, test,

	divide, advise, categorise, reflect, appraise, criticise, justify, verify, support, predict, hypothesise, discuss, investigate, evaluate.
Analysing	*Main Ideas* - Naming of concepts. - Development of technical terms, tied back to discipline/subject paradigms. - Pivotal point for mapping the macro-sequence - From the concrete to the abstract, the complex to the conceptual, the particular to the general. - Inductive reasoning.
Applying	*Investigation/Inquiry* - Social research, action, experience. - Application of concepts. - From critical (how can the concept be applied? used?) to creative (experience in using the concept and making one's own social knowledge). - Deductive reasoning (from abstract to concrete). - From critical inquiry (e.g. research into a certain field, encountering more texts) to creative production (e.g. drafting, conferencing, editing, publishing). - Critical e.g.s {as above} - Creative e.g. (primary): Give your opinion, solve, tell a story, give a speech, role play, build, report, visit, experiment, try out, advise, imagine, suggest, investigate, model, draw, write, map, meet. - Creative e.g. (secondary): Invent, change, modify, construct, produce, make, solve, use, illustrate, combine, compile, compose, create, devise, design, organise, plan, re-organise, reconstruct, rewrite, imagine, role play, write, give your opinion.
KNOWLEDGE OUTCOMES	*Reflection/Think Again* - Student self-evaluation and teacher evaluation - Key question: can the concepts/learnings be used meaningfully? (Less important than whether they can be defined abstractly.) - Applying concept in another/new context.

The Evidence-Critique-Impact Model

The Evidence-Critique Impact model was first developed with Andrew Scown for the M.Ed. in Educational Leadership and Management, Faculty of Education, Language and Community Services, RMIT University (Cope & Kalantzis, 2001; Scown, 2004).

Table No. 5.6: Evidence-Critique-Impact Model

Learning by Design	ECI Pedagogy
Experiencing	*Evidence* means: working with raw information and everyday experiences, as found in the real world-observation, data collection, reflection on personal experience. Using *Evidence* involves one or several of the following processes of knowing and learning: - Reflecting on your own experience, the evidence you already have to work with based on your own practical knowledge, and/or any other personal life experiences relevant to the topic. - Immersion in information: statistical information, historical documents, case studies, interviews that recount personal experience, media reports, financial data etc. - Empirical knowledge: the world of apparent facts; information that has been presented as correct. - The immediately visible world, the world of commonsense experiences, the everyday lifeworld. - Collection of raw data. - Situated knowledge: knowledge that we know is useful because we can see it works, or knowledge based on what we can see doesn't work. - Observation: watching, seeing, perceiving, noting things that are happening in concrete life experience.
Conceptualising Analysing	*Critique* means: working with generalising concepts and theories which describe underlying structures and processes in the real world, plus critically reflecting upon the social, economic, cultural and political interests served by those structures and processes. Applying Critique involves one or several of the following processes of knowing and learning: - Reflective interpretation of Evidence. - Generalising from evidence by using concepts and abstractions: words that describe general ideas, or processes that are wider than one specific instance. - Analysing underlying patterns, such as systems or structures, which might not be immediately self-evident; making things overt that are covert in everyday situated experience. - Professional knowledge, as embedded in specialist professional discourses. - Interpreting the meaning of evidence from the context in which it is to be found. - Locating knowledge or actions in their historical, social, economic or cultural setting. - Critical framing: explaining the purposes of a particular piece of knowledge or human activity by reference to its organisational or environmental setting: its cultural location, the individual and group interests involved, and its uses and consequences. - Critically evaluating and comparing different purposes and different effects of a particular way of seeing things or way of acting. - Comparative and cross-cultural analysis: comparing and

	contrasting the ways comparable things are done in different settings. - Analysis of politics in its broadest sense: the exertion of power, or the establishment of relationships of governance and consent.
Applying	*Impact* means: acting on knowledge, applying new learnings to the real world, innovating and reflecting on the change process. Making an Impact involves one or several of the following processes of knowing and learning: - Application, appropriation and engagement: knowing and knowing-through-learning that is directly useful in and for the real world - Making knowledge work in the real world, putting knowledge to work; knowledge that is pragmatic; knowledge that is effective. - Turning knowledge of the evidence, plus critique into knowledge that can be used to get something done. - Having a real impact on the world, either by implementing a framework of knowledge or action transferred with little change from one context to another, or by creating new or transformed frameworks of knowledge or action for new settings. - Process design: using knowledge to create systems and structures that work. - Experimenting with new behaviours: developing and strengthening capabilities. - Risk assessment and risk taking - Transfer: taking knowledge and generalisations from one setting and to another; adapting knowledge and processes to realworld settings. - Transformation of one's context: changing one's organizational and environmental conditions. - Transformation of self-having engaged in learning process, learners can never ever be the same again. More than passive or purely cognitive knowledge, self-transforming knowledge involves a development in values, a re-creation of personal meanings and the design of new personal frameworks for making sense of the world. - Learning that has made an Impact is also learning that has transformed the learner. - Evaluation of impacts, reflective practice. - Good sense which is deeper than commonsense; action in the world based on broadly and deeply knowing the world; knowledge that transcends immediate experience in the everyday lifeworld. - Strengthening, re-focusing and extending existing relationships.

The components of the Learning by Design schema are emphatically not a sequence-to-be followed. They are not a pedagogy in the singular, but a kind of meta-pedagogy, a schema against which any possible pedagogy can be mapped. The teacher can still do traditional pedagogy, and mapping against the Learning by Design schema, will show that it tends to emphasise conceptual learning, naming facts and stringing together the abstract theories (of history, of physics, of grammar) that constitute supposedly definitive disciplinary knowledge. And they may note that this pedagogy is at the expense of experiential, critical and applied knowledge processes. Or the teacher may be more comfortable with progressivist pedagogy, which is big on experiential and applied learning but often at the expense of the higher order conceptual and analytical knowledge processes. The Learning by Design schema does not tell the teacher what to do (in the way that Bloom's taxonomy does, or Kolb's Model of experiential learning). Rather, it tells the teacher what they are doing—which knowledge processes a particular sequence of learning processes uses. This presents the teacher with a choice, either to justify the learning processes they are using (this learner, this class, this subject, this school, my preferred teaching style) or, in a suggestive way by comparison with their teaching against a range of possible knowledge processes, to expand their range of knowledge processes in a particular learning experience. The result of the first choice is that the teacher is not so much 'doing' the Learning by Design pedagogy. In fact, they are 'doing Bloom', 'doing Kolb' or doing whatever they normally do. The difference is that they are now being explicit about the range of knowledge processes they are using, and this alone may be sufficient to lead them to make the second choice, to supplement their pedagogy from a broader range of possibilities.

The *Learning by Design* pedagogical schema is the result of numerous iterations in the research context—working out what seems to describe the things teachers do in their classrooms, what provides them with a useful scaffold for planning their students' learning, how can they turn their plans and programs into a documentary resource, and how they can share their experiences of teaching. In Part 2 of this book, teacher/researcher participants describe this third source of inspiration for the theory of pedagogy presented here.

CHAPTER 6

Measuring Learning

Traditionally, assessment in schools has focused on examinations and tests. However this approach to measuring learning is not adequate for the purposes of New Learning, where education is less about individuals accumulating a library of facts and regurgitating received theories and is more about shaping the kind of person who will need to be knowledgeable in a much broader and deeper sense.

This chapter presents a schema for the ongoing evaluation of knowledge processes that can be integrated into planned learning experiences. The schema enables the tracking of each of the knowledge processes: Experiencing, Conceptualising, Analysing and Applying. It also enables the tracking of how well a learner is moving from the competence to think and act with assistance; to the competence to think and act independently and the competence to perform collaboratively. In this schema, the capacity to make and share knowledge with others is considered the most difficult and a higher order level of competence because it involves, communication, negotiation and sensitivity as well as sound knowledge about a subject or task.

TESTING TIMES

Traditional assessment worked this way: Education authorities listed the contents-to-be-covered in the syllabus; the text books followed the syllabus; the teachers in the classroom did their chalk-and-talk in a way which was faithful to the syllabus and the textbook; and finally the students did the tests, demonstrating (by their right or wrong answers to a content-focused questions) what they had learnt or not. More than just the end point of the learning process, however, the tests drove the system. They were the measure of all value—the value of individual students, the value of their teachers and the knowledge which the tests adjudged to be known or not known.

The 'back-to-basics' people have for some time wanted us to return to old style testing, and in most places in the world their political pressure has to a greater or lesser degree borne fruit. Regular, universal, standardised testing puts accountability back into the system, they say. It gives parents and learners clear information about how the learner is going. It makes teachers and educational institutions perform.

Actually, the new-old tests take education back to a time when the whole educational effort was focused on exam technique and the kinds of 'correct' answers which (after spending a considerable amount of mental effort into divining the intentions of the examiners) seem to produce the 'best' results. They are individualised (measuring what's in a single person's head) when real-world learning is increasingly collaborative and knowledge is seen to be possessed by groups and organisations (relying on the information and recording systems which constitute corporate memory, instead of relying on what's in individuals' heads). They rely on memory when knowledge is increasingly supported by ever-present props (books to look up, people to ask, help menus to search and help desks to contact). And they measure certain limited kinds of intelligence. Indeed, these are just those kinds of intelligence which thrive on what tests measure. Tests are an excellent measure of a person's ability to do tests, and often not much else.

This kind of test-driven education certainly produced some people who had demonstrably learnt things, and the test results were the evidence of this learning. But they were things which were too often narrow, decontextualised, abstract and fragmented into subject areas artificially created by the education system. More than anything, standardised testing produced compliant learners, people who would accept what was presented to them as correct, and who had passively learnt off by heart knowledge which could not readily be reapplied in new and different contexts. They may have been superficially knowledgeable (facts, theories, correct usages), but they did not have knowledge of sufficient depth for a life of difference and change.

Application of what has been learned, as well as the discovery of new ways of knowing and acting, are vital in an era that thrives on innovation and is inherently complex. The new learning of today and in the near future will be less about imparting defined knowledge and skills and more about shaping a kind of person: somebody who knows what they don't know; knows how to learn what they need to know; knows how to create knowledge through problem solving; knows how to create knowledge by drawing on informational and human resources around them; knows how to make knowledge collaboratively; knows how to nurture, mentor, and teach others; and knows how to document and pass on personal knowledge (Kalantzis & Cope, 2001a). These kinds of capacities are at a much higher level than what was measurable by old-style tests of fact and theory.

From the point of view of difference and diversity, they key problem is that the tests of traditional curriculum favour the kind of person who does well in tests. They fail people who do not. The two classes of people reflect two different kinds of lifeworld experience. One lifeworld, perennially it seems, produces people well suited temperamentally to traditional curriculum, and they seem to succeed. The alternative is not simply any other lifeworld, but every other lifeworld, and by and large, people from these places seem to fail.

Tests tend not to tell the teacher anything they do not already know about their students. Their purposes are more often political than they are pedagogical. When aligned to resource distribution (rewards and punishment for school success or failure), the testing agenda is even more misguided. Not to mention the expense—the huge amounts of money being thrown at testing, and the resources devoted by schools to teaching to the tests in order to get the best performance results and meet their accountability targets. The resources would be better spent on teacher professional development and designing strategies for capturing and disseminating teacher best practice, including sophisticated assessment strategies that arise from and relate directly to the curriculum, and that value teacher professional judgement.

The terrible irony of this moment is that, precisely when old style tests are least relevant, we are nevertheless relentlessly falling back on their supposedly definite clarity. This is partly because many of our political leaders cannot imagine an educational future which goes much beyond their own experiences of schooling. And so, in our attempt to address new problems, we find ourselves using old solutions.

The quest in recent years for accountability and commensurability has focused global attention on producing education outcomes which are simple to interpret, tangible and transparent, and easily comparable. This is done in the interests of individual learners, who are seen to benefit from a culture of competition, and from the accretion of knowledge committed to their individual memories. It is also done in the name of those whose delivery and rationalisation of education resources is justified by figures which are comparable and easily interpreted. Assessment is also justified in the name of parents who, it is argued, increasingly demand extensive information about the progress of their children. According to the prevailing wisdom, regular, universal, standardised testing provides accountability to the system, easily digestible information to parents, and regularly updated knowledge of the progress and relative competencies of individual students.

The effects of this outlook extend beyond assessment techniques to the curriculum taught. Indeed, the increase in standardised testing reflects, and further promotes, curriculum models which are focused around the so-called basics of numeracy and literacy. Dominant extant assessment regimes are reinforcing these old basics, but the very concepts of numeracy and literacy, and the skills required by students, are themselves changing dramatically in the knowledge society. Assessment techniques therefore need to be altered, in many cases quite radically, to promote new learning and to measure more accurately the skills required for success in the twenty-first century.

Outlining these required skills is important, and can only be done by situating education in the context of the new economy. New learning certainly requires assessment, in order to inform students, parents and prospective employers of the knowledge learnt by a person. However, new assessment techniques mean redefining what is meant by terms such as competence, ability, capacity and intelligence. Indeed, they even involve changing the measure, from the replicated sameness of outcomes anticipated by standardised testing, to similar or comparable outcomes amongst learners whose life experiences, interests and thinking styles are invariably very different. Standardised testing measures whether its one-size content knowledge has fitted all (which it never can, and in fact measures the similarity of some students to the single set of assumptions about knowledge and thinking). New learning, by contrast, is taking students in the direction of comparable levels of personal autonomy, self determination and access to social resources in the worlds of work, citizenship and personal life.

A 'new basics' is emerging, demanding skills and competencies which cannot be measured by testing regimes focused on the old basics. A complex, diverse society, in which knowledge has become the engine of national development and self-fulfilment, requires a much more multifaceted approach to tracking and reporting the educational achievements of individuals and educational institutions.

NEW LEARNING, NEW FORMS OF ASSESSMENT

If old-style tests are not always the best measure, how do we know when learning is effective? In practical terms, traditional or standardised tests:

- are good at testing what tests test, and not always so good at assessing what a learner knows; and
- even when they do assess what a learner knows, they are not particularly good at assessing that learner's capacity to know; and

- they compare apples with apples, but not with apples and oranges, when we live in an increasingly critical way in a word of apples and oranges (highly varied learning styles or preferred ways of knowing and diverse life experiences, cultures or types of person). So what do we do instead?

The *Learning by Design* approach suggests three measures of learning outcomes: assessing individual learners (at the level of pedagogy or Learning Elements); program evaluation (at the level of curriculum or Learning Frameworks); and organisational performance evaluation and research (at the level of education, or Learning Communities). Its practical focus is on how to evaluate the effectiveness of the pedagogical, curriculum and management choices made in the teaching and learning process.

At the level of pedagogy, a number of assessment techniques will become increasingly relevant to measuring the attributes of persons who will be most effective in the new economy and most valuable as citizens.

- *Project assessment,* based on indepth tasks which involve task plan, complex collation of material and presentation would measure broad knowledgability and a flexible solutions orientation to knowledge. It would also enable some measurement of multiple intelligences, be they communicative, analytical or creative.
- *Performance assessment,* based on the planning, doing and completion of a task, would measure a wide range of skills, including organisation and problem-solving.
- *Group assessment,* of the collective work of a whole learning group, or of the collaborative capacities of individual group members, would be an important means of measuring the collaborative skills so important in the new economy.
- *Portfolio assessment,* through documenting the body of works undertaken, unique life experiences and other learning achievements, would enable personal experiences and perspectives to be included, and thus in a deeper way, the individual strengths of diverse individuals (Kalantzis, Cope, & Harvey, 2003).

The *Learning by Design* Framework takes a holistic and integrated

- approach to assessment. Key principles underlying its approach to measuring Learning Outcomes include:
- It's not (just) the test at the end.

- Measure the 'new basics' and not the old: Multiliteracies, collaboration skills, problem solving, creativity-imagination innovation.
- Evaluate performance over a whole Learning Element, or a special assessment task (such as a concluding joint or individual project) which tests the full range of knowledge processes required in the Learning Element.
- Assess personal knowledge and performance: experiential, conceptual, analytical and applied.
- Assess individuals in a group context: the ability to make productive social connections (to texts and people, and collaboratively constructed knowledge).
- Corroborate results with formal peer review (open, one-way blind, two-way blind, moderated).
- Make qualitative judgements to justify quantitative ratings.
- Build individual portfolios (e.g. digital portfolios) where the proof of the result is in the portfolio as much as the rating.

Following is a criterion-reference framework for the ongoing evaluation of the knowledge processes that are the core of a Learning Element. In this framework, the capacity to make and share knowledge with others is considered the most difficult and highest order level of competence because it involves, communication, negotiation and sensitivity as well as sound knowledge of a subject or familiarity with a task.

Learning by Design: Criteria for Measuring Learning Outcomes

The student demonstrates that she or he:

PERFORMANCE LEVELS KNOWLEDGE PROCESSES	LEVEL 1: *Assisted Competence:* *Needs explicit instruction or support from the teacher or peers to be able to undertake the task or activity.*	LEVEL 2: *Autonomous Competence:* *can figure out how to undertake the task or activity by themselves, and complete it successfully (their own work, or a part of a joint piece of work).*	LEVEL 3: *Collaborative Competence:* *can work effectively with others, including people with less or different knowledge and expertise than themselves, to produce an excellent piece of work (their own, or a joint piece of work).*
Experiencing: The Known	Needs prompts from the teacher or peers to make the connection between their own everyday life experience and the learning task. *Rating:* 0-5	Can figure out for themselves the connection between their own everyday life experience and the learning task. *Rating:* 3-7	Is able to demonstrate to others the connections between the learning task at hand, and their own or the other person's everyday life experience. *Rating:* 5-10
Experiencing: The New	Needs scaffolds by the teacher or peers to make sense of an unfamiliar text, place, activity or group of people. *Rating:* 0-5	Is able to make enough sense on their own of an unfamiliar text, place, activity or group setting to be able to understand its general gist. *Rating:* 3-7	Is able to engage in and with an unfamiliar text, place, activity or group in such a way that the actively interact with it or add meaning based on their own perspective, knowledge and experience. *Rating:* 5-10
Conceptualising: By Naming	Once explained to them, is able to use a concept appropriately in context, and generalize	Is able to work out for themselves the meaning of a concept from the context of its use or by looking up its	Is able to define a concept in terms of other concepts, and explain that concept to other people with an accurate,

	effectively using this concept. *Rating:* 0-5	meaning, and then use that concept to make an abstraction. *Rating:* 3-7	simplifying definition and by providing clear examples. *Rating:* 5-10
Conceptualising: With Theory	Is able to see the connection between two or more concepts once this is pointed out to them. *Rating:* 0-5	Is able to work out for themselves the connections between concepts in a theory. *Rating:* 3-7	Is able to put concepts together in a theory and explain that theory to another person. *Rating:* 5-10
Analysing: Functionally	Is able to understand, once pointed out to them, the general function or purpose of a piece of knowledge, text or human activity, or causal connections. *Rating:* 0-5	Is able to analyse causal connections for themselves. *Rating:* 3-7	Is able to work with others to figure out and demonstrate the way they see causal connections to people who may not see them the same way. *Rating:* 5-10
Analysing: Critically	Is able to comprehend, once explained to them, some of the obvious human interests and agendas behind a text, action or piece of knowledge. *Rating:* 0-5	Can construct a plausible interpretation of the underlying motives, agendas and interests driving a text, action or piece of knowledge. *Rating:* 3-7	Can corroborate from multiple sources an analysis or develop a group understanding of, the explicit and implicit motives, agendas and actions. *Rating:* 5-10

Applying: Appropriately	Is able, in a supportive and structured environment, to communicate or act in ways which conform to conventions or textual genres. *Rating:* 0-5	Is able independently and without explicit scaffolds oi nstructions, to communicate or act in ways which conform to conventions or textual genres. *Rating:* 3-7	Masters a convention or a genre to the point where they become fullyfledged members of a new community of practice. *Rating:* 5-10
Applying: Creatively	Is able, in a supportive and structured environment, to put together in a meaningful way, two or more conventional forms of communication or action. *Rating:* 0-5	Is able independently and without explicit scaffolds or instructions, to put together in a meaningful way, two or more conventional forms of communication or action. *Rating:* 3-7	Can create a hybrid text, action or group environment which involves a genuinely original combination of knowledge, actions and ways of communicating. *Rating:* 5-10
MULTILITERACIES		Effectiveness in communication of meaning and use of multiple modes of meaning (e.g. linguistic, visual, audio, spatial, gestural) *Rating:* 0-20	
			Maximum Possible Rating: 100

CHAPTER 7

The Learning by Design Framework

A critical question for the *Learning by Design* approach is the pedagogical quality of elearning as directly compared with traditional classroom environments. What are the 'pedagogical moves' characteristic of each domain?

This chapter addresses these broad questions, as well as the particularities of how learning is recorded, shared and reflected upon, in the classroom, or to meet curriculum, systems or community requirements. The particular tools of the *Learning by Design* framework—which will enable schools to document and share learning experiences-are explored, including the Learning Element template, which is key to the learning architecture of *Learning by Design*. The Learning Element has been devised to document the knowledge processes outlined in Chapters 5 and 6, and has also been designed to address and negotiate learner diversity. Building on the Learning Element are the Learning Framework (for documenting curriculum) and the Learning Community (documenting the programs and organisational arrangements of a learning institution).

DIGITAL DILEMMAS

If tests are one area in which there is evidence of a return to traditional curriculum, another is the area of 'elearning'. This is counterintuitive, at first glance anyway. What could be more future-oriented than learning on a computer, or better still, a networked computer?

In a pedagogical sense, however, there is nothing necessarily new about computer-assisted and online learning environments. In fact, they can be a place for the revival of the worst of old learning environments: didactic, lock-step and assessed by an impassive private audience, in this case the computer calculating the 'results' of learning and reporting these to the student and the teacher. Indeed, elearning may well be worse than the old environments—more dogmatically univocal, linear and arbitrarily judgmental than even the most rigid of traditional teachers.

There can be little doubt that computer mediated learning ('elearning') is destined to become a larger part of the educational experience of children in the years to come (Castells, 2001; Cuban, 2001; Lankshear, Snynder, & Green, 2000;

Snyder, 2002). The rationale for its introduction range from the need to immerse children in the ubiquitous information and communications technologies of our times, to the purported inherent qualities of elearning environments (Cope & Kalantzis, 2004b; Gilster, 1997; Mitchell, 1995).

Throughout the two decades since they were introduced in significant numbers in schools and homes, there has been constant debate about the value of computer-mediated learning. Does computer-mediated learning enhance or extend traditional classroom-based learning? How similar or different is it to classroom based learning? The theoretical foundation of this question is the presupposition in activity theory that the nature of an activity is in part determined by the tools used in that activity . Repeatedly, the research results bring us back to the question of pedagogy—what kinds of pedagogical processes make for effective learning, with and without technology mediation, and how can technology be harnessed to meet pedagogical objectives? To what extent and in what ways does computer mediated learning influence pedagogy? What impact does any identifiable shift in pedagogy have on influencing learning outcomes? We do not assume that technologies per se can influence learning outcomes. However, shifts in pedagogy which may be the direct or indirect effect of technology use, can have such an influence (Chandler-Olcott & Mahar, 2003).

Since the widespread availability of the personal computer, a large amount of 'educational' material was available, ranging from environments of great pedagogical sophistication, such as Seymour Papert's Logo project, with its radical translation of mathematics and logic into an environment where children in effect learnt a form of programming (Papert, 1994), to (at the other end of the spectrum) games which purported in their marketing to parents to have 'educational value'.

The debate about the role of computers in education has intensified with more widespread access and the rapid emergence of the Internet from the mid 1990s. The Internet and networking technologies more generally, represent a significant development in the use of computers in education, adding communications tools that were not initially a feature of personal computers, as well as the potential to access enormous amounts of information, much of which might once have been sourced from libraries. If the widespread adoption of personal computers from the mid 1980s and then the Internet from the mid 1990s were two initial stages in the history of computers-in-education, then we are now at the cusp what we would argue is a third important stage. In this stage, it seems that traditional learning content may increasingly and at least in part be displaced by elearning resources (such as the Australian Learning Federation's emerging resource bank of 'learning objects'). Moreover, the communications and file sharing potentials of networked computing will open new possibilities for content creation by teachers and collaborative work by learners. The *Learning by Design* approach explores the emerging possibilities of this third stage in the history of computers in education.

Information and communications infrastructures are clearly a central part of the development of a 'knowledge society', not only from the point of view of preparing students for a world of work where networked computers are pervasive, but also from the point of view of community participation, citizenship and learning. Learners who are excluded from the new information spaces, will clearly be socially and culturally as well as economically disadvantaged.

However, as always, monumental technological and social changes such as the digital revolution are deeply fraught. On the one hand, critics argue that they add yet another dimension to inequality in the form of the digital divide (Castells, 2000; Gilster, 1997; Light, 2001). They also analyse what they consider to be the anti-humane aspects of the new technologies, the 'grey ecologies' of 'telepresence' in which we are tethered to machines, addicted to their 'electronic dazzlement' and but separated from our fellow humans (Virilio, 1997). Applying this generalised critique into classrooms, already advantaged learners increase their privilege by their access to computers and the Internet, but maybe at the expense of the qualitative human interactions that characterise powerful learning in traditional non-elearning classrooms. The critics of elearning also rightly point to the fact that much of the dedicated educational material is lock step and highly individualised (one user/one screen), appearing to be innovative in the 'dazzlement' of the medium, whilst in fact representing pedagogies that are of dubious quality. Although filling the learning space, they do not represent effective or powerful learning. At best, elearning is as good as the pedagogies that teachers would have used anyway (Windschitl & Sahl, 2002).

Digital 'Learning Objects', for instance, appear to be one of the dazzling innovations of the new elearning world. These are e-learning activities which exploit the interactive and multimodal potentials of computers. They are built on the constructivist principles of learner engagement and demand high levels of learner interaction, or so we are told, and with such regularity that constructivism has nearly become an article of faith amongst the converts to elearning.

As often as they provide an exciting glimpse of the future, however, learning objects can also be a depressing reminder of the past. This is when they represent a form of curriculum development akin to old-style generic and centrally produced textbook publishing. Their creation often requires huge upfront investment, and computer coders rather than teachers are required to do the work. Some learning objects cost hundreds of thousands of dollars per hour of learner interaction to develop. The result, from a curriculum point of view, is frequently less than satisfactory. Instead of teachers actively being engaged in instructional design, they once again become recipients of learning resources that have been instructionally designed for them, by somebody else who knows better. And to justify the investment, the objects have to be sufficiently generic to reach a mass audience. As a consequence learning resources are created that do not engage with the panoply of lifeworld differences—local learning settings, groups of students and individual learners.

Often, the dazzle of learning objects is not so much in the pedagogy as it is in their colour and movement. The old textbook had a page with a diagram and text showing the phases of the moon; now the students can see the earth and the moon turning, and they might even be able to use their mouse to turn the orrery depicted on the screen. The only difference is that a still object has become a moving object. Pedagogically, this is an insignificant step. The dazzle is particularly deceptive when, behind the colour and movement, there is a traditional pedagogy—multiple choice questions with the computer scoring how well the student has learnt their planetary facts.

This is not to dismiss learning objects. Some things they do well: drills, simulations and the presentation of vivid moving images. And when learning objects are structured like computer games, they also have the virtue of requiring the learner to be 'in' the narrative, not unlike the video games whose allure is to place the player at the centre of the story. There is much in elearning that is ingenious and inherently attractive.

Still, difficulties remain. Learning objects are dependent on computer access which all-too neatly sorts students onto one side or other of the digital divide, not just between one school and another but also between learners who have computers at home and those who don't. This kind of learning is also machine dependent—if you're not tethered to the machine, you're not going to benefit from the learning object.

A more optimistic literature points to the social and educational possibilities of the new information and communications technologies. This literature points to the capacity of these technologies to galvanise communities of practice, handing over some of the means of cultural expression and communication from the expensive and highly centralised broadcast media of twentieth century modernity to smaller communities (via websites, digital printing, mp3 music, digital video). The digital media are relatively easy to access and relatively cheap.

The potential is to transform schools into 'knowledge-producing communities'. Instead of being the recipients of transmitted knowledge (syllabuses, textbooks, 'information' resources), schools might become places where teachers and learners develop school-based knowledge banks, and where traditional classrooms, dominated as they are much of the time by teacher talk, are replaced by open schools in which groups of students work autonomously and collaboratively on knowledge projects within a structured 'content management' environment (Kalantzis & Cope, 2004a; Yelland, 1998, 1999).

Celebrated US educationalist, Larry Cuban, published a book in 2001 with the provocative title *Oversold and Underused: Computers in the Classroom* (Cuban, 2001). His conclusion was that computers were just another fad, rather like school milk or school meals of the past, a seeming cure-all for a range of educational ills, but a in reality a fraudulent smokescreen which had achieved little or nothing of educational value. However, in the concluding pages of the book, he makes a remarkable prediction. It is one with which, as improbable as it may seem today, it is hard to disagree. 'I predict that the slow revolution in technology access, fuelled by popular support and continuing as long as there is economic prosperity, will eventually yield exactly what the promoters have sought: every student, like every worker, will eventually have a personal computer. But no fundamental change in teaching practices will occur' (pp.195-196).

When this eventuality does arrive, there may indeed be no fundamental change in teaching practices, but perhaps there could be, and perhaps there should be. It is this 'could' and 'should' which are the focal points of the *Learning by Design* approach. We want to examine what is different or new in elearning environments, and particularly the 'third stage' digital environments to which we alluded above, and what if any difference this makes to learner outcomes.

As for this latter question, we want to leave open the possibility that, at least in some respects, they may be better than traditional classrooms. Traditional 'classroom discourse' was built around a peculiar discursive play between one teacher and thirty-odd learners, bounded by four walls. It was, for simple logistical reasons, limited much of the time to teacher-centred didactic talk, and the teacher posing leading questions to one learner at a time. The result was a lot of silence for a most of the learners for most of the time (Cazden, 2001).

The counterpoint to this reading of the traditional classroom has been a growing research literature which has attempted to demonstrate that computers can assist student learning in powerful ways in the level of personal interaction they require, the customisation of learning experiences or simply by exposing students to one of the foundational technologies and communications media of our times. This case is mainly centred around the theory of constructivism (Bereiter, 1994; Ferguson, 2001). Comparing these computermediated environments with traditional classrooms, one might even go so far as to claim that the classroom is an outmoded human and learning architecture, problematic from the start, and one which much of the time has not lived up to the promise of education.

The learning environments of which we have called 'transformative curriculum' can certainly be created without fancy technologies—with good curriculum design, on paper and with intensive oral interaction. Ideal uses of technology use mixed media, employing the Internet and computers as but one element in a learning environment whilst also providing channel alternatives—print, oral communication, and task-focused group interaction.

What matters most is the design of learning, and the curriculum architecture in which learning sits. What is the source of curriculum? How is it designed to mesh with the differences amongst learner lifeworld experiences and subjectivities? What is the nature of teacher-teacher, teacher-learner and learner-learner interaction in the fabrication and realisation of curriculum?

Digital learning objects are just another 'input', in much the same way that the chapter of a textbook might be used as an input. Learning design is much more than the construction of inputs. It connects a knowing expert—the teacher as knowledge worker—and learners with all manner of interests and purposes. The inputs are incidental to this process. The real issue is one of engagement, and this will only occur in conditions of belonging and transformation, where the engagement carries the learner, one step at a time, distances that are appropriate to their starting point. None of this is inherent in the inputs, and that applies to a learning object as much as it does to a textbook chapter. The keys are the level of engagement, the datum of the learner's lifeworld, the dynamics of motivation, the time spent on task (sustained engagement), the success in expanding horizons and the effects of personal transformation.

The principal practical questions for curriculum are how to develop and share a broad range of curriculum units capable of engaging with widely different student interests and needs (rather than generic 'activities'), how to track 'performance' measured as distance travelled (relative to the learner rather than the input), and how to account for the learner's learning to the learners themselves, to the parents, to the school, to the education system and to the broader community.

Notwithstanding the limitations of learning objects, the digital technologies in their most recent phase of development do afford some exciting opportunities in developing transformative curriculum. Imagine, for instance, if teachers wrote up their lessons on an epublishing platform, which provided clear scaffolds for writing up curriculum and allowed them to share their work with other teachers in and beyond their own department or even their own school, with their students and with the wider learning community. This would not require computer access for all, as documents could simply be downloaded and printed out by individual users, or multiple copies produced through a print-on-demand interface. Then it would be possible to create curriculum which genuinely engaged with local lifeworlds, and without every teacher having to reinvent the wheel. This could include material on local history, local communities and the local natural environment, or learning though literacy texts reflecting a moment in time or a narrow slice of peer, popular or media culture.

It would also be possible to build an ever-growing bank of lessons which catered to the needs of different groups of students within the school, depending on interest, ability level and the like. Then individual students and groups of students could work through units of work that suited them, and at their own pace. This could also be a space for any place, any time learning, as well as learning collaboratively with and through peers and the community. It could unshackle learning from the linear and monological topic-by-topic, chapter-by-chapter curriculum in which teacher talk can succeed at little more than reaching for the unhappy medium that is the middle of the class. It could be the beginnings of a curriculum the genuinely catered to difference.

This is precisely what the *Learning by Design* approach has set out to achieve, and the story of this experiment is told on Part 2 of this book.

NEW TIMES, NEW LEARNING, NEW TOOLS

The *Learning by Design* approach has developed a series of tools which enable schools to document and share learning experiences and resources. At the heart of this initiative is the 'Learning Element' tool. In practical terms, this is a Microsoft Word template which will save back to XML (Extensible Markup Language). Using the emerging technologies of 'the semantic web', the Learning Element document can be printed out as a conventional paper resource, published to the web or saved as a digital 'Learning Object' into any standards-compliant Learning Management System or e-learning software environment.

The Learning Element is a hybrid curriculum form. With parallel teacher and learner sides to every page, it encourages the teacher to think through what each learning experience does both in teacher professional discourse (the left hand side of the page) and in terms of classroom talk (the right hand side of the page). The Learning Element is both a instrument for curriculum planning and a learning resource. It is possible to hide the teacher side of the page, and give the Learning Element to individual learners so they can undertake self-paced instruction, or to groups of learners working together on a collaborative activity. For classrooms where there is deep diversity amongst learners, this is a way to cater for that diversity.

After the Learning Element has been worked through, the teacher may choose to rewrite in the light of the teaching/learning experience, including perhaps and text and images which provide a record the tangible actualities of teaching. As teachers record the best of their teaching practice, their Learning Elements can be published into a web-based digital portfolio of their best work and thus shared with other teachers, and the wider school community. When they themselves, or another teacher, comes to use the Learning Element another time, they have an open text which can be adapted, modified and improved.

By this means, schools will be able to develop locally-engaged learning resources which draw on local community concerns. They will also be able to work collaboratively with 'outside' sources of local knowledge to create locally engaged knowledge, of use also perhaps beyond the school walls. In addition to the documentation templates, it is the ambition of the *Learning by Design* approach to provide every learner, every teacher and every community-based knowledge collaborator with a self-maintainable personal website (including blogging, personal portfolio and content sharing and publication functions) as well as cascading community publishing sites (the class, the school-community project, the inter-school initiative etc.). Such an ambition lies at the heart of the 'CGPublisher' software development initiative (Common Ground, 2003-2005a). The Learning Element is just one of the digital artefacts that can be published through this online environment. The result is a learning architecture that supports the school as an a knowledge-producing community, building the professional capacities of teachers to be 'learning designers' and 'learning managers' within and beyond the walls of the classroom and the school.

The aim of the *Learning by Design* approach is to develop innovative modes of learning, enabled by the information and communications technologies but not dominated by them. As argued in the first part of this chapter, we have witnessed successive technology waves come and go within the education sector, with little long term impact on the improvement of learning. At least part of the cause, in our estimation, is that technology solutions have been largely modelled on

The Learning by Design Framework 93

outdated pedagogical models—of students as passive receptors of knowledge, who are then primarily tasked with reproduction of that of knowledge in classroom activities and the assessment process. The *Learning by Design* approach envisions technology as an enabler of more dynamic and engaging pedagogical models, where students are instead involved directly with the creation and sharing of knowledge, and teachers in the creation of curriculum more closely engaged with the local community. By these means, schools, teachers, students and community members will be directly involved in collaboratively researching, collaborating and publishing their learning.

The result will be a kind of 'knowledge management' for schools, in which information and communication technologies are a medium through which schools can develop a capacity for producing their own knowledge—including, for instance, a bank of Learning Elements which have been tried and tested in local conditions and which have proved engaging to learners. In this endeavour, technology is the enabler not the driver—it creates the capacity for teachers to develop and share their teaching with each other in the form of a professional curriculum and learning resource bank and with their learners and the community through web-based learning management and web publishing systems. Learners work collaboratively in this environment (sharing common files through a server-based content management system). They can also publish their work, changing the predominantly vertical in-class communications pattern from submission to an audience of one (typically, the assessing teacher) to lateral communications to all members of the learning community. This is in stark contrast to more common uses of information and communication technologies in education, which all too often, and despite better intentions, treat students as passive receptacles of knowledge, in many respects much like a knowledge flow created by the traditional textbook. Schools which are knowledge-producing communities, by contrast, are learning environments which are capable of generating and maintaining their knowledge, and developing in students a passion for knowledge creation and knowledge sharing.

Such a knowledge infrastructure has three aspects:

- *Content Creation* – tools for students and teachers to create content.
- *Content Management* – tools for students and teachers to organise, locate, retrieve and update content.
- *Content Dissemination* – tools for sharing content with other schools, parents and the general public.

THE LEARNING BY DESIGN TOOLS

The *Learning by Design* tools include open and flexible templates for planning and documenting at three levels:

- *Learning Element:* documenting pedagogy in the form of a teacher and/or learner oriented text. A coherent learning experience on a single topic.
- *Learning Framework:* documenting curriculum in the form of one or more alternative learning pathways across a number of Learning Elements.
- *Learning Community:* documenting the programs and organisational arrangements of an institution of learning.

Outside of these three levels of documentation but supporting them, there may also be *Learning Sources*. A Learning Source is something that is referred to in a Learning Element, Learning Framework or Learning Community document. This could include images, short texts, chapters of books, digital learning objects, multimedia resources, databases, websites and the like, uploaded and archived or, in the case of external digital sources, hyperlinked to a Learning Element, Learning Framework or Learning Community document.

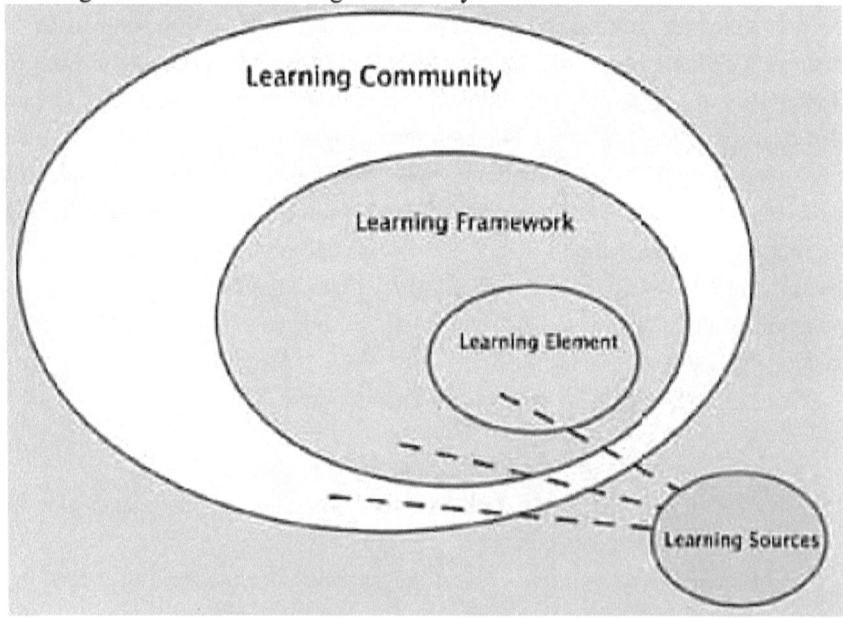

Figure 7.1: *Learning by Design,* Levels of Documentation

The *Learning by Design* tools provide templates for documenting choices made at each level. The documentation can be for personal use only, for sharing with selected others or for public communication. The templates can be used to:

- Document and manage lesson plans and teaching programs.
- Collaborate with colleagues to produce innovative learning experiences.
- Reflect on choices made to enable learning.
- Developing school-based learning materials as well as other forms of documentation of the learning community such as policies and overall programs.

The following table spells out the connections between the theory of learning outlined in Chapter 4 and the levels of documentation in the *Learning by Design* framework:

Table 7.1 Documenting Pedagogy, Curriculum, and Education

Pedagogy	Learning Element
Learning is a process of knowing, and knowing is a form of action. In learning, a knower positions themselves in relation to the knowable, and engages (by experiencing, conceptualising, analysing or applying, for instance). A learner brings their own person to the knowing, their subjectivity. When engagement occurs, they become a more or less transformed person. Their horizons of knowing and acting have been expanded. Pedagogy is the science and practice of the dynamics of knowing. Assessment is the measure of pedagogy: telling of the shape and extent of the knower's transformation.	Documenting pedagogy: A Learning Element is a coherent bundle of learning activities and tasks, such as a lesson or a short string of lessons. A Learning Element can be documented as a teacher resource, a learner resource, or both in parallel. It is the equivalent of a textbook chapter or lesson plan.

Curriculum	Learning Framework
In places of formal and systematic teaching and learning, pedagogy occurs within larger frameworks in which the processes of engagement are given structure and order, often defined by content and methodology, hence the distinctive 'disciplines', such as 'literacy', 'numeracy', 'science', 'history', 'social studies', 'economics' or 'physical education'. Evaluation is the measure of the effectiveness of curriculum.	Documenting Curriculum: A Learning ramework ties together a coherent bundle of Learning Elements, such as a whole course, a subject, a discipline-based area of knowledge or training program. It can be documented as a teacher resource, a learner resource, or both in parallel. It is the equivalent of a student textbook, teacher curriculum resource book or teaching program plan.
Education	**Learning Community**
Learning happens in community settings, sometimes specially designed as such (institutions of early childhood, school, technical/vocational, university and adult learning), and sometimes takes informal or semiformal forms within settings whose primary rationale is commercial or communal (such as workplaces, community groups, households or public places as locations of learning). Research tells us how and how well education works in a particular setting.	Documenting Education: A Learning Community document might write up innovative practices, research results and evaluation outcomes in a learning community, or the application and evaluation of a program consisting of a bundle of Learning Frameworks.

LEARNING ELEMENT: AT THE LEVEL OF PEDAGOGY

Practically speaking, the *Learning by Design* framework is a set of publishing tools by means of which teachers can document the choices made in the construction of learning experiences, and capture curriculum content so that it can be shared with learners and other teachers. It is an attempt to develop a vocabulary of learning that can be used by teachers for the documentation of locally developed, difference-sensitive curriculum.

The Learning Element template, for instance, provides a documentation scaffold which suggests that the teacher might write up a learning experience so that it can be accessed by learners (as a student resource) and other educators (as a teacher resource). These tools use digital publishing technologies to deliver open, flexible, collaborative spaces for teachers to make explicit the choices they make as they meet a particular or set of learning goals.

The Learning by Design Framework

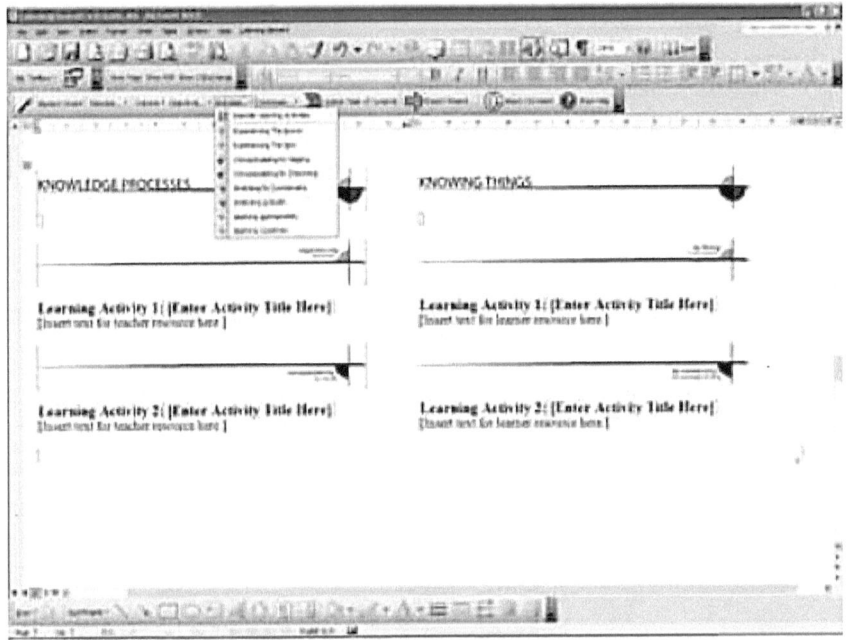

Figure 7.2: Screengrab of a Learning Element Template.

Pull down menus allow the teacher to choose any combination of knowledge processes, and in any sequence. They then write learning activities which bring that knowledge process to practical, pedagogical life, including text, image, web links (all of which can be printed out), or, for seamless onscreen transitions embedded learning objects, moving image, audio sources etc.

This means that:

- The teacher-author is creating a learning resource that can be made available in both print and electronic formats.
- The author is guided by a series of wizards, toolbars and menus.
- The pedagogy embedded in these tools is not prescriptive—it can reflect very different subject matters, teaching approaches and learning styles.
- This resource can be saved as a 'learning object' and inserted into any standards-compliant learning management system.
- Pre-made 'learning objects' can be embedded within the Learning Element, thus providing a way for teachers to create customised learning experiences based on freely or commercially available digital learning objects.

- The Learning Element is accompanied by metadata suitable for library cataloguing, digital resource discovery and web syndication.

And as a consequence:

- Teachers have an easy-to-use planning tool and framework for creating learning resources—electronic and print.
- Teachers become creators sharable learning content.
- Professional knowledge is transformed from personal knowledge to common knowledge.
- New kinds of 'efficiency' are achieved—in some respects this is more work, but in other respects it is less.
- Transparency and accountability are heightened—online management of learning, with greater visibility of expectations and processes for learners, parents, schools, education systems. The Learning Element level consists of core knowledge processes.

Wrapped around these knowledge processes are 'learning focus', 'knowledge objectives', 'knowledge outcomes' and 'learning pathways':

Table 7.2: At the Pedagogical Level—The Structure of a Learning Element

LEARNING ELEMENT: A coherent bundle of learning experiences, learning tasks or activities, such as a lesson or a short string of lessons	
LEARNING FOCUS	Information about where the Learning Element fits in to the curriculum
Knowledge Domain	The subject or discipline area
Scope of Learning	The topic or theme.
Learning Level	The age or year level of the learners.
Prior Knowledge	What the learners already know, or are expected to know in order to be able to work on this Learning Element. For example, prior experience, concepts, analyses or applications, as defined by the teacher or the learner, taking into account the diversity of learners.

KNOWLEDGE OBJECTIVES	The intended learning outcomes. For example, 'as a result of working their way through this Learning Element, a learner or a group of learners will be able to ...' May include objectives in relation to Experiential Knowledge (learning goals to be realized in demonstrable behaviours), Conceptual Knowledge (learning goals to be realised in conceptual, theoretical or cognitive capacities), Analytical Knowledge (learning goals to be realized as understanding of underlying dynamic and critical appraisal capacities) and Applied Knowledge (learning goals to be realised through problem solving, action and performance).
KNOWLEDGE PROCESSES	Different ways of knowing reflected in different types of learning activity, in which the sequence and balance may vary according to subject matter, preferred learning styles etc. The knowledge processes are filled out by content, expressing the depth and breadth and breadth of learning.
Experiencing	Learning activities focused primarily on personal knowledge, concrete experience, evidence, data. **... the Known**: Drawing on the learner's prior knowledge, life experience and community background as a learning resource. *Some Process Orientations:* Identify, Retrieve, Recall, Exemplify, Clarify, Analyse, Check, Locate. **... the New**: Immersion in new knowledge, experience and community settings which connect with the learner to the extent that the new makes enough sense for learning to occur. *Some Process Orientations:* Restate, Illustrate, Summarise, Verify.
Conceptualising	Learning activities focused primarily on abstract concepts and theoretical synthesis. **... by Naming**: Defining and applying concepts. *Some Process Orientations:* Define, Name, Give Examples, Classify. **... with Theory**: Linking concepts into a language of generalisation, or visual representation of conceptual relations. *Some Process Orientations:* Generalise, Synthesise, Abstract, Structure, Organise, Hypothesise, Model, Map, Overview.

Analysing	Learning activities focused primarily on analysing and interpreting functions, interests and perspectives in knowledge. **... Functionally**: Identifying the role and function of knowledge. What does it do? *Some Process Orientations:* Compare, Contrast, Explain. **... Critically**: Analysing purposes and human intentions involved in knowledge. Who is it for? Interpreting personal and cultural perspectives involved in knowledge. What point of view does it represent? *Some Process Orientations:* Infer, Interpret, Conclude, Deconstruct, Critique, Judge, Assess, Appraise, Argue, Differentiate, Discriminate, Distinguish, Evaluate.
Applying	Learning activities focused primarily on applying knowledge, creating meanings and making a practical impact on the world. **... Appropriately:** Applying knowledge in an appropriate way to a typical situation. *Some Process Orientations:* Apply, Use, Solve, Implement, Generate, Plan, Produce, Justify, Reconstruct. **... Creatively**: Creating new knowledge; taking knowledge from one or more settings, and adapting it to a different setting. *Some Process Orientations:* Transfer, Translate, Design, Construct, Invent, Create, Imagine.
KNOWLEDGE OUTCOMES	Processes for assessing the knowledge learners have acquired (experiential, conceptual, analytical and applied). Might include learner self-assessment, peer assessment, teacher professional assessment, instructional designer assessment such as an assessment task built into the Learning Element.
LEARNING PATHWAYS	Suggested follow-on activities and learning experiences, which might involve learner pathway preferences, teacher pathway recommendations, instructional designer pathway recommendations or pathway co-design as an outcome of negotiation of what to learn next.

To take the learning objectives and learning assessment areas, first: in each of these areas two fundamental questions may be raised—who defines the objectives and outcomes, and what are they? The 'who' question might be answered as the learners themselves, the teacher or the instructional designer (the author of the Learning Element, for instance)—or it might be an outcome of collaboration and negotiation between one or more of these parties, each of whom as an 'interest' in the Learning Element. The 'what' question might be framed in terms of the knowledge processes—as knowledge objectives before engaging in the knowledge processes and as knowledge outcomes as assessed during or after the engagement with the knowledge processes.

Wrapped around knowledge objectives, knowledge processes and knowledge outcomes are entry and exit points into a Learning Element. The learning focus defines the knowledge domain (subject or discipline area), scope of learning (theme or topic), learning level (stage, year or age) and prior knowledge. This last

The Learning by Design Framework 101

area could be defined in terms of the Knowledge Processes. It could provide a basis for learning which stays within the learner's zone of proximal development (belonging in the learning), and also provide a measure at the point of assessment of the extent to which the envelope of that zone has been broadened (learning as transformation).

The exit point of a Learning Element raises the question of learning pathways, or what the next Learning Element will be. In fact, there are two questions: who determines the pathway, and what the pathway is. The 'who' question might be answered by the learner (what they'd like to do next), the teacher (when the learning is program driven) or the instructional designer ('now move on to Chapter 4'). Or the pathway might be determined by the negotiated process of pathway co-design.

The *Learning by Design* Framework presents this as a range of possibilities at the Learning Element level, not at all prescriptive and ordered in no necessary sequence. Different choices of elements and different sequences will determine the particular pedagogical flavour of a set of learning experiences. For instance, a traditional curriculum might make it clear that learning objectives are those determined by the instructional designer or teacher, rather than negotiated with learners; the knowledge objectives might be best categorised as conceptualising; the knowledge processes may primarily involve factual experiencing the new and the theorising required of a particular academic discipline; the knowledge outcomes may be assessed by means of a test, either one that comes with the course materials in the form of an assessment task developed by an instructional designer or a teacher generated test.

And all this may well be for the best (or worst) of reasons, related to the nature of the subject matter, the learning styles of the students or the 'rigorous academic' branding of the educational institution, for instance. Progressivist curriculum will have different emphases. And transformative curriculum will traverse a broader pedagogical range.

The Learning Element schema reflects the way in which the *Learning by Design* tag-concepts might be represented in a teacher resource. The tags perform the function of 'marking up' the pedagogy, and as such are made visible as section headings, labels or pedagogical flags. *Learning by Design* speaks of learning in the professional language of teaching.

In the case of a learner resource, the tag-concepts may need simplification if they are to be intelligible to particular groups of learners. When simplified, they still describe the same underlying aspects of learning. The following paraphrase of the *Learning by Design* concept-tags has been pitched at about the middle of the primary school.

Table 7.3: Learning Element Tags with Translation to Approximately Mid-primary Level

LEARNING ELEMENT	LEARNING SPACE
LEARNING FOCUS	WHAT WE"RE LEARNING
Knowledge Domain	*Our Subject*
Scope of Learning	*Our Topic*
Learning Level	*Our Class*
Prior Knowledge	*What We Already Know*
Prior Experience	Places I Have Been
Prior Concepts	Things I Have Thought About
Prior Analyses	Views I Have
Prior Applications	Things I Have Done
KNOWLEDGE OBJECTIVES	FINDING OUT
	By bring
Experimental Objectives	*By Connecting*
Conceptual Objectives	*By Thinking About*
Analytical Objectives	*By Doing Things*
Applied Objectives	
KNOWLEDGE PROCESSES	KNOWING THINGS
	By Being
Experiencing	In Your World
Experiencing the Known	In new Worlds
Experiencing the New	*By Connecting*
Conceptualizing	The Same Type of Thing
Conceptualizing by Naming	Different Types of Things
	By Thinking About
Conceptualizing by Theory	What Something Does
Analysing	Who Something is For
Identifying Functionally	*By Doing Things*
Identifying Critically	The Right Way
Applying	In Interesting Ways
Applying Appropriately	
Applying Creatively	
KNOWLEDGE OUTCOMES	HOW WELL HAVE YOU LEARNT?
Experiential Outcomes	*By Being*
Conceptual Outcomes	*By Connecting*
Analytical Outcomes	*By Thinking About Things*
Applied Outcomes	

When written up as an explicit and shareable document describing the features of a coherent and momentarily complete learning experience, a Learning Element may cover the following issues, represented as headings or 'tags':

A Learning Element

LEARNING FOCUS

Preliminary information about where the Learning Element fits in to the curriculum, including:
Knowledge Domain: The subject or discipline area.
Scope of Learning: The topic or theme.
Learning Level: The age or year level of the learners.
Prior Knowledge: What the learners already know, or are expected to know in order to be able to work on this Learning Element.

KNOWLEDGE OBJECTIVES

The outcomes intended from the learning experience.

KNOWLEDGE PROCESSES

Different ways of knowing reflected in different types of learning activity, in which the sequence and balance may vary according to subject matter, preferred learning styles etc. The knowledge processes are filled out by content, expressing the depth and breadth and breadth of learning.

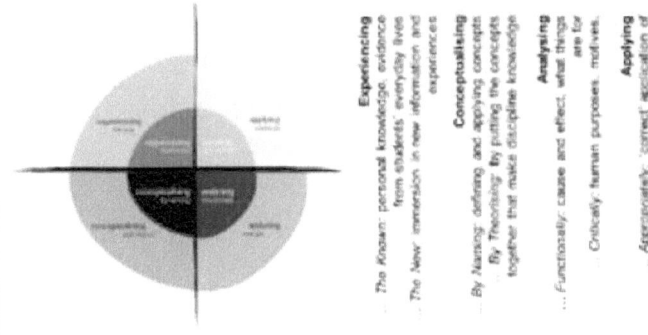

KNOWLEDGE OUTCOMES

Assessing what has been learnt: teacher assessed, peer assessed and learner self-assessed perspectives.

LEARNING PATHWAYS

One or a range of suggested follow-on Learning Elements.

Pedagogy at Work

What does the *Learning by Design* framework mean in practice? Following are some examples of tasks that may be appropriate to a particular knowledge process:

Experiencing

... *The Known* -bring in, show or talk about something/somewhere familiar or 'easy'—listen, view, watch, visit.
... *The New* -introduce something less familiar, but which makes sense just by immersion—listening, watching, viewing, visiting etc.

Conceptualising

...*By Naming* -make a glossary, label a diagram, sort or categorise like and unlike things. ... *With Theory* -draw a concept map, diagram or a write a theory which puts the concepts together.

Analysing

... *Functionally* -write an explanation, draw a technical or functional diagram, create a storyboard, make a model.
...*Critically* -hold debate on a social issue connected with a piece of knowledge, predict consequences of knowing/not knowing, write a thoughtful review.

Applying

... *Appropriately* -write, draw, act out in the 'correct way', solve a problem.
...*Creatively* -use the knowledge you have learnt in an innovative way or applied to a different setting, suggest a new problem, translated into a different mix of 'modalities' of meaning.

The range of tasks or activity types involved each of these knowledge processes may encompass the following—documented in detail in the *Learning by Design* Guide (Kalantzis & Cope, 2005):

Experiencing: The Known

- Literacy Experiences: Receptive Activities
- Multiliteracies Experiences: Receptive Activities
- Image Documentary
- News Story
- Video or Audio Interview
- 'Stream of Consciousness' Recollection
- Brainstorming
- Survey
- Observation
- Passion Project
- Knowledge Journey
- Socratic Dialogue

Experiencing: The New

- Literacy Experiences: Receptive Activities
- Reciprocal Teaching
- Summarising
- Frames
- Multiliteracies Experiences: Receptive Activities
- Into Unfamiliar Territory: An Image Documentary, News Story, Video or Audio Interview, Survey, Observation or Knowledge Journey
- Think-Pair-Share
- Co-operative Learning
- 'On the Road' Stream of Consciousnesses Reflections on New Experiences

Conceptualising: By Naming

- Literacy Concepts: Develop a Metalanguage
- Multiliteracies Concepts: Develop a Metalanguage

- Glossary
- Concept Organiser
- Naming an Image and its Parts
- Classify by Concept
- Cross-Classification
- Concept Clarification • Inductive Reasoning

conceptualising
by naming

Conceptualising: With Theory

- Literacy and Multiliteracies Theories
- Mind Map
- Taxonomy
- Theory-Making
- Deductive Reasoning
- Modelling

conceptualising
with theory

Analysing: Functionally

- Literacy and Multiliteracies Analyses
- Y Chart -Observational
- Cause and Effect Pattern Organiser
- Event Modelling
- Timeline
- Flow Diagram
- Storyboard
- Comparison Chart
- Venn Diagram
- Comparison Matrix
- Analogy
- Metaphor
- Structural Analysis
- Instructions

The Learning by Design Framework 107

Critical Literacy and Multiliteracies

- Y Chart -Evaluative
- Critical Assessment Tool
- Cost-Benefit Analysis
- SWOT Analysis
- Risk Assessment
- Critique: A Writing Frame
- Debate
- Moot Court
- Polling

Applying: Appropriately

- Literacy Applications: Productive Activities
- Multiliteracies Applications: Productive Activities
- Problem Solving
- Experiment
- Hypothesis Testing
- Prediction

Applying: Creatively

- Literacy Applications: Productive Activities
- Multiliteracies Applications: Productive Activities
- Kinaesthesia
- Knowledge Transfer
- Problem Defining
- Action Research
- Scenario Cafe

- Conflict Resolution
- Decision Making Strategy
- Invention
- Lateral Thinking
- Personal Action Plan

The following pages provide some illustrations of how the knowledge processes play out in four classrooms with teachers involved in the Multiliteracies project: an early literacy/science class in Bamaga (Cape York), Queensland; a junior secondary science class in Townsville, Queensland; a middle years social studies class in Keilor Downs, Melbourne; and a junior secondary English class in Townsville, Queensland.

COCONUTS: EARLY LITERACY/SCIENCE CLASS, BAMAGA (CAPE YORK), QUEENSLAND

Knowledge Processes

Experiencing

The Known
- Coconut trees pervasive in the local environment.

Conceptualising

By Naming
- Naming 'sid' (not a commonsense name for coconut), 'sut', 'rut'.
- Scientific labelling: multimodal naming.

With Theory
- Connecting the concepts and generalising: 'Da rut i go andaun'.

Analysing

Functionally

- Why do we need to know about coconuts? (Dangers when growing in public places.)

Critically

- Facing pages of text: Torres Strait Kriol (right) and 'standard English' (not shown). When and to whom do you speak about coconuts in Kriol?

When and to whom in English? (The council workers about moving dangerous ripe coconuts from a tree.)

Applying

Appropriately
- The scientific text (right).

Creatively
- Find out more about coconuts from your parents (Kriol).

Visit the council and find out about the ways in which they manage the danger of falling coconuts (Council English).

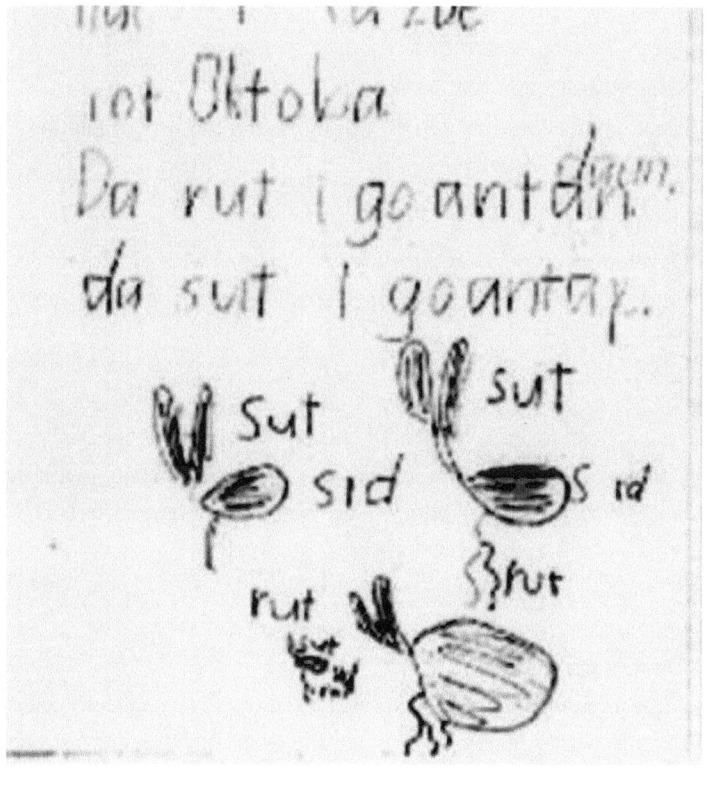

Junior Secondary Science Class, Townsville, Queensland

Knowledge Processes

Experiencing

The Known
- Everyday uses of electricity: what does it do in our lives?

The New
- Cyclone simulation: what would happen if there was no electricity for a while?
- Experimentation with simple circuits.

Conceptualising

By Naming
- Scientific concepts: current etc.
- Electrician's concepts: circuit diagrams, and the way of naming the parts symbolically, visually.

With Theory
- Developing a scientific theory which explains what electricity is.
- Putting the electrician's concepts together into a circuit diagram.

Analysing

Critically
- Contrast everyday domestic descriptions of electricity, with scientific and electrician's descriptions. How and why are they different?

Applying

Creatively
- Create a burglar alarm.
- Draw a circuit diagram to explain how it works to an electrician.
- Explain what's happening in scientific terms on a science program
- Provide your parents an introduction in everyday language on how the alarm works.

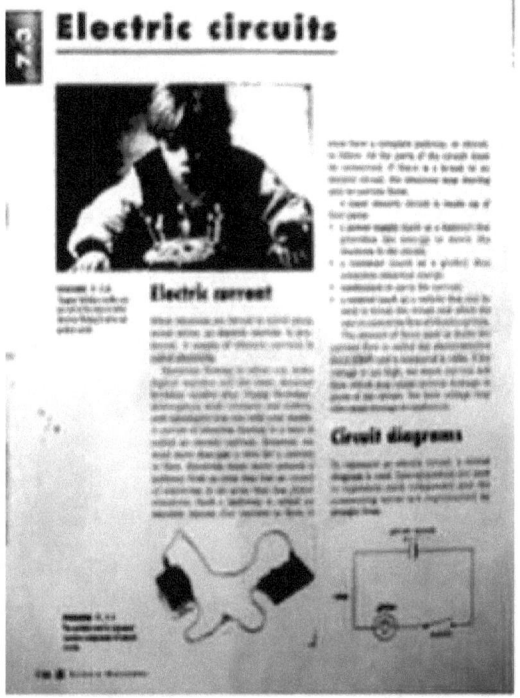

MIDDLE YEARS SOCIAL STUDIES CLASS, KEILOR DOWNS, MELBOURNE

Knowledge Processes

Experiencing

The New
- Visit to local Council to investigate local government elections.

Conceptualising

By Naming
- Framing (how the image is of the candidate is represented).
- Authorisation (a specific part of an election leaflet)

With Theory
- Putting the concepts together to describe the characteristic features of a

Analysing

Functionally
- What the political flyer tries to achieve, its purpose.

Critically
- Selectively says good things about a candidate.

Applying

Appropriately
- Create a political flyer.

Marie and her year 5 class.

Junior Secondary English Class, Townsville, Queensland

Knowledge Processes

Experiencing

The Known
- Bring in your favourite CD.

The New
- Listen to a piece of popular music in an unfamiliar genre.
- Read magazine reviews of music: magazines for different genres.
- Survey other students on favourite music genre.

Conceptualising

By Naming
- Text features: lyrics.
- Musical features.
- Visual features: video clip.

With Theory
- How the various features of meaning work together to create a song in particular genre.

Analysing

Critically
- What kinds of people listen to what kinds of music: heavy metal, hip hop, techno, folk etc?
- How do the record companies market music? How well do they serve the interests of artists?

Applying

Appropriately
- Write a music review.

Creatively
- Write song lyrics, music, perform, film video clip.

NEGOTIATING LEARNER DIVERSITY

The Learning Element architecture touches on the ever-present realities of learner diversity in a number of ways:

- The Learning Element consists of two parallel texts—a teacher resource side (which talks the professional discourse of teaching) and a learner resource side (which speaks directly to the learner in a written form of the language of the classroom). The teacher resource side can be hidden, and just the learner resource side presented to learners, either in electronic or printed form. This serves as a kind of menu for self-managed learner activity, be that self-paced individual learning, or group learning. Drawing on a bank of Learning Elements—either from the teacher's own repertoire or shared with them by other teachers—it is possible to have individual students or groups of students within a class working on different Learning Elements at the same time, depending on their prior knowledge, interests and learning objectives.
- The Learning Element does not presuppose necessary entry points. At its beginning, it asks the question of prior learning. What does the learner already know? Who they already are? How will this particular Learning

Element be of value to them and potentially transformative? From learner to learner, and from group to group, the answers to this question are inevitably going to be various. This is a key in to answering the question of who in the class is going to do which Learning Element and when. Unlike classrooms of old, there is no requirement that every learner is on the same page at the same time.

- Nor does the Learning Element presuppose a particular destination at the exit point. The Learning Pathways question at the end of the Learning Element is something like, 'given who the learner is, what's the next transformative experience, what seems to follow for them?' Given learner diversity, the answer to this, too, will likely be various.

- Even when a whole class is working their way through the same Learning Element, it touches on diverse lifeworld experiences in a number of places and in a number of ways. For instance, Experiencing the Known brings in student experiences which will inevitably be different, and that difference will be introduced there as part of the learning experience. Experiencing the New involves an awareness of the relative distance or strangeness of a new realm of knowledge or action in relation to the datum point of learner identity and knowledge—new experiences can be only just so strange but intelligible to be of value as a learning experience (Vygotsky's 'zone of proximal development'). This will vary from learner to learner. Analysing Critically measures the human interests behind a piece of knowledge or moment of action, and this will necessarily be assessed from the learner's own subjective standpoint. Applying Appropriately takes the learner back to their own 'real' life, and its own particularity. And Applying Creatively is a conscious journey into to new realms, a transformative process in which the reference point is always who the learner already is and their multifarious experiences.

- The overall approach to learner diversity is not one which simply respects the diversity that exists—along the lines of that patronising version of multiculturalism which would preserve different cultures in aspic. Rather it sees diversity as a dynamic thing and learning as the stuff of transformation. It is a journey in which Conceptualising and Analysing adds depth and breadth dimensions to the otherwise flat and often mundane world of Experiencing, such that, when you return to that world in moments of Applying, you discover that the world is not the same, and that you, the learner, are no longer the same person.

LEARNING FRAMEWORK: AT THE LEVEL OF CURRICULUM

The Learning Framework level of documentation pieces Learning Elements together into a coherent program of learning. The heart of this level is the Learning Elements map, a place where Learning Elements are ordered. Typically, traditional curriculum ordered Learning Elements in a linear way, topic by topic, week by week, chapter by chapter. The *Learning by Design* Framework is perfectly capable of this kind of mapping, which might simply take the form of a numbered list.

However in learning communities of difference, a Learning Elements map may be a place where students and teachers negotiate alternative navigation paths, depending on the dynamics of lifeworld difference. Learners might access Learning Elements which suit their needs, interests and abilities, and which stretch these in just the right measure.

The Learning Elements map may be preceded by the preliminaries of curriculum focus, such as defining the curriculum domain (the subject or discipline), the scope of curriculum, the curriculum level and the learning group profile. It may also be preceded by an outline of intended curriculum outcomes, and these could be defined in terms of learner identified outcomes, teacher identified outcomes, instructional designer recommended outcomes or collaboratively resulting in negotiated outcomes.

And the Learning Elements map may be followed by an outline of the processes of curriculum evaluation, or an overall analysis of whether the Learning Framework meets its objectives. This may involve learners, teachers or independent outsiders. Here, the key question to be addressed is to what extent did it meet the aspirations articulated in the intended learning outcomes?

Finally, there's the question of curriculum pathways: what would be an appropriate follow-on Learning Framework or subject within the scope of an overall learning program?

Table 7.4: At the Curriculum Level—The Structure of a Learning Framework

LEARNING FRAMEWORK - CURRICULUM
CURRICULUM FOCUS *Curriculum Domain* *Scope of Curriculum* *Curriculum Level* *Prior Learning*
CURRICULUM OBJECTIVES *Learner Identified Objectives* *Teacher Identified Objectives* *Co-Designed Objectives*
LEARNING ELEMENTS MAP *Instructional Designer Recommended Pathways* *Learner Preferred Pathways* *Co-Designed Pathways*
CURRICULUM EVALUATION *Learner Evaluated Outcomes* *Peer and Outsider-Evaluated Outcomes* *Instructional Designer Recommended Evaluation Tasks*
CURRICULUM PATHWAYS

LEARNING COMMUNITY: AT THE LEVEL OF EDUCATION

Documentation at the Learning Community level may have a variety of purposes, from vision statements, to policies, to overall programs. One kind of Learning Community documentation could be broadly reflective of an educational organisation, or an educational innovation. Key areas to cover in such documentation may include: What is the educational focus: organisation profile, community profile, systems profile, learner group profile and available resources? What are the broad educational objectives in terms of vision and intended outcomes? What is the nature of the particular education intervention that is being documented, be that a Learning Frameworks map in the case of documenting an existing or new learning program, or an educational action plan in the case of an organisational development, community capacity building or school-based research? In the case of an educational action plan, aspects of the documentation process may include descriptions of methodology, community involvement, action stages and the evaluation strategy for the intervention. At the end of the process, actual educational outcomes can be documented, as well as educational pathways—such as recommendations for possible follow-on interventions.

Table 7.5: At the Educational Level—The Structure of a Learning Community Document

LEARNING COMMUNITY - EDUCATION
EDUCATIONAL FOCUS ***Organisation Profile*** ***Community Profile*** ***Systems Profile*** ***Learner Group Profile*** ***Resources***
EDUCATIONAL OBJECTIVES ***Educational Vision*** ***Educational Outcomes***
EDUCATIONAL INTERVENTION ***Learning Frameworks Map*** ***Educational Action Plan*** *Methodology* *Community Involvement* *Stages* *Evaluation Strategy*
EDUCATIONAL OUTCOMES
EDUCATIONAL PATHWAYS

PUTTING THE *LEARNING BY DESIGN* FRAMEWORK INTO PRACTICE

Learning by Design is not prescriptive. It is not a singular and definitive answer to the perennial question of the structure of effective learning. Rather it is a series of building blocks for creating pedagogies, curricula and learning communities, empathically in the plural. Pedagogies, curricula and learning communities written up using the *Learning by Design* Framework can and will vary according to the nature of a discipline, the learning styles of a student and the learning philosophies of a school or a teacher. *Learning by Design* is no more than a series of flags or headings to assist in the process of documenting learning, and share these beyond the otherwise largely ephemeral experience of classroom pedagogy, curriculum implementation or the life of an educational community.

An instructional designer, teacher, educational administrator or learner can use these tags as a kind of scaffold as they document and publish their learning innovation, instructional design or learning experience. Any of these tags can be used, in any combination and in any order. This is not to say that any and all combinations of tags will produce equally effective or valid learning experiences or adequately document the design of educational interventions in a particular learning community. Rather, it is to emphasise the fact that *Learning by Design* is no more than a set of recombinable concepts which will allow alternative frameworks for documenting innovation and curriculum. It is an open language for documenting a wide range of possible pedagogies, possible curricula and possible educational interventions.

Following are a number of key principles underlying *Learning by Design*:

- The *Learning by Design* framework is not prescriptive. Rather, it is a language of education, curriculum and pedagogy. It aims to name as comprehensively as possible, and in as open a fashion as possible, the various aspects of learning and learning communities.
- At the Learning Element level, the *Learning by Design* framework does not prescribe or even recommend a correct pedagogy. Rather, it provides a language by means of which the defining features of pedagogy—any pedagogy, every pedagogy—can be distinguished and named. It can name the prominent aspects of traditional curriculum, and indeed help identify it as such—a curriculum which is heavily skewed to one kind of experiential learning (immersion in new empirical experience) and conceptual learning (the concept definitions and theories that tie a discipline together). It can do the same with progressivist pedagogy, which is often heavily skewed towards the experiential. In certain circumstances, these choices of pedagogy may be entirely appropriate and defensible—as in the cases of Koranic learning and the subject matter of elementary particle physics already mentioned in Chapter 4.
- The *Learning by Design* framework consists of a number of concept-tags: labels that can be applied to the different parts of learning content or the stages of a learning experience. Although they are laid out in a particular way for clarity of exposition, there is no rigid order or essential sequence to these concept tags.
- The *Learning by Design* framework serves a number of practical functions. It works as a scaffold for writing up learning processes for the purpose of sharing these with other teachers, learners and communities. In the most practical of senses, the concept tags can be cut and pasted as structural markers into publishable documents. *Learning by Design* sets out to make the stages or aspects of the learning process transparent. It aims to add structure and rigour, not only to the documentation process, but to the processes of curriculum development and delivery.
- The *Learning by Design* framework provides definitions of each concept-tag in a dictionary of learning concepts. Synonyms of each concept can be mapped into the major approaches to pedagogy by means

of conceptual 'crosswalks'. For instance, *Learning by Design* tag-concepts have been mapped one by one against their synonyms in Bloom's taxonomy (Anderson & Krathwohl, 2001) and Kolb's theory of experiential learning (Kolb, 1984). This process continues as the research continues. In other words, *Learning by Design* can be used as a way of 'doing' Bloom's taxonomy or Kolb's experiential learning, or whatever pedagogy a teacher chooses to use in a particular learning setting. For that matter, you could 'do' rigorously traditional forms of curriculum, such as Direct Instruction, mapping these also against *Learning by Design*—and that mapping would reveal the narrowness of their pedagogical range.

- The *Learning by Design* framework serves as a kind of checklist. What are the emphases of a particular set of learning activities? And are these sufficient to meet the needs of learners and to convey the breadth of discipline-specific subject matter? Could these be extended? Such a checklist might well (but not necessarily) point to the possibility of extending learning in the direction of a transformative curriculum. Transformative curriculum involves the appropriate and where feasible balanced use of a variety experiential, conceptual, analytical and applied knowledge processes.

In sum, *Learning by Design* provides tools at three levels.

- At the Learning Community Level it provides tools by means of which learning organisations (such as schools, further and higher education institutions) or units within learning organisations (such as divisions, departments, faculties) can document educational innovation, programs, research and evaluation.
- At the Learning Framework level, it provides tools for the documentation of curriculum—programs of learning at the level of courses, subjects or individual customised learning. This is a space in which instructional designers, curriculum developers and educators wishing to publish their curriculum innovations to the wider world, may choose to work.

And at the Learning Element level, it provides some basic concepts for the documentation of pedagogy—the microdynamics of learning experiences, tasks or activities. This is a space in which teachers and curriculum designers can document and publish their work. It is also a space in which learners may be able to document their learnings for the purposes of building a portfolio of their learning experience and sharing them with each other. These three forms of documentation can be nested within each other—a Learning Element within the context of a Learning Framework, and this within the context of a Learning Community. Effective documentation, however, can occur at each of these three levels separately, or at all three levels, or in combinations of levels.

Table 7.6: Documenting Pedagogy, Curriculum and Education

1. Pedagogy – the HOW of formal learning. The way that learning activities are selected and designed and experienced in any learning encounter. This is at the heart of learning and has the greatest impact on the performance/outcomes of the learner.
The micro designs of learning activities: The knowledge processes of *Pedagogy*.
For example, a sequence of learning activities such as a lesson, a group of lessons, a chapter in a textbook—A LEARNING ELEMENT.
2. Curriculum – the WHAT of formal learning. Subject choices, content material, discipline fields and orientation to knowledge. These decisions are important for social, economic and political reasons and change in focus from time to time.
The macro designs of learning programs, subjects and disciplines: The framework of *Curriculum*.
For example, a subject for a term or a year, a whole program of teaching or textbook that 'covers the course'— A LEARNING FRAMEWORK.
3. Education – the WHY of formal learning. The goals and expectations of range of stakeholders, for example, learner, teacher, school, community district, government and so on.
The social designs of learning communities: The institution of *Education*.
For example, the vision, plans and curriculum offerings of a school, and research into or evaluation of the performance of a school— A LEARNING COMMUNITY.

CHAPTER 8

Creating Common Educational Knowledge

The *Learning by Design* approach also draws upon the emerging theory of 'knowledge management' (Cope & Kalantzis, 2002; B. Martin, 2002; Scarbrough, 2001; Stewart, 1998). This theory raises key questions pertinent to schools, including:

- How can planning and documentation processes be improved, particularly in a networked digital communications environment?
- To what extent can tacit professional knowledge be made explicit, and to what ends (such as sharing professional knowledge in the 'learning organisation', transparency and accountability with learners and parents)?
- To what extent can systematic reflection on pedagogy in the planning and documentation process improve teaching and learner outcomes?

This chapter considers how the *Learning by Design* framework can be implemented, as a knowledge management project that is akin to publishing processes.

Managing Pedagogical, Curriculum and Educational Knowledge

All human groups—be they families, community groups, businesses or educational organisations—work with knowledge as a matter of course. As defined in Chapter 5, knowledge is the connection between the stuff of the mind and the stuff of the world. It is not just thinking. Knowledge is also acting and meaning.

With knowing, comes learning. In the context of the everyday learning in the lifeworld, knowing and learning are more or less implicit, organic and deeply embedded. They are an unconscious part of everyday practices. There is minimal need for explicit articulation and little or no need for documentation. Knowledge is pervasive but unmanaged; learning is everywhere but not pedagogical, curricular or educational.

Knowledge management is the systematic, conscious and explicit process of capturing and documenting knowledge (Cope & Kalantzis, 2002). Institutions of learning manage knowledge in a number of ways: as course prospectuses, annual reports, curriculum outlines and lesson plans, for instance. However, much of this documentation is for a limited audience—and in the case of a lesson plan, it may be so limited as to serve the teacher's everyday needs and meet minimal performance review requirements. Rarely would this knowledge be captured in such a way as to fill the space of the textbook in the case of learner resources, or the space of a teaching resource book in the case of teacher resources. The effect is either that, on the one hand, localised knowledge stays with the individual teacher or, on the other hand, the space of the learning experience is filled with generic commercially published textbook and teacher resource material which may be inappropriate to local conditions or the range of learners in the classroom.

People may know things, and this is implicit in their practice. This knowledge, however, is of limited value in and of itself. It is of restricted value if it is not transferred or transferable to other people within a community of common interest. Knowledge management involves the transformation of personal knowledge into common knowledge through a process of communication.

Personal knowledge may well be founded on a profound personal or professional understanding of an area of practice, such as pedagogy, curriculum or education. However, it remains ephemeral if it is left implicit, internalised and individualised. This is called tacit knowledge because it resides in individual minds and frequently remains unarticulated (B. Martin, 2002; Polanyi, 1962).

Common knowledge, on the other hand, is knowledge that is collaboratively constructed and socially shared. Wheels are not reinvented. Lessons from mistakes are learnt once. The knowledge of the organisation or community is not dangerously depleted when a key person departs. Common knowledge, however, requires high levels of communication or knowledge transfer. In organisations where knowledge is managed well, common knowledge is formally documented in a process strikingly akin to publishing. The resulting 'published product' is explicit, externalised, shared social knowledge.

The literature on 'knowledge management' describes the ways in which system and rigour—active learning by design—might be added to the knowledge which is implicit and informally learnt within organisations (Cope & Kalantzis, 2002; Davenport & Prusak, 2000; Scarbrough, 2001). Our theoretical starting point here is the emerging literature on knowledge management. This literature is one aspect of a wider theorisation of the emergence of an 'information society'

(Castells, 2000, 2001). More specifically, the 'knowledge management' literature speaks of the ways in which any organisations or communities of practice transform tacit, personal knowledge into explicit, common organisational or professional knowledge (Cope & Kalantzis, 2002; Davenport & Prusak, 2000; Scarbrough, 2001; Stewart, 1998; Wenger, 1999; Wenger, McDermott, & Snyder, 2002).

First, to allay a commonsense assumption: all-too-often, 'knowledge management' means IT solutions and these take the form of out-of-the-box IT systems, or content management systems, or groupware. To be sure, the new technologies have the capacity to enable and transform knowledge. They also have an enormous capacity to enable informal learning, both for novices and partially knowledgeable collaborators. But more than IT, knowledge is also the stuff of incessant talk, collaborative working relationships, personalised stories and constant learning.

With or without technology assistance, knowledge management involves transforming personal knowledge into common knowledge, implicit and individual knowledge into explicit and shared understandings and everyday common sense into systematic designs. It is also the business of codifying these designs as information architectures, paradigms or disciplines. The knowledge management transition in this expanded sense stands in a direct parallel with the transition from everyday informal learning to systematised formal learning that characterises disciplinary knowledge.

Not that this transition leaves the world of tacit and individual subjectivity behind as a poor cousin to something that might be mistakenly considered to be knowledge proper, in the same way that formal learning can never supersede the rich situatedness of informal learning. On the contrary, herein lies the raw material of intuitive professional judgement and creative problem solving. The shape of things sometimes can sometimes be felt in an intuitive way before it can be explicitly articulated.

This is a new task for the knowledge or learning organisation. However, the extra work of organising knowledge should create less work overall. This is the basis of the 'learning organisation' the sum of whose knowledge is greater than the individual components of knowledge in the heads of individuals (Senge, 1990).

Knowledge management or organisational learning involves:

- *Capturing Data:* the rudimentary work of collecting the raw material of everyday experience. This raw material is captured in the form of

numbers, names, lists, texts, images and the like. These data are direct representations of the world in the form of discrete, unanalysed, uninterrupted 'facts'.
- *Systematising Information:* the work of categorising, verifying, aggregating, sorting, calculating and summarising data. Numerical data becomes financial information once entered into a financial management system; data on individual customers becomes customer-base information once entered into a database; data in the form of digital content documents become information when they are filed and made accessible in a digital repository.
- *Synthesising Knowledge:* the work of drawing conclusions from information, critically evaluating the relevance and significance of information, and applying the conclusions drawn from this interpretative and evaluative work to everyday life situations. These processes involve cognitive processes of abstraction (making generalisations which encompass numerous particulars), inference (drawing conclusions), interpreting (drawing together significant information from a mass of information), critique (assessing the validity and truth claims of information) and transfer (applying conclusions drawn in one situation to other possible situations). They also involve the active processes of application of knowledge to the world—testing, implementing and evaluating. At the point of application, the cycle commences again: capturing data, systematising information and creating further knowledge.

Knowledge management is not simply about the creation of an abstract resource — something created by the processing of data into information and information into knowledge — it is also a set of social relations and a process of communication. Knowledge management involves the transformation of personal knowledge into common knowledge through the processes of communication and organisational learning. Knowledge is of limited value in and of itself. People may know things, but this knowledge is of restricted worth if it is not transferable and transferred to other people within a community of common interest. Every moment of learning is, or is potentially, a moment of teaching and learning.

Personal knowledge, moreover, may be well founded on the rigours of data capture, information systematisation and knowledge synthesis. It may well be based on a fully accredited formal qualification. However, it remains ephemeral if it is left internalised, individualised and implicit in a person's practical capacities.

Common knowledge, however, requires high levels of communication or knowledge transfer. In fact, it involves systematising processes of learning across the organisation. In knowledge organisations, common knowledge is also formally documented in a process strikingly akin to the creation and teaching of disciplinary knowledge. It is explicit, externalised, shared, social knowledge.

The business of transforming personal knowledge into common knowledge involves a number of processes of definition and refinement, and these processes of refinement reflect the characteristic features of publishing:

- *Information* Architectures: Effective communication occurs within recognisable information designs. In the Learning by Design approach, three flexible information architectures have been developed for the documentation of a Learning Element (describing pedagogy), a Learning Framework (describing curriculum) and a Learning Community (describing education). Information architectures are characteristically represented as schemas. The schema of a book, for instance, consists of a cover, title page, copyright page, table of contents, parts, chapters, chapter sections and subsections, appendices, bibliography and the like. Although there are enormous variations between books (novels, picture books, technical books, textbooks etc.), they are all recognisable (and thus readily 'readable') because we know what to expect from the book as an information architecture. So it is with learning. There are certain characteristic features of learning and these can be represented schematically or paradigmatically. This level of clarity, however, does not mean that within the overall paradigm of learning there might not be enormous variations in pedagogy, curriculum in education. Indeed, the schema may well reveal significant variations.
- *Collaboration:* Authoritative texts are almost invariably created socially, the product not only of their authors but also of collaborators who play various commissioning, editorial, referee and publication roles. Commissioning: a head of the social science department (publisher) might suggest that a teacher (author) write up the Learning Element on the migration experience. Editorial: the head then comments on various drafts. Referee: other members of the department, and an external educational consultant, all look at draft and make comments. Publication: when the work is completed, and is deemed to be of a standard worthy of publication into the bank of Learning Elements being developed by the Social Science department, it is published to the web

for access by other departmental members, learners, parents and maybe also the wider world. The quality of the text is in the careful social construction that has gone into it.
- *Validation:* Authoritative texts are the product of delegation (only the members of the Social Science Department at the school can publish into their bank of Learning Elements, and in this case a particular teacher was invited to write up their Learning Element). They are also published at the end of a quality-filtering process, and with the authority of a person or group who wishes to maintain the integrity of the developing knowledge bank.
- *Access:* Knowledge is then made available on the basis of 'permissions'—to the audiences for whom the documents in which it is embodied were designed. In the case of a school, teacher resources may be made available only to teachers, and learner resources to teachers, learners or parents. Or they might be made available to the through the web to the wide world, free or at a cost.

These publishing processes can be layered from level to level: the school council as publisher of Learning Community documentation authored by working groups of parents, teachers or administrators as authors; the school programs committee as publisher of Learning Framework documentation authored by teachers or school departments; school departments or curriculum project groups as publishers of Learning Elements authored by teachers; and teachers as publishers of student resources authored by learners themselves.

At any and every level, publishing is a metaphor for the documentation of knowledge in recognisably regular yet flexibly variable information architectures, using processes of collaboration for content development and the validation of quality, and providing access according to the intentions of the parties to the publishing process.

Networked computers and the Internet may well be handy tools in this process, but the key difference between knowledge management processes and the practices of making web pages or sending emails is the collaboration factor. Neither web pages nor emails require collaboration—and in this sense they are simply a transmission medium. Knowledge management requires systematic processes of collaboration, and it is not until the web is used to facilitate systematic collaboration that it truly becomes a publishing medium.

These are the formal, documentary aspects of knowledge management within an organisation. These are tremendously important as highly considered, focused distillations of knowledge, all designed for transfer of knowledge through effective communication. At the level of the organisation they replicate the processes of creating scientific, technical or domain-specific knowledge across the profession itself. They turn the organisation into a knowledge producing community, as well as an entity which derives and replicates received professional knowledge. And they turn the organisation from a group of learned professionals into an active learning organisation which is also a dynamic teaching organisation.

This, however, is not to ignore the informal processes of knowledge transfer, of taking what is implicit in personal knowledge and creating common knowledge through one-on-one interactions, often orally—such as mentoring or simply scaffolding learning on a personal basis. These informal processes can include novice-to-expert queries, team meetings, stories, informal conversations and private advice. These interactions will mostly be ad hoc, for the most practical of reasons. They are instantaneous and inexpensive forms of knowledge transfer, and powerfully connected to practical and immediate learning needs. The question remains, to what extent can these teacherly qualities be systematised, promoted and taught? And to what extent can the informal domain can be linked into formal knowledge management systems through expertise directories, help lines, training programs or documented planning forums? Dynamic knowledge management rests on multichannel communications and multiple modes of learning in which a rich informal culture of knowledge transfer is supplemented with a formal program of knowledge management which distils and makes accessible essential professional knowledge.

IMPLEMENTING THE LEARNING BY DESIGN FRAMEWORK

Earlier in this volume, we touched briefly on the potentials of the new, digitised information and communications technology, a subject we have addressed at greater length elsewhere (Cope & Kalantzis, 2004a, 2004b). Needless to say, the debate about the digital future swings between the breathless optimism of the technologists to bleak views of the baleful consequences of the 'grey ecologies' of machine-mediated telepresence and the digital divide (Virilio, 1997). We would argue that much which is regarded as new, such as the 'virtual', hypertextuality and non-linear reading (Chartier, 1998, 2001; Gilster, 1997; Mitchell, 1995), does little more than make more efficient the epistemological modes of text that developed in the centuries immediately following the invention of print in 1450.

However, genuinely new potentials emerge with the multimodality (text, still and moving image, sound) intrinsic to digital convergence, its economies of scale and its highly distributed character. Older centralised, 'transmission' models of knowledge and learning are being be replaced in part by the collaborative work in knowledge producing communities—be this in organisations, professions or institutions of learning.

There is nothing in elearning, however, which is meaningfully different to learning without the 'e'. It's just that a distributed digital information and communications infrastructure will facilitate the blurring of the boundaries between the formal and the informal domains, and between tacit knowledge designs and actively designed knowledge management systems. The new technologies just make it easier to do what we would have wanted to do anyway, but there is no inherent message in their medium.

The first phase of 'elearning' was concerned to use the digital medium as a new way of delivering content to learners in the form, for instance, of digital 'learning objects'—effectively textbooks that move. The second phase attempts a more fundamental shift in the human relationships of learning and the directions of the knowledge flows. It can work with minimal computer access, but foreshadows a time, perhaps five or ten years hence, when every learner will have a laptop computer and possibly a range of other digital content creation and communications devices. Working in the digital medium will likely become as ubiquitous as the pen and paper of the traditional classroom. This is already the case in a few schools, but the full educational potentials of the digital technologies have as yet nowhere been realised.

Here is a scenario for the near future, closer to the vision of 'knowledge management':

- Students will use continuously networked computers to source a wide range of educational and general resources.
- Teachers will create and publish modular Learning Elements which students can access and work through at their own pace, individually or in groups, and negotiate alternative learning pathways with their teachers.
- Students will do their work in private collaboration spaces, invite in other creators to access the same files the case of (increasingly important) collaborative work; the teacher will act as a 'publisher' of this work, reviewing and commenting on drafts until a final work is ready to be published simultaneously to the class website as well as the student's personal website.

- Every student will have their own website, which serves both as a digital portfolio of published works, and a 'weblog' which performs an identity-defining function (images, diary, personal biography etc.).

This will fundamentally change the human and knowledge relations of learning:

- Learners will be autonomous and responsible, working at their own pace and following learning pathways determined by their own prior knowledge and lines of interest.
- Collaborations and joint work will be easily managed and using devices such as emails mirrored in a web-based spool of messages so that each time a collaborator makes a change to a work, and capturing the conversations and negotiations around the evolution of a work.
- The audience for a student work will be increasingly lateral, communicated not just to the teacher but also to fellow students, the wider learning community and parents.
- The direction of knowledge flows will be bottom-up less than top-down: learners will use a variety of sources to build their own knowledge and teachers will translate broad curriculum goals into locally engaged curriculum.
- Learning will be localised, relevant and engaged, connecting with the learner's social environment, personal interests and experience, whilst making powerful links between local or specific knowledge and global or general knowledge.
- From being the objects of broadcast knowledge (textbooks to learning objects) schools will become knowledge creating communities.

How, then, can schools become knowledge producing communities and not just receivers and transmitters of knowledge? What might be the value of using the *Learning by Design* framework? Following are some features of the *Designs for Learning* framework:

- Authentic, relevant, local, community-linked, engaged learning.
- Rigorous management of school, teacher and learner intellectual property.
- Peer-to-peer classroom interactions: from teacher talk to learner collaborations.
- From knowledge purchasers and receivers to knowledge producing communities.

Creating Common Educational Knowledge 131

- Private and public spaces.
- Open-ness and transparency in learning communities.
- Rich assessment: digital portfolios as a record of learning.

The *Learning by Design* approach, in the case study presented, uses CGPublisher as its content management platform (Common Ground, 2003-2005a). CGPublisher consists of two spaces:

- A private space where works are stored and people collaborate to draft and edit these works; and
- Public websites, where these works are published, and personal websites for the authors and publisher websites where all the community's works is published.

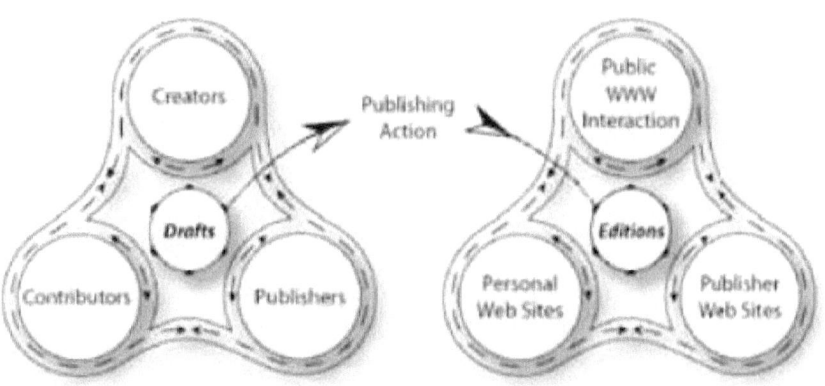

Figure 8.1: A Publishing Model for Knowledge Producing Schools

Publishing sites can be nested within publishing sites, as illustrated by the following example:

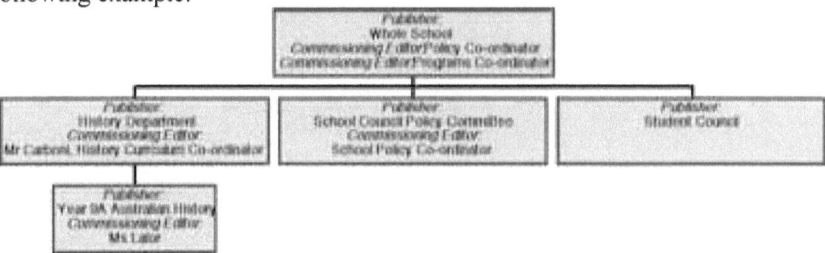

Figure 8.2: Nested Publishers within Publishers, Communities within Communities

At a school level, a cascading series of publishing sites might be interlinked as follows. The implementation strategy can harness either or both of top-down energies (digital knowledge management) or bottom-up (build upon on the energies of students by giving them personal websites, from which they can build collaborations with other students, teachers can subsequently take on a 'publisher' role etc.).

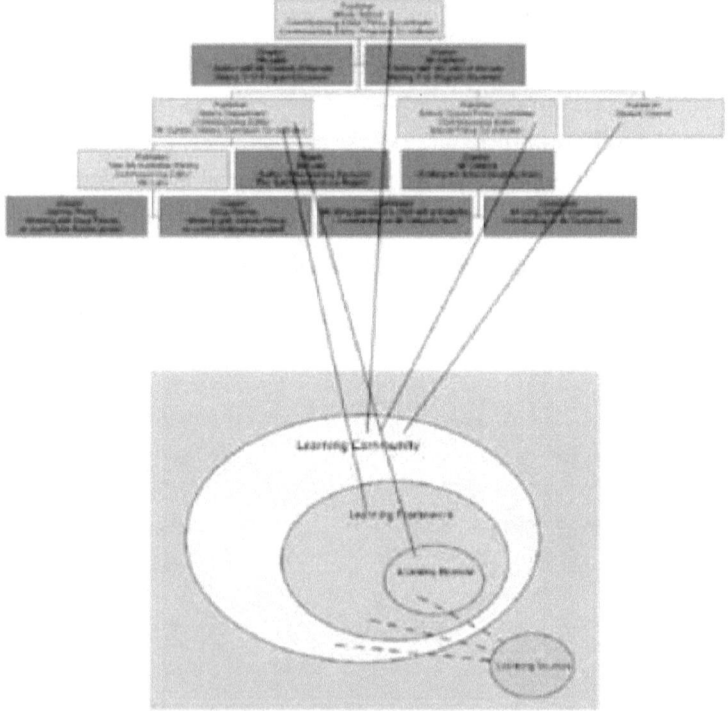

Figure 8.3: Levels of Publishing Activity and Different Forms of Documentation in a School (Key: Blue = Publisher Sites; Green = Creator Sites)

How, in a practical sense, might the *Learning by Design* Framework work? CGPublisher is the knowledge management tool being used by the *Learning by Design* research and development project. Teachers work in Microsoft Word templates which give stylistic consistency to their work, and publish these to 'bookstores' within CGPublisher. Within the templates, they cut the concept-tags and paste them in whichever combination and order suits the needs of their learners and the particular body of knowledge their learners are addressing. These templates give explicit pedagogical shape to the curriculum they are writing up. CGPublisher also provides a collaborative space within which co-authors can work together, and works can be commissioned, refereed, reviewed, copy-edited and approved for publication.

In terms of technology requirements, implementation of CGPublisher requires no more than a networked computer with a web browser and a word processing program. Within this environment, the Learning by Design templates are authoring tools, with templates representing each of three levels of documentation—Learning Community, Learning Framework and Learning Element. These word templates can be published within the broader CGPublisher online content management system, in which any kind of downloadable or printable file or template format may be used.

The *Learning by Design* templates simultaneously provide two kinds of structural support (and in both cases, the templates are flexible and suggestive rather than rigid and insistent):

1. *Presentational:* by providing text/style formats and page designs which will look good and work well for print and ebook rendering.
2. *Structural:* by providing prompts relating to possible information architectures for published material documenting pedagogy, curriculum or educational interventions.

The designs for learning created at the local level can be published to the web, becoming part of the teacher's portfolio of published works on their personal website, as well as becoming part of the ever-expanding knowledge bank of the school or educational jurisdiction.

The operational aim of both CGPublisher and the *Learning by Design* templates is to make publishers of people and organisations with knowledge, content and experience who would not otherwise be in a position to publish. Its aim is to turn the 'commonsense' of everyday practice into explicit and well presented documentation.

One of the less remarked but profoundly significant aspects of the new communications environment is digital printing . Herein lies a means of using the digital revolution to cross the digital divide. Nor does every learner have to be tethered to computer to enjoy the benefits of digitisation. One computer may serve many teachers and learners. The computer can a means by curriculum is documented and published, and also a place from which multiple copies of a resource can be printed, either to a network printer or by remote order to a printing company—which may even be able to print and bind a piece of work to professional standards as a paperback book. CGPublisher supports both ebook (electronically downloadable) and pbook (printable) formats, as well as any other electronic file format (audio, video, digital still image, multimedia). The medium is cheap and accessible, both from the point of view of creators and consumers.

CGPublisher sets up an environment which emulates traditional publishing, with all its quality control and checking filters. Nothing simply gets published. Rather, it sets up a series of publishing relationships involving author, referee, editorial and publishing roles. Texts are socially constructed and systematically evaluated before they 'go live'—and when they do, they go live in two places: on the publisher website as well as the author's personal website.

Thus, within an educational setting, there may be many layers of author (creator) and publisher (approval) relationships. In a classroom, the publisher may be the teacher (one publisher site representing the best of the class's work, with multiple author sites for each of the learners and to which their work is published once approved by the publisher/teacher). Or the publisher of Learning Elements and Learning Frameworks might be the school department, and the authors the teachers who are writing up their best teaching/learning programs. Or the publisher of a Learning Community document might be the school, once the final draft produced by the authors, parents or working group has been approved. Or the publisher of any of these kinds of documents authored by members of schools might be the education system, or a consultant working within the system.

The benefits of adopting this publishing approach to educational content development are as follows:

- *Empowerment:* Conferring power to teachers and schools or other learning institutions by giving them the capacity to document, archive and disseminate (commercially or for free) their best work.
- *Content development:* providing teachers and learning institutions with a publishing process management tool (conceptualisation, copyright agreement, manuscript development and publication in an online bookstore) managed by delegated publishing editors within the learning institution.
- *Flexibility and modularity:* allowing for the publication of units of work as small as a Learning Element.
- *Local relevance:* creating materials relevant to local community and individual learner needs.
- *Diversity:* building up a modularised knowledge bank which allows considerable flexibility in learning paths, from class to class and even learner to learner.

- *Knowledge management:* building, archiving and publishing a progressively expanding knowledge bank, preserving corporate or learning community memory for access by new teachers and learning community members.
- *Knowledge efficiencies:* reducing the inherent tendency of teachers to 'reinvent the wheel' in school-based curriculum, whilst at the same time reducing the teacher and the school's dependency on commercially published textbooks.
- *Transparency:* with parental as well as teacher and student access to material documented and published by the school.
- *Access:* with all published material downloadable either as ebook or printed from source files for distribution to people without immediate computer access.
- *Progression:* creating a pathway for ongoing experimentation and integration of emerging online activities and resources with conventional curriculum resource development processes.
- *Commercialisation:* providing teachers and schools with a platform through which to sell their best work to the wider world, and thus commercialise school-based intellectual property. (CGPublisher manages ecommerce and digital rights.)

In these ways, digital technologies (print, screen, the Internet) can form the basis of new learning environments which allow diversified engagement with learning more appropriate to the range of students' interests and capacities; they can facilitate the creation of non-linear curricula; and they can support the creation of a publishing environment in which the readership of student work is a community of peers as well as a public audience of family and community.

It is the purpose of the *Learning by Design* Framework and CGPublisher to provide tools with which to capture the ephemeral, to articulate the tacit, to transform personal-professional knowledge into common knowledge. They also build on the premise that knowledge is social and knowledge construction is best approached collaboratively.

A take up strategy for such an approach to education might be to:

- Start small: scalability, from a personal website, to becoming a publisher, to linking publishers—then it's a matter of growing the user base from the:

- Bottom-up: the personal websites are infectious, and these create self-expanding horizons as the communication and collaboration potentials open up; or alternative, the impetus for taking on this kind of a model might be:
- Top-down: the need of content management systems to put order into the digital chaos, unlock islands of content and put a community or even dollar value the school's intellectual property.

Two key concepts underlie this approach to educational knowledge management: paradigm and narrative. Paradigm consists of the concepts used to define the processes of pedagogy, curriculum and education. These are metalanguage of sorts, a language by means of which it is possible to speak explicitly about the language of learning. The 'tags' within the *Learning by Design* templates speak this language. They are also accompanied by 'crosswalks'—a thesaurus of tag synonyms—by means of which it is possible to 'do' any pedagogy within the same templates.

Narrative is what actually happens in the development or realisation of the learning design laid out within a Learning Element, Learning Framework or Learning Community document. It is how the 'movements' in a Learning Element play themselves out for a particular resource writer, teacher or learner, or how they hang together in the case of a particular theme within a particular discipline. In this sense, paradigm is by no means prescriptive. It provides not so much a structure for knowledge, but open possibilities in which learning takes its own narrative course—for the realisation of pedagogies, curricula and educational alternatives emphatically in the plural, and thus knowledges, equally in the plural.

The results should include transparency and accountability— making learning processes visible to professional co-workers, learners and the wider community. They should create efficiencies in stringent times, making more work in the first instance but less work in the longer run, where knowledge is captured, reapplied and revised. And they should also add a layer of quality assurance, as knowledge is made official through a filtering system of commissioning, drafting, collaborative writing, refereeing, reviewing, editing and approving for publication.

What does all this managing of knowledge do? It creates a different kind of educational organisation. This organisation is one in which certain kinds of knowledge rise to higher levels of validity. This is the knowledge that has been collaboratively constructed, is widely informed, is cross-referenced—and these processes give it a collegial or organisational imprimatur. This knowledge becomes authoritative to the extent that the processes of knowledge construction are made transparent. And the unidirectional (top-bottom, expert-novice, organisation-customer) transmission of knowledge is replaced by knowledge as dialogue.

This, then, is an outline of a knowledge management agenda for education. Its overall aims are to change the sources of knowledge and the direction of content flows, to create greater transparency in learning communities and to broaden the professional repertoires of educators. And in terms of the themes with which this volume opened, one of the overarching aims is to provide a space for the creation of learning environments which are sensitive to difference, and which programmatically deploy diversity as a strategy for educational and social access.

In this last task lies a paradox. On the one hand, we may be agnostic about lifeworld origins, yet we are interested in access and diversity—and some lifeworlds deny one or both of these possibilities. Translating this paradox into the domain of education, on the one hand out of respect for difference we may be agnostic about different forms of pedagogy, curriculum and education—differences in the ways in which the knowledge processes or 'learning movements' are orchestrated, and the thematic and disciplinary narratives they embody. On the other hand, we are interested in an agenda of transformation which does not remain satisfied with differences the way they are. It strongly implies that a broader and more modulated repertoire of learning movements is preferable, and that learning should take learners into new and potentially transformational places.

NEW LEARNING: REALISING THE VISION

This volume has worked across two knowledge and learning domains, the informal/tacit, and the formal/explicit. The former has a design, the latter is 'by design'. Our project as educators is to make informal learning somewhat more 'by design'. This is when as theorists and practitioners we need to venture beyond the walls of schools, technical colleges and universities, to examine the dynamics of knowledge and learning in workplaces, professions and other communities of practice. And on the return journey, we may be able to bring the engaged situatedness of informal learning and tacit knowledge to bear on formal learning, and so make education in its traditional forms more to the point and more relevant.

Which brings us to the core theoretical frame of reference: the distinction between the everyday lifeworld and 'science', as made by Husserl (Husserl, 1970). This is a distinction which we have elaborated upon, extended and modified elsewhere (Cope & Kalantzis, 2000a). We would like to propose that we define our discipline as a science of learning, not in the narrower sense of that word which predominates in today's Anglophone world, but in the broader sense of the word in other European languages, as a process of systematic inquiry. In counterdistinction to the relative unconscious, unreflexive knowledge in and of the lifeworld, such a science of learning sets out to interpret designs which are beyond and beneath the everyday, amorphous pragmatics of the lifeworld. It brings these designs to consciousness and on this basis develops agendas for action. Our project in the science of learning no less than to develop an understanding of system and method in learning, not just in conventional learning settings, but those everyday lifeworld settings where so much learning occurs. Today's teaching profession is alive with possibilities for such a science.

Translating this broad vision into educational pragmatics, the new classroom will have no fixed walls. It will involve groups of learners of any size, small and large. Students will be able to learn at home and in the community as well as at school; they will be able to work in self-managing learning teams (supported by Learning Elements, and navigating their way through Learning Frameworks) and create collaborative works; they will be knowledge makers as much as they are knowledge receivers.

Schools whose learning is by design in the broad senses discussed in this volume will:

- Harness and build upon the energies of learners and reduce the dependence on teacher direction.
- Be more transparent and accountable: teacher-designed curriculum (Learning Elements and Learning Frameworks) will be fully visible to learners and parents; and student work will be published to rich web-based digital portfolios, demonstrating what the learner has done and knows, in preference to a single numerical score.
- Foster lateral communications between learners, increasingly using peers as tutors, reviewers and assessors of student work.
- Maintain audit trails which make collaborative and autonomous work practical and viable, as well as reducing the incentive to plagiarise.
- Foster digital literacy, not as something that schools will need to teach any more than they would have needed to teach SMS messaging to young people; rather this learning will most likely be from peers, help menus or trial and error.

- Manage more effectively the intellectual capital of schools, building knowledge banks of locally engaged but broadly shareable teacher professional knowledge—developing, in other words, a system of knowledge management.
- Build a culture of professional co-operation and teamwork, capturing professional knowledge and instructional designs, and sharing these as common organisational knowledge.
- Blur the physical and institutional boundaries between school and the wider world of family, community and workplace.
- Develop integrated patterns of institutional subsidiarity and federalism, with government and systemic guidelines flexibly interpreted at the local level alongside transparent accountability and quality assurance processes.
- Use fully multimodal content creation and communications strategies, supporting linguistic, visual and audio modes, with works varying from written texts, to still and moving images, spoken voice and music, multimedia, datasets, software applications etc.
- Support learner diversity: engagement with varied interests, identities and experiences; allow self-paced learning; and facilitate alternative learning pathways within an overall learning environment.

... and so, these schools will be more effective in achieving optimal outcomes for all learners.

Part II
Learning in Practice

CHAPTER 9

Learning by Design: A Marriage of Theory and Practice

Peter Burrows

The profession of teaching is in the throws of a tumultuous transition —teachers, from most disciplines, must learn to understand new and emerging technologies and media, and develop skills in these areas. Luke argues that we are at a moment 'where the kids know more about the technologies than we do—where their mastery of practices and, indeed, mastery of new forms of reason, bypasses ours'.

Teachers now must cope with more diverse student groups— students with a variety of dispositions, sensibilities and learning needs and they must do this while caught up in a generational shift as baby-boomers retire and new teachers enter the profession.

How are teachers to manage this transition? Are the pedagogical practices of the past appropriate to the present or the future? How will new teachers be supported, guided and mentored through this transitionary period? How can the pedagogical expertise of older teachers be shared with new teachers?

In earlier chapters Mary Kalantzis and Bill Cope eloquently set out the theory of *Learning by Design*, where considerations of pedagogy prevail, and they identify the close relationship between *Learning by Design* and the theory of Multiliteracies. In later chapters the *Learning by Design* project-consultants Anne Cloonan, Mary Neville and Rita van Haren explore the ways in which the theories of *Learning by Design* and Multiliteracies were enacted in classrooms in Queensland, Victoria and the Australian Capital Territory (ACT). In these chapters the relationship between Multiliteracies, *Learning by Design* and State educational agendas is also explored.

In the following three chapters the aim of the author is to draw lessons for the future of teaching and learning from the RMIT University funded Learning by Design Project, lessons which will help policy-makers and teachers manage the above-mentioned transition. The author also aims to help the reader understand how the quite complex theories of Learning by Design and Multiliteracies were married and dialogically transformed into practice via conversations between theorists, project-consultants, school principals and teacher-practitioners and through the use of a pedagogical-designframework-and-heuristic (pedagogical framework). This framework took the form of a structured, though open and flexible, Microsoft Word template, which teachers from a range of disciplines including english, science and maths used for planning and documenting their classroom practice.

A marriage of theory and practice was created where, together, theorists and practitioners figured out new ways of teaching. The products of these new ways of teaching were powerful, more inclusive learning experiences documented as Learning Elements inside the *Learning by Design* pedagogical framework and shared via a web-publishing medium. The dialogic that emerged from this marriage was both supported by, and manifested in, the various iterations of the framework and in the diverse range of Learning Elements created by teachers. (The reader is encouraged to explore the richness and diversity of these Learning Elements first-hand by visiting the web-site: www.L-by-D.com) In this way the *Learning by Design* pedagogical framework acted to prompt and expand teachers' repertoires of practice as well as providing them with a means to document and share that practice with other teachers. For the theory-makers, Kalantzis and Cope this has meant iterating ever more rigorous theory informed by teacher practice.

In these three chapters the *Learning by Design* Project is explored via an examination of the roles played by the various actors as the project unfolded:

- the children whose diverse needs prompted and stimulated other actors;
- the direct and hands-on involvement of the 'theory-makersdesigners', their theory and pedagogical framework;
- the principals and school leaders whose leadership and support were central to the enactment of Multiliteracies and *Learning by Design*;
- the experienced and multi-talented pedagogical mentors (project-consultants) engaged to support teachers in state-based trials;
- the teachers as theory-enactors involved in transforming *Learning by Design* and Multiliteracies theory into classroom practice;
- and, the teachers as author-publishers of *Learning by Design*, sharing their practices and experiences with others.

The themes, findings and lessons explored in the following chapters are the result of research carried out by the author for RMIT University's *Learning by Design* project. The research data assembled for the project included material from semi-structured interviews and focus groups/forums with the teacher participants and project-consultants, and impact statements which participants completed at the end of their involvement in the project. The themes discussed in the chapter dealing with the leadership role of principals emerged from an analysis of nine responses to an open-ended questionnaire emailed to principals involved in the project, a telephone interview with one of these principals, and via field notes taken during discussions with the project-consultants.

The research is informed by the collaborative practitioner research model that incorporates teachers as co-researchers (Nofke & Stephenson, 1995). In other studies, permutations of this approach have been successfully used to identify learning outcomes, confirm understandings about teaching and learning and have enabled teachers as researchers to 'identify and speculate on new findings with regard to links between teaching practice, school organisation and student learning' (Cherednichenko, Davies, Kruger, & O'Rourke, 2001, p. 2).

The project was designed to test and refine pedagogical theory in the field; provide participants with extended professional learning, focusing on improving practice; and to be of direct benefit to the participating teachers and their schools – this has meant the research has had both action research and action learning orientations.

The next section of this chapter begins with an outline of the project and the role played by the theory-makers, an elaboration of the roles played by children in the project, and a review of the leadership role played by school principals. This is followed by chapters that explore the roles of the project-consultants and the teachers and includes an identification of the factors necessary for developing teacher-practitioners who are fluent in the language of Multiliteracies, adept at applying the theory in context appropriate ways and concludes with a discussion of the future of *Learning by Design*.

DESIGNING RICHER, MORE INCLUSIVE TEACHING PRACTICES

In this section the background and objectives of the *Learning by Design* project are explored along with the role played by theory-makers, Kalantzis and Cope.

The influence children have had on the *Learning by Design* project is also examined, as is the leadership role played by school principals.

Key insights in this section relate to:

- the emergence of more diverse and inclusive teaching practices (designs for learning) resulting in an expanded pedagogical repertoire;
- an appreciation of the role of the pedagogical framework in prompting such developments,

- evidence that the framework has acted as a heuristic prompting teachers to discover for themselves aspects of their practice which had formerly been tacit;
- an expectation that the richer, more diverse practices encouraged by the framework will mean more students will experience classroom success and feelings of belonging;
- an acknowledgment of the leading role played by school principals.

BACKGROUND TO LEARNING BY DESIGN

Building on the central notions of learning by design and designs for learning the project leaders, Kalantzis and Cope, developed pedagogical theories and practices to inform such designs. This was with the goal of improving learning experiences for a diverse range of potential learners, making such experiences more meaningful and inclusive. Their approach was informed in particular by Multiliteracies theory, which they helped conceive .

The project leaders designed and unfolded a project that offered selected K-12 teachers:

- a series of professional learning workshops supported by a printed guide/workbook covering key aspects of the theory of Multiliteracies and the emerging theory of *Learning by Design*;
- a pedagogical framework in the form of a template in the ubiquitously available Microsoft Word to be used for planning and documenting classroom practice;
- a web-publishing medium for teachers to share their practice with others;
- ongoing support from state-based pedagogical mentors (project-consultants), Anne Cloonan, Mary Neville and Rita van Haren (who are also contributing-authors to this volume).

The professional learning workshops and printed guide were aimed at helping teachers understand ideas associated with the theory of Multiliteracies and multimodal teaching and how they might apply these understandings via a range of knowledge processes and pedagogies – i.e. via situated practice (learning through experiencing); overt instruction (learning by conceptualising); critical framing (learning by analysing and critiquing); and via transformed practice (learning by applying).

The pedagogical framework was provided to teachers as a means of reflexively thinking through the design of their curriculum and pedagogies, irrespective of the focus of that curriculum, from both the students' and their own perspectives. It prompted teachers, whether they were teaching English, arts, SOSE, science, maths or any other subject to employ a mix of knowledge processes and to document their planning and practices (designs for learning). Documenting encouraged teachers to reflect on their pedagogical choices. In the language of *Learning by Design*, these documented designs were called Learning Elements.

The movement from Multiliteracies theory and *Learning by Design* to classroom practice was underpinned by support from local pedagogical mentors—the project-consultants—who, whilst also *learning alongside* the teachers, acted as sounding boards, advisers and guides.

The overarching goal of the *Learning by Design* Project has been to transform the pedagogical practice of the teachers involved – to expand their professional repertoire and to encourage them to make their planning and pedagogical decisions more deliberative, mindful and transparent.

This goal reflects the view that the professional capacity of teachers is critical to the learning experience of children—more influential than socio-economic background or the curriculum—and that pedagogical know-how is at the heart of this professional capacity. Quality of pedagogy is said to account for twenty percent or more of the variance in learning outcomes between children, hence the project emphasis on developing pedagogical expertise. This is reflected in a series of inter-related project objectives which are elaborated in the following section.

OBJECTIVES OF THE LEARNING BY DESIGN PROJECT

Although it is difficult to disaggregate or deconstruct the inherently interdependent threads which, weaved together, *are* 'The *Learning by Design* Project', this list of objectives illuminates the fundamental orientation of the work:

- a wider recognition of the diverse learning needs of both students and teachers and the promotion of theories and practices that support those needs;
- an improved understanding of concepts associated with the theory of Multiliteracies and a capacity to adapt ideas associated with the theory to different teaching and learning contexts;
- an enhanced awareness of multimodal teaching techniques and practices and an improved capacity to teach in multimodal ways using, where appropriate, digital technologies;

- an improved understanding of a variety of pedagogical approaches and knowledge processes and an improved capacity to mindfully and appropriately use and apply these different processes;
- the capturing, documenting and sharing of ideas, teaching techniques and designs, curriculum and pedagogical practices, that might otherwise remain unexpressed and undocumented;
- the publishing of this professional knowledge amongst a community of peer-practitioners in order to support, inform and inspire those practitioners;
- an expansion of teachers' professional repertoires of practice while helping them develop an acuity, and the confidence, to combine and synthesise these practices in context appropriate ways;
- to improve the level of skills and knowledge of students in order that they might achieve their aspirations and meaningfully participate in the peer-groups and local communities to which they belong and contribute to the societies in which they live and work.

The reader should note the reinforcing loop created between the first and last objective—highlighting the central place students and their needs occupy in the remit of the project. This is informed by the knowledge that a significant challenge facing teachers today is a need to create learning environments which engage the sensibilities of students who are increasingly immersed in sensorially rich digital environments and multimodal settings. The role of students in the Learning by Design project is covered in the following section.

THE ROLE OF STUDENTS

At the author's first meeting with ACT project-consultant Rita van Haren, she made the observation that 'the students are the starting point for *Learning by Design*'. She went on to explain that this was because *Learning by Design* accommodated diverse needs and different learning preferences 'you can't treat all children as if they were the same' she said. This idea is supported by Comber and Kamler (2005) who note that children today have learning needs and ways of knowing that are more diverse than their parents and grandparents, while Cope and Kalantzis identify children as being situated in environments characterized by 'local diversity and global connectedness'.

The varied learning needs of children was evident in the diverse school populaces of project schools—one school had students from 25 different countries while another, the Mater Hospital Special School in Brisbane, provided educational services to hospitalized students and day-patients from Prep to Year 12, covering a wide range of backgrounds and abilities/disabilities. Another of the Brisbane-based schools was described by the teacher as being 'multicultural with no single predominant culture', the children were described as ranging from 'high achieving, to students who have disengaged from classroom learning experiences...originating from one child high socio-economic families to low socio-economic situations.' Such schools provided appropriate environments for exploring the theories of Multiliteracies and *Learning by Design* allowing for a variety of pedagogies and modes of meaning-making to be investigated.

In Anne Cloonan's chapter the expansion in modes of meaning-making and what it might mean to be literate is made apparent via her observations of a toddler's confident use of various technologies. The world in which children live today is qualitatively more complex and sensorially more demanding and clamorous than in earlier periods. Children need to make meaning of this more complex cultural and sensorial world and need to be able to express and articulate themselves via a variety of 'modes'—linguistic, visual, audio, spatial and gestural.

A clear outcome of this phenomenon for Kalantzis and Cope was that the curricula and pedagogical practices of the past were no longer sufficient—they recognised that linguistic literacy remained important but would no longer be enough. They identified a need for children to be 'multiliterate', taking account of a 'multiplicity of communications channels and media' and recognising that 'written-linguistic modes of meaning are part and parcel of visual, audio and spatial patterns of meaning'. They also identified the way in which *being literate* related to a variety of social languages—languages that related to being part of, belonging to, a specific social, technical or professional group. The existence of these various social languages, and the 'part and parcel' nature of the relationship between the written-linguistic and other modes of meaning-making, suggest it would be short-sighted for teachers to concentrate on one and exclude others.

This reframing and expansion of the meaning of literacy into multiliteracies has important implications for teacher relationships with students and for student confidence and self-image. Comber and Kamler (2005) write about a generation of teachers that have 'been inducted into counterproductive discourses that constitute certain students as 'deficit'', that is, that posit some students as somehow deficient relative to their peers.

The research for the *Learning by Design* project indicates that use of the pedagogical framework expands teachers' repertoire of practices creating conditions for learning that are more likely to be inclusive of the needs of a diverse range of students. The evidence of expanded repertoires can be found in the variety of practices documented in the published Learning Elements (www.L-by-D.com) and in the comments of the teachers. A Brisbane-based teacher, writing about the effects of her involvement in the project identified a shift in her practice: 'questioning and discussing with students the multimodal aspects of all texts has now become a natural part of the interaction between students and texts in my classroom'.

Another teacher suggested that the expansion in her practice was a consequence of 'going into their worlds more… (the pedagogical framework) helped me to consider what the students were bringing… their experiences… and to figure out ways to enable them…help them to relate these experiences to what they were learning.'

Another teacher believed that it was her responsibility as a teacher to provide students:

> with enough opportunities and direction to engage in their world, in as informed a (way) as possible… to have our classrooms reflect lots of the changes that have happened in our society, and also teach them… allow our students to develop ways of critically dealing with all these new texts which constantly surround and challenge them.

This teacher saw the pedagogical framework and the professional development associated with being involved in the project as both prompting and providing a means to fulfil these responsibilities.

A consequence of the teachers expanded repertoire of practices are increased opportunities for students to express themselves in different modes—this may mean that more students will experience success and the feelings of belonging that are crucial to learning . This was certainly evident in the accounts of teachers who presented at forums in Brisbane and the ACT. A Brisbane-based teacher spoke of the dramatic shift in the level of engagement of a number of students who had previously been regarded as having had 'problems with paying attention'. A Canberra-based teacher described her involvement in the *Learning by Design* project as 'exciting…it makes teaching and learning very exciting… (there is) less of that focus on pen and paper, you begin to engage with those kids that don't want to use pen and paper'.

The prospect of teaching and learning that is 'exciting' is important for a number of reasons—it suggests teachers who are engaged and interested in their work and offers the promise of students who are similarly interested and engaged. Teaching that is made exciting may be particularly important in a context where some teachers in an aging workforce may need to be mobilised for what Allan Luke calls 'one further pedagogical hurrah'.

Widespread adoption of the principles of *Learning by Design* and sustained use of the pedagogical framework explored in this chapter are expected to lead to a more positive orientation by teachers to students, thereby reducing talk of 'deficits' and the labeling of children as 'deficient'.

These ideas about students and what it means for them to be multiliterate has provided the impetus for the *Learning by Design* project and for the design of the pedagogical framework. The framework prompts teachers to reflectively consider the diverse needs of their students, the pedagogical alternatives available to them, and to make context appropriate decisions about their practice.

THE ROLE OF THE THEORY-MAKERS, THEIR THEORY AND PEDAGOGICAL FRAMEWORK

The concept of *learning by design* casts teachers as mindful and deliberative designers of learning experiences rather than consumers or purveyors of pre-fabricated content.

Kalantzis and Cope discuss their conception of 'design' in earlier chapters—but to briefly reiterate, they identify an ambiguity in the definition of design wherein one possible meaning is related to the morphology or existence of invisible inner structures within various entities. Inherent relationships of cause and effect may be characteristic of such entities but these relationships are often implicit rather than consciously fabricated. They argue that this conception of design is evident in teaching in so far as all teaching practices can be seen to lead to some kind of outcome that is a consequence of those practices. Such teaching may also reflect 'designs' associated with socialisation, culture or habit and therefore may be taken for granted or overlooked. Inherent in this conception of design as it relates to teaching is an implied benefit of becoming more aware (mindful) of such designs and their consequences, and making them explicit.

Alongside this conception they posit the more familiar notion of design as an act of fabrication, representing both a product of conscious thinking and something concrete or enacted. This conception of 'design' and 'learning by design' suggests personal agency, mindfulness and premeditation. Such designs when associated with learning are characteristic of the formal curriculum and educational forms with which we are familiar and represent self-conscious choices and personal initiative.

Each of these conceptions of design has informed the *Learning by Design* project—teachers becoming cognizant of their current and former practices/pedagogies and the consequences thereof, and becoming more deliberative and premeditative about planning their current and future practices and pedagogies. The orchestrated achievement of this mindfulness is at the heart of the Kalantzis and Cope theory and is central to the design of their pedagogical framework—the framework itself is literally an embodiment of the theory of *Learning by Design*.

However, equally important has been the direct involvement in the project of the two high profile and well respected theory-makers themselves, catalysing and engendering support and interest amongst the project participants and institution decision-makers. That one of these theory-makers, Mary Kalantzis, was a Research Professor, Chair of Education at RMIT University and head of the Council of Deans of Education added weight and credibility to the project. One of the state-based project-consultants observed that: 'the teachers were really impressed, I was really impressed, that these internationally recognised figures were coming to speak to us, to spend two days working with us... it was unbelievable.'

Mary Kalantzis and Bill Cope began their respective careers as teachers and teacher-researchers—this is reflected in their thinking and theory-making which is grounded by considerations of practice. The theory of Multiliteracies and the idea of *Learning by Design* are the product of more than twenty years of research and collaboration with others, driven by a concern for the diverse needs of learners and a desire for theory that could be enacted.

Drawing on Multiliteracies theory, and with this concern for learners and for theory enactment, Kalantzis and Cope have designed a pedagogical-framework-and-heuristic that they offer to teachers 'inside' a Microsoft Word template. They chose a Word template to present their framework because it was a relatively simple, widely available and accessible technology likely to be used by many teachers. (The framework-in-use, as manifested in the teacher-published exemplars, can be found in the chapters that follow and at www.L-by-D.com.) The completed framework, which in the language of *Learning by Design* is called a Learning Element, is in a form that can easily be 'published' and shared with others. Moreover, this meant that any teacher, or group of collaborating teachers, with access to Word and basic computing skills, using the pedagogical 'tags' in the framework to guide and prompt them, could use the framework to document and share their planning and practice.

Some teachers immediately recognised the value of this capacity to share ideas and know-how with their peers:

- ...we need to be able to share our professional learnings and our professional practices... I believe a lot of our skills are far too compartmentalised, particularly in the secondary sector... within departments, within staffrooms, within classrooms, and I think if we have a common planning tool, a common language of the way we talk about our pedagogy that we can share the expertise and make sure all kids get the benefit of some of these good teaching practices.

Beyond providing a means to share knowledge, the framework also acted as a heuristic in that teachers could discover for themselves aspects of their practice which had formerly been tacit, including preferences for some knowledge processes and pedagogical approaches over others—teachers became aware of their 'hidden' designs. 'I suddenly realised', said one of the Canberra-based teachers, 'that almost all of my teaching was focussed on learning concepts... a little bit of learning by experience but almost no real-world application of what we were studying... or analysis... or critique. I was shocked by this at first...' A Brisbane-based teacher, on a slightly different tack, offered 'I am obviously not good at analysing what happens in a lesson critically and in detail...so specifically planning for these knowledge processes in lessons is really crucial if learning is really to happen.'

Many teachers interviewed recognised the value of being prompted, via the pedagogical framework, to consider a variety of knowledge processes. One teacher saw the framework as providing a means of stimulating analysis and reflection:

> It is really a way of making sure that we keep on being at that edge of good practice, keep looking at what we need to do and keep questioning why we are doing it, and if we are doing it in the best way, and if the kids are getting the best outcomes out of it for the effort that they are putting through, so yes, I think it is really useful as a tool for analysis and reflection...

Another teacher, talking about the framework, remarked that 'the design of it encourages you to use a variety of strategies to engage with students and to get them to respond...it gets you to think about what you are doing and why'.

The framework thus prompted teachers to become more mindful and premeditated about their teaching practice—to understand learning as an outcome of a considered, reflectively thought-through design process—to recognise teaching as *learning by design*.

To support the pedagogical framework Kalantzis and Cope developed a two day professional learning workshop and a printed guide/workbook to explain and contextualise the theory and to show teachers how to use the framework. Teachers were asked to consider what 'good teaching' looked like and how it was enacted—they were shown how such teaching practices could be mapped against the pedagogical tags in the framework.

These professional learning workshops and the printed guide/workbook were crucial in terms of setting the scene and introducing the teachers to the language of Multiliteracies. Many teachers would not really understand key terms in this language until much later. At the time of writing, some continue to grapple with the *slippery* meanings of some terms as translated into practice. Anne Cloonan has much to say about this positive struggle for understanding in a later chapter—the indications are that the somewhat slippery nature of conceptual ideas in *Learning by Design* have been a positive factor as teachers slowly made meaning of these ideas in practice and between themselves.

It appears that the difficulty teachers experienced in resolving the meaning of terms such as *experiencing the new* and *conceptualising by naming* served to foster a discourse and engagement amongst them as they wrestled with what the terms meant and how their practices mapped to these concepts. This created opportunities for teachers to closely consider their practice—one teacher commented 'I found I was asking myself questions like: 'What am I really doing?' and 'What do I want to achieve from what I am doing?' It really got me thinking!' Another teacher, commenting on the work she had been doing with a group of teachers remarked that 'we worked out the meaning of these terms together…it gave our work a focus…we would sit around the computer (as they planned their Learning Element) and discuss and argue about what we thought the terms meant.'

Kalantzis and Cope, have in effect established and promoted a professional language and therefore the possibility for a professional literacy—a literacy of pedagogy, collaboration and considered classroom practice. In the context of the project, teachers learned to *talk with each other* about their practice, using this new language, while creating thoughtful and considered *designs for learning* which they tested in their classrooms. These enacted designs became the subject of presentations to, and discussions with peers, incorporating reflections about the process and the experience of using the framework.

The designs for learning were guided, prompted, documented and eventually shared using the pedagogical framework, at first in closed-group forums and later, in their final guise as Learning Elements, via an internet-based publishing medium. (www.L-by-D.com)

The theory-makers Kalantzis and Cope have played a central role in establishing a suitable ground for the project through the specific qualities of their theory and the hands-on nature of their involvement. Adam Phillips, writing about philosopher William James, notes 'theories matter for James according to their use. They are not destinations, they are our means of transport.' The theories of Kalantzis and Cope have provided a means of transport for practitioners to transform pedagogical ideas into practice.

In the following section the role played by the school principals is explored.

LEADING THE WAY—THE ROLE OF THE SCHOOL PRINCIPALS

The data for this section was gathered from responses to a series of questions that were sent via email to the school principals involved in the *Learning by Design* project. Nine responded via email, a tenth principal talked with the author via telephone. All of the principals that responded to this request were from either Queensland or the ACT.

It became apparent, both during the research and from the responses to the above-mentioned questions, that the various school principals played a crucial role in providing leadership and support. As noted by one principal, '{it is} crucial because of my role in setting goals and direction for the school and maintaining constancy of purpose (and because) I am able to ensure that the project is adequately resourced'.

One of the Canberra-based principals noted that he had

> ...approved and endorsed the adoption of the process as a major plank of our continuous improvement strategy. I have worked with other senior staff in the school and cluster to articulate to staff the rationale for adopting the *Learning by Design* template as our framework for curriculum planning and implementation (and) have explained the link between the *Learning by Design* project and our school strategic goals.

So, leadership was communicated via what principals said in meetings and professional development sessions with teachers, as noted by one of the Queensland principals 'raising awareness, and generating a professional dialogue around the ideas of Learning by Design and Multiliteracies'. Their commitment to the project was tangibly demonstrated via funding support. As one principal observed, 'funding enabled time off-line for teachers to attend professional development, plan in-service strategies and share learning with other teachers'. School funding allowed relief to be provided for teachers to attend workshops and to plan and design their Learning Elements.

In a later chapter, Mary Neville writes about there being a climate for pedagogical change and renewal in Queensland—this same climate for change was also evident in the ACT. Moreover, there appeared to be a predisposition for the kind of theories and practices offered by *Learning by Design* and a belief that these theories and practices were extensions of existing school or state initiatives:

> The principles of the *Learning by Design* project were aligned with the direction (in which) my school was heading and it was presented as a framework for planning for success. (...) *Learning by Design* is a natural progression for our school. We have been planning integrated units of study over the past few years; however, our challenge was to plan for more in-depth understanding of real-life issues. We had been trialling the Kath Murdoch inquiry approach and felt that *Learning by Design* was the next step along the journey.

Another principal identified that *Learning by Design* had been 'very relevant to (our) whole-school literacy focus, the embedding of ICTs and reinforcing the strength of Innovation and Technology as two of our college's cornerstones.' A Queensland-based principal suggested that it had complemented their Literate Futures focus and 'aligned very well with our curriculum practices...*Learning by Design* supports flexible curriculum design, real life application, variety and inclusive practices'.

One of the ACT principals recognised links between his school's focus on the various domains of learning outlined in the Queenslandsourced Productive Pedagogies and the *Learning by Design* pedagogical framework:

> We have adopted the *Learning by Design* template as our planning format because the knowledge processes and the multimodal emphasis are judged to be excellent vehicles for achieving Intellectual Quality and the other domains of the Productive Pedagogies.

This was echoed by another of the ACT principals who noted that 'our initial focus was through Productive Pedagogies and improving teacher practice', adding that '*Learning by Design* provides a valuable framework for teachers to plan within.'

The five principals involved in the *Learning by Design* project in the ACT were part of a cluster of four primary schools, Bonython, Charles Conder, Gordon and Tharwa Primary Schools, with most of the children from these schools destined for Lanyon High School, the remaining school in the cluster. Apart from the country-based Tharwa Primary School, which is more than one hundred years old, the other schools in the cluster all began operating in the 1990s. The teacher mobility policy of the ACT Department of Education means there is a high turnover of staff throughout the cluster with many beginning teachers employed. Demographically many of the students are latchkey children from homes where both parents work to repay often hefty mortgages. Scholastically there is a wide and uneven pattern of success against formal department assessments, with students at Lanyon High School for example, performing below the territory averages for literacy and numeracy.

The schools in this group form 'the Lanyon cluster of schools' and the five principals work as a team. They meet regularly to discuss strategies and tactics for improving the educational outcomes of their respective schools and for students in the cluster more generally literacy and numeracy are high priority areas.

The work of this group of principals is instructive. Their approach to improving literacy and numeracy across the cluster was innovative and involved a uniquely powerful combination of strategies. Their various innovations and direct support created an environment well suited to the trial and elaboration of the pedagogical framework and enactment of Multiliteracies theory.

The leadership of these principals anticipated and paved the way for *Learning by Design* and the pedagogical framework. For example, recognising and responding to literacy and numeracy outcomes below the ACT average, the principals applied for and were granted funds to support the professional development of teachers in the cluster. They recognised a need for a specialist role with an exclusive focus on literacy, numeracy and pedagogy—someone that could help build the professional skills of teachers. They proposed, and were successful in establishing, a full-time position at the level of deputy principal to fulfil this role and to work with teachers in schools across the cluster.

Such a position, at this level, they believed would allow the recruitment of a suitably qualified person and would send a clear and unambiguous message to staff in the cluster about the importance of literacy, numeracy and pedagogy. They believed that such a role would deliver substantive improvements in student outcomes not possible via other means.

The cluster leadership group were successful in convincing the director of education of the need and efficacy of such a role. It was duly advertised and filled by Rita van Haren, an acknowledged expert in literacy and 'teaching teachers to teach literacy'.

The manner in which the principals in the Lanyon Cluster, together with the newly appointed deputy principal, pursued the goal of improving literacy outcomes is also instructive—they cast their research net to find out what was going on elsewhere, in Australia and overseas, to improve teaching and learning, and in particular, literacy levels. They explored the Education Queensland publication 'Productive Pedagogies', where the focus was on the professional learning of teachers and in particular pedagogical practice. They formulated plans and tactics based on their research and began to enact their local, context-specific, literacy and numeracy strategy.

All of this thinking, researching, discussing and planning around literacy, professional learning and pedagogy meant that the leadership group of the Lanyon Cluster, including the new deputy principal, were well primed for an introduction to Multiliteracies, *Learning by Design* and the pedagogical framework. This created the conditions necessary to support the project—a leadership group keen to address teaching and learning outcomes while supporting teacher professional development, actively looking for a means to achieve this, a history of innovation and preparedness to try new ideas, a full-time literacy and pedagogy practitioner in a senior leadership role, funds to release teachers for professional learning, departmental support and a leadership group keen and enthusiastic to see what might be possible.

The leadership and enthusiasm of the Lanyon cluster principals was manifested in multiple ways—attending the workshops conducted by Kalantzis and Cope, alongside teachers from the cluster; vocalising their support for the project at meetings and staff forums; showing interest in the work of those teachers involved in the project; engaging in a sustained discourse around the idea of *learning by design* with their teachers and each other; and working closely with Rita van Haren a person dedicated to the role of teacher professional development, pedagogical improvement and literacy and numeracy outcomes.

In summing up his experiences of involvement in the project one of the Lanyon cluster principals noted:

> I really appreciate the opportunity to be involved in this project. It has provided a stimulus and a vehicle for accelerating the improvement of pedagogy in the school and in the Lanyon cluster. While staff often find

the *Learning by Design* approach to be demanding I believe they are increasingly able to see the value of it and that their competence will grow as they continue to use and implement it. I am pleased that we adopted it as our whole-school approach and that we are all working on implementing it together.

The principals involved in the project played a central role in leading and supporting the diffusion of theories and practices associated with Multiliteracies and *Learning by Design*.

While the theory-makers established the theoretical foundations for the project, and were instrumental in its design and management, the professional development of teachers and the learning needs of children were the focus for the work.

In the following chapter the role played by the project-consultants is elaborated.

CHAPTER 10

The Emergence of Pedagogical Mentors: The Project-consultants

Peter Burrows

In this chapter the influence of the project-consultants on teacher-participants is explored. Their emerging role as pedagogical mentors is investigated and the focus that was exhibited in each one's work is illuminated and examined.

Key insights and lessons in this chapter relate to:

- The benefits of providing teachers with local, accessible and sustained pedagogical leadership;
- There is a need for concentrated hands-on support and feedback for many teachers at the beginning of their engagement with Multiliteracies and *Learning by Design*;
- A potential model for this support is offered which provides for widespread diffusion of the pedagogical practices associated with Multiliteracies and *Learning by Design*;
- Multimodal 'texts' (linguistic, visual, audio, gestural and spatial) provide teachers with an easy to comprehend introduction to the theory and practice of Multiliteracies and *Learning by Design*;
- There is a need to further explore the potential to develop such 'texts' for deployment via the internet so that they might be more widely shared;
- The consultants' engagement with the project led to the development of key pedagogical expertise which directly benefited both themselves and their constituencies.

BACKGROUND

The *Learning by Design* project-consultants together with the teacher-participants have been involved in an 'action research' endeavour where:

> ...unlike traditional research, action research begins not with a research question but with the muddle of daily work, with the moments that stand out from the general flow....

This conception of action research as conscious engagement with 'the muddle of daily work' is consistent with the teachers' use of the pedagogical framework to plan, organise and make explicit their practices. These practices, many of which had previously been unexamined and taken-for-granted suddenly became apparent to the teachers using the framework and available for consideration and reflection. For example, a Canberra-based teacher remarked 'I suddenly realised that almost all of my teaching was focussed on learning concepts... almost no real-world application of what we were studying.'

> Teacher/action research is about discovering ourselves, about uncovering our assumptions – assumptions about learning, about teaching, about values and beliefs.
>
> An important first step, therefore, in becoming a teacher/action researcher is to enter into an exploration of how we compose our own practice. What beliefs underlie what we choose to do in the classroom? What counts as "data"? What might we do differently?

The *Learning by Design* pedagogical framework helped teachers to uncover their assumptions about learning as manifested in their practices – they were prompted by the framework to explore how they composed their practice and to think about how they might teach differently.

However, a crucial influence in the development of this mindfulness has been the work of the project-consultants who helped teachers translate the theories and philosophies of Multiliteracies, multimodalities and the multiple pedagogies and knowledge processes of *Learning by Design* into significant shifts in practice.

This translation work was crucial in the sense that the consultants were, in each case, credible and influential figures whose opinions and ideas were respected by the teachers with whom they worked. The consultants came with a strong practice-base, grounded in extensive teaching experience; they were avid readers of educational and pedagogical theory and had been engaged in a broad range of professional development activities, both for themselves and in the delivery and facilitation of such activities for others. Two of the consultants had been simultaneously involved in Learning by *Design*-related Masters of Education projects. One of the consultants modestly described her contribution as 'that little bit of help'. Another of the consultants described what she did as 'helping teachers learn how to do this' but the comments of the teachers with whom they worked suggests a more significant contribution.

The data analysed for this chapter was drawn from comments made by teachers in interviews, during focus groups, from impact stories and via field-notes the author kept whenever he met with the project-consultants. The meetings the author had with the project-consultants took the form of extended conversations often spanning three or more hours. The field-notes included verbatim quotes, paraphrased comments and the author's observations and reflections.

The work of Anne Cloonan, Mary Neville and Rita van Haren manifested a number of shared practical concerns and interests. Each consultant was committed to contributing to the professional development of the teachers they worked with and to their own professional learning. Each was committed to the notion of thoughtful and premeditated pedagogical practice and to the idea of fairer and more inclusive learning experiences for children.

However, each approached the project and their role in markedly different ways and although it is somewhat reductive to talk in terms of each consultant having a specific focus—because each addressed their project responsibilities in complex and multi-layered ways— individual themes emerged from the data.

In the case of Anne Cloonan the focus became *teaching teachers to teach* via the pedagogies of *Learning by Design*—for Anne teaching teachers also meant learning *with* teachers.

Mary Neville's focus was concerned with *engendering widespread reform* through the systematic diffusion of Multiliteracies theory and *Learning by Design* practices via a pool of teacher-disseminators.

The work of Rita van Haren can be seen as providing sustained *pedagogical leadership* to 155 teachers from a geographical cluster of five schools, more than 80 of whom have engaged with the *Learning by Design* theory and supporting framework.

The project-consultants did not begin working on the project as pedagogical experts or pedagogical mentors, although each was a highly experienced teacher operating in a role where they were, in one way or another, supporting the professional and pedagogical development of a cadre of teachers. Neither were they directly recruited to the project. Rather the project-consultants found their way to *Learning by Design* serendipitously and became pedagogical experts as they grappled with the theory and began to engage with and use the pedagogical framework, *learning alongside* the teachers they were supporting. They became pedagogical mentors as a consequence of their involvement in the project, via their relationships with each other, the teachers with whom they were working and through their regular contacts with the project leaders Kalantzis and Cope. Mary Kalantzis played an active part in the professional learning of Cloonan and Neville in that she was supervising both consultants in *Learning by Design* related Masters of Education.

Some of the highlights of the project-consultants' work included:

- the making of four, award-winning, twenty-minute professional development videos that document and explain the theory of Multiliteracies and the ideas and practices of *Learning by Design* (Anne Cloonan);
- the creation of the means for the systematic diffusion of *Learning by Design* theory and practice via a pool of teacher-disseminators (Mary Neville);
- the development of a cadre of more than 80 teachers across a cluster of schools who together represent a body of Multiliteraciesknowledge and practical *Learning by Design* expertise (Rita van Haren).
- Over the period of the project their various roles and contributions included;
- providing one-on-one and team mentoring;
- giving individual feedback, encouragement and support to teacher-participants;
- facilitating professional development forums and workshops for teachers;
- reviewing, providing feedback and editing drafts of the teachers' Learning Elements;
- broadening the base of pedagogical knowledge and expertise via the teachers with whom they worked;
- gathering research data via interviews, focus groups and impact statements;
- liaising with school principals, school leaders and project leaders;
- devising and implementing context specific project-plans;
- writing project-related articles in professional publications, books and journals;
- presenting project findings at professional conferences;
- *developing themselves as outstanding resources* for their respective constituencies.

This final point is perhaps the most important because it implies that each institutional supporter of *Learning by Design* has a deployable legacy of knowledge, practice and expertise as a consequence of that support.

In the following three sections the work of the individual project-consultants is explored in more detail.

RITA VAN HAREN: PEDAGOGICAL LEADER AND CRITICAL FRIEND

As mentioned in a previous chapter the five schools involved in the *Learning by Design* project in the ACT were part of a cluster of four primary schools and one high school known as 'the Lanyon cluster of schools'. At the time of the project Rita van Haren held the unique position of deputy principal responsible for literacy, numeracy and pedagogy across the five schools in the Lanyon Cluster, as well as being the *Learning by Design* project-consultant.

Observations of Rita at work and analysis of the data indicate that her clear and unambiguous interest could be located at the intersection between pedagogy and teacher professional learning *as a means of better addressing the diverse needs of students*. For Rita involvement in the *Learning by Design* project provided a way to make teaching more inclusive—for Rita the knowledge processes and the *Learning by Design* framework encouraged teachers to address the question 'What are the pedagogical strategies that I need to include all students?'.

In one of the conversations Rita had with the author she observed that:

> Using the (pedagogical framework) meant that teachers had to articulate the pedagogies they were actually using... (the framework) provided an organisational structure for planning and thinking about pedagogy... teachers were planning, not for the sake of documenting but for identifying what they were doing in the classroom...

However, whilst inclusivity and pedagogy were Rita's passions, it was her 'excellent leadership (and) building capacity in schools', as noted by one of the school principals with whom she worked, that were the hallmarks of her work. This leadership and capacity building were realised via hands-on involvement, encouragement, coaching and direct support of the teacher-participants. This provided the means by which her inclusivity agenda and pedagogical focus were translated into meaningful practice.

One of the teachers at a focus group described Rita as 'our critical friend' someone who was 'bringing people on board'. The teacher explained that the idea of 'critical friend' was part of the language of teachers in the Lanyon cluster and indicated a respected mentor and guide – someone who could be expected to 'ask difficult but thought-provoking questions', someone who was anticipated to contribute to one's professional development, '...a critical friend...and Rita has been just that', the teacher concluded.

Another teacher in the same session said of Rita. 'She's a bit contagious...it was her enthusiasm and commitment that drew me in...' While one of the principals in the cluster, commenting on Rita's influence observed that, '...we are really focusing on literacy and pedagogy in the cluster and Rita has played a big part in establishing and sustaining that focus, she has really led the way.' Another principal observed that 'the strength of the project was having someone like Rita driving the project in each of our schools', further noting that 'change in attitude as much as practice is a long process and needs continual injection of time to allow people to work with the new framework.' He saw this as one of the important roles that Rita fulfilled:

> The support of our cluster deputy principal has been invaluable and the links with the national project have added legitimacy to our efforts and enhanced the quality of our outcomes.

Rita worked alongside teachers as they grappled with the pedagogical framework, as they struggled to make sense of the concepts and ideas presented in the framework, and as they attempted to map their planning and practices to these concepts. In a sense Rita acted as a reassuring bridge between the unfamiliar concepts of *Learning by Design* and the teachers' practices, as described here by one of the Canberra-based teachers:

> When we first saw the document (pedagogical framework) we broke into a sweat... but Rita really helped us...we worked it out together and now we have this document (a completed Learning Element)...it's working for us because we can see a value in what we are doing. Rita helped us to see that we are all learners with this and because of that you can take a risk and not feel silly.

Whilst Rita's contribution can, in part, be attributed to her unique position as a deputy principal responsible for literacy, numeracy and pedagogy in the Lanyon Cluster—and therefore a consequence of her undivided attention – there were clearly other important factors. Her personal drive and dedication to the goals of improving teacher pedagogical practice and student literacy and numeracy outcomes, and her canniness in realising these goals, were also significant drivers.

For example, Rita recognised the changing context in which teachers were working and she promoted use of the pedagogical framework as a means for teachers to review and reflect on their practice:

> ...teachers are still influenced by their formative education...this is necessary but not sufficient, things have changed, students have changed. When someone says that they are already doing this, I ask them to articulate the pedagogy they are using... I ask them to use the template (pedagogical framework) for this...to map their practices onto the template.

Rita, as observed by the author, approached her role with vigour and enthusiasm. Her strong grasp of pedagogical theory and the application of that theory, based on many years experience, personal research and reflection, was manifested in her engagement with project-teachers, many of whom recognised her expertise: 'Rita really helped us with the theory...for me the message I kept getting (from Rita) was... that this is a set of professional skills that we are learning not a bag of tricks'.

> Another teacher, responding to a question about how comfortable she felt with the theory offered the comment: ...we were really lost and confused at the beginning...it all just seemed like so much jargon to us, a foreign language almost... but Rita was there to help us through that... I don't know if we would have persisted with it if she had not been there to encourage and support us at the beginning.

In an earlier conversation with the author Rita had observed 'I did not want them to be scared of it because it is our professional language'. Rita also recognised the initial negative response to the theory:

> ...for the teachers it really seemed like jargon at first but now they are using the language and using it confidently...many of them understand and can talk about the various knowledge processes... it has become a shared professional language, a language of pedagogy and that is really exciting.

Rita's grasp of the theory, the mapping of that theory to practice, and her capacity to articulate that understanding in a language and manner appropriate to the teachers with whom she worked, as evidenced in the meetings with teacher-participants observed by the author, was exemplary. Her capacity to engage with teachers and to sustain that engagement was also manifested in these meetings. The professional standard of the Learning Elements produced by the teachers in the Lanyon Cluster, as reviewed and edited by Rita, is further evidence of the effective translation of theory into practice (www.L-by-D.com).

Rita however did not believe that success should be measured by the number of completed Learning Elements, 'I am not concerned abut how many Learning Elements we have completed (published) I just want them to go through the process... it's experiencing the process that is really crucial, that's where the professional learning takes place'.

That is not to say that Rita did not see the Learning Elements as important – she recognised that these documents could be used to induct and support beginning teachers 'showing them how we work here...getting them onboard quickly' and as a means of bringing teachers together in collaboration, in one case bringing seven teachers together – but for Rita the *Learning by Design process* was central to the pedagogical and professional development of the teachers in her cluster.

Perhaps most significantly, Rita approached the task of promoting and supporting Multiliteracies and *Learning by Design* by keeping the focus on pedagogies and on teacher professional learning via an ongoing discourse. As she pointed out 'it's about getting it onto the agenda, keeping it there... getting people to think and talk about their pedagogy ...and when people are ready they come to it'.

The author observed that Rita, in the midst of her 'process' of engagement with teachers, made meta-use of and applied the various knowledge processes from the pedagogical framework to help them understand that framework. That is, Rita called on each of the knowledge processes—*situated* practice (learning through experiencing); over*t* instructio*n* (learning by conceptualising); critica*l* framin*g* (learning by analysing and critiquing); and transforme*d practice* (learning by applying) – in helping teachers learn *about* the pedagogical framework and how to apply the knowledge processes in their work.

This meant that Rita's practice (theory-in-use) was closely aligned with the theory promoted and articulated in the framework (espoused theory) – this provided her work with a strong (albeit, perhaps intuitive) sense of credibility and coherence.

The combination of this intuitive credibility in the way in which the work was unfolded and Rita's sustained support and encouragement of the teachers throughout the project were instrumental in helping a broad range of teachers from across five schools engage with, and enact the theory. It would be difficult to imagine such outcomes in the Lanyon Cluster of Schools without the leadership and support of the pedagogical mentoring provided by Rita van Haren.

It is worth reiterating that as a consequence of Rita's efforts more than 80 teachers in the Lanyon Cluster have used the *Learning by Design* pedagogical framework – many of these more than once; some teachers who joined the project at the beginning are up to their fourth use of the framework.

MARY NEVILLE: A FOCUS ON REFORM VIA SYSTEMATIC DIFFUSION OF THEORY AND PRACTICE

'S..A..T… Sat! Have I got the letters in the right place? Say the word…say the word…'

'Sat!' The children chime in together.

The scene is Mary Neville's office. The voices of the teacher and the children are heard clearly through the adjoining partition wall. As Mary comes in from the corridor she is followed through the open door by the sound of many children talking, the sounds overlap and are at once familiar. The author is rushed back to his own primary school days.

'When your office is located next to a school classroom you go with the flow, after all the school is for the kids', said Mary, 'I was a teacher for such a long time that it just seems natural to me.'

The ensuing conversation, the author's first in-person meeting with Mary Neville, is peppered with terms that indicate her focus, many of these terms are repeated throughout the conversation and are later recognisable as themes in her work:

> …systemic initiatives… whole school… decentralised… learn on the job… systemic initiatives… professional learning… systemic initiatives… whole school learning… sustained influence on schools… people to support… help teachers analyse their teaching… a shift in practice… a deeper influence with less people… build capacity in the schools… multiliteracies whole school focus… networking… the absence of a centre… build more capacity, that's the plan… schools have choices…

The focus for Mary Neville—beyond that of providing teacher professional learning—was the systematic diffusion of the theory and practice of Multiliteracies and the idea of *Learning by Design* via a pool of teacher-disseminators. 'The issue for me was how to translate this to other teachers, how to build capacity in the schools', Mary said. This focus can be construed as a concern with broadly based reforms of teacher practice.

The Queensland Education model of distributed school-level decision-making in regards to curriculum, pedagogy and teacher professional learningwas takenupbyMaryinthe ways in whichshe organised and facilitated the project which she initiated in 2003. Mary could see that if the project were to be successful there needed to be a distributed pool of 'experts' working directly in schools with other teachers. This meant that participants for the Brisbane project were recruited via a competitive process involving a call for 'expressions of interest'. Teachers had to apply in writing to be part of the project, supporting their application with a rationale for their involvement, and an undertaking to build capacity for Multiliteracies pedagogy in their schools. The complete list of selection criteria was as follows;

- Specify your willingness to build capacity for Multiliteracies pedagogy in your school and briefly describe an intra school plan for sharing your project;
- Demonstrate how the development of Multiliteracies across the curriculum is linked to the school's Whole-school Literacy Strategy—in particular, plans for supporting professional development using the Teaching of Reading in a Multiliterate World CD-ROM Professional Development package;
- Demonstrate the extent to which your school works as a professional learning community or has plans to further develop a learning community within the school.

'The teachers who wanted to be involved in the project were willing, interested and reflective…good teachers are reflective', Mary observed. This competitive process, the focus on the dissemination of Multiliteracies theory and practice, and encouragement of teachers-aslearners in a professional community meant that the teachers involved in the Brisbane project were, without exception, self-motivated people with an interest in the project goals, and a commitment to their own professional development. Some teachers recruited to this group were so self-sufficient that, unlike some teachers in other locations, they needed little help in interpreting the terminology used in the pedagogical framework and less support in translating their designs into practice.

Support for the *Learning by Design* project amongst teachers was underpinned by a Queensland Education focus on Multiliteracies. For example, one Brisbane-based teacher when asked about how he became interested in the project responded:

> ...because multiliteracies is one of the New Basics... so that's what got us going...it's just the fact that Queensland is onto this stuff and its in the air and in the syllabus and part of the agenda...

The combination of a pre-existing interest in Multiliteracies, department-level support and hand-picked teachers meant that the foundations were in place in Queensland to apply the theory of Multiliteracies and *Learning by Design*. At first though some teachers had a narrow idea of what was intended: 'I had to define what was meant by multiliteracies and that it was not just about IT', Mary observed, 'some teachers were caught up in this idea of it being about computers and learning to use computers...the problem of multiliteracies was solved by adding multimedia or multimodal to what they were already doing, a digital makeover ...but this misses the point completely'.

The author observed and participated in a full day forum where the project-teachers presented and discussed their work—the forum was also intended, Mary said, 'as an opportunity for teachers to reflect on their professional learning'. It became evident at this forum that the Brisbane Learning by Design teachers were talented professionals who were passionate about their teaching. The manifestations of their practice, the completed Learning Elements presented at this forum— examples of which can be found at www.L-by-D.com—were rich, engaging and stimulated a prolonged and animated discussion between the teachers.

Rather than write at length about these 'products' of the project, the reader is invited to explore Mary Neville's chapter later in this volume and to examine the Learning Elements published by the Brisbane-based teachers at www.L-by-D.com.

Some readers might conclude that the Queensland process of competitive selection suggests that the *Learning by Design* project-teachers were the 'cream of the crop'. Such readers might wonder whether perhaps these teachers were documenting work that would have been produced anyway. Whether this is so, or not, such work is now extensively documented and in a form which can be shared with others – this is an important point as other teachers now have access to these teaching exemplars. In a sense if it were the case that these teachers would have taught in these ways regardless of their involvement in the project it perhaps demonstrates the theory of *Learning by Design*; that is, that good teaching is the result of a considered design and it is rich and multifaceted, promotes multiliteracies in students, acknowledges multimodal meaning-making and employs a range of knowledge processes and pedagogies. The author formed the impression that while the teachers were already thoughtful and adept practitioners, their engagement in the project added another dimension to their teaching and provided them with a language to discuss and share their practice.

The forum presentations and discussions indicated that each of the Brisbane-based teachers had meaningfully engaged with the theory and had demonstrated a good working knowledge of how the theory could be enacted.

Mary Neville provided the teachers at the forum with peer-review forms adapted from a Kalantzis and Cope (2004a) design included in the publication *Designs for Learning*. These forms encouraged teachers to use the *Learning by Design* knowledge processes to reflect on the work being presented and to provide each other with specific and considered feedback. A facsimile of the form has been reproduced here—it was an insightful initiative that created opportunities for reflective, 'double-loop learning' as teachers were prompted to think about key aspects of the theory in light of both their own practice and the practice of others. This peer-review form provides a useful *Learning by Design* heuristic for others to adapt and use.

Name of Work Being Reviewed

	Comments	Rating
Diversity What has the person learnt and expressed about the students' diverse life experiences? How has the person built on these diverse experiences to create improved learning outcomes for students?	{ } They felt this aspect was difficult { } They used students' everyday experiences as starting points { } They know enough about diversity to be able to help other people understand it.	0-10
Multiliteracies What has the person learnt and expressed about the multiliteracies in her/his learning element. How have multiple modes of meaning been addressed in the learning activities?	{ } They felt this aspect was difficult { } They incorporated multimodal literacies into the learning experiences. { } They know enough about Multiliteracies to be able to help other people understand it.	0-10

Knowledge Processes *(Experiencing, Conceptualising, Analysing, Applying)* Does the person provide a variety of knowledge processes throughout the learning element? Do they demonstrate an understanding of the differences between each knowledge process and the benefits of each one?	{ } They felt this aspect was difficult { } They can do it with help { } They can interpret the knowledge processes by themselves. { } They know enough about this approach to pedagogy to be able to help other people understand it.	0-10
Learning Element How well have the learning experiences been selected and designed? How well have students engaged in the learning experiences?	For example...from evidence in student work samples...outcomes the person described...	0-10

Any general comments and suggestions? (Feel free to go over the page)
You may wish to check how fairly you have rated this work with another rater.

Mary's use of the peer-review form is a demonstration of, and consistent with, the decentralised model of teaching in Queensland and provides an insight into Mary's understanding of key aspects of *Learning by Design*. The reader will also see repeated indicators of Mary Neville's focus on dissemination of the theory and practice of *Learning by Design* in the form itself: 'They know enough about this approach to pedagogy to be able to help other people understand it'. The notion of the teachers being proficient enough to help others is central to Mary's work.

All of the participants at the forum received copies of feedback from their peers and from Mary. The form both mimicked and reinforced aspects of the pedagogical framework in that it helped to structure and organise participant's thinking and responses in useful and appropriate ways while reinforcing the theory. Participants learned more about the knowledge process and the theory of *Learning by Design* as they considered each presentation in the context of the prompts.

An examination of the teachers' use of the feedback forms indicated that most teachers had entered into the spirit of the process providing both constructive criticism and suggestions for future practice. For example one teacher offered the following feedback to a peer: 'Used an incident in the classroom – great idea related to interests of all kids. Good understanding of knowledge processes evident through detailed progression and range of experiences.' Another teacher offered the same peer: 'your work has such an expansive, thought-through quality—meticulous attention to how. Lots of examples of the different pedagogical takes blended, overlapping and separately deployed—a strong sense of tacit mastery of the pedagogies.' Yet another teacher offered 'clear understanding of the students and their needs and experiences...excellent modelling of practices...superb depth of knowledge.'

Receiving immediate written feedback from peers provided each teacher with multiple perspectives on their work.

The professional quality of the teacher presentations, the high standard of their individual Learning Elements and the sustained discussion between teachers at the Brisbane forum created an impression that this approach to the dissemination of Multiliteracies theory and the pedagogies of Learning by Design had been effective. This was evident in the professional capacities of the project-teachers as manifested at the forum and in the various Learning Elements they presented. This was further supported by responses in the impact statements written by the Brisbane-based teachers following the end of their participation in the project – each, as a requirement of their involvement, outlined the contributions they were making to the dissemination of Multiliteracies and Learning by Design in their respective schools.

It is important to note that this outcome was a consequence of Mary Neville's project design and the congruence of that design with the broader agenda and policies of Queensland Education—this is covered in more detail in Mary Neville's chapter later in this volume.

ANNE CLOONAN: TEACHING TEACHERS TO TEACH USING THE PEDAGOGIES OF LEARNING BY DESIGN

Anne Cloonan's focus, although not without parallel in the work of Rita van Haren and Mary Neville, could be seen to be about *teaching teachers to teach* using multimodal texts and the pedagogies of *Learning by Design*. This approach centred on developing a practical understanding of teaching and pedagogy through the lenses of Multiliteracies and *Learning by Design*.

In Anne's case this 'understanding' was both engendered and communicated via the making of four multimodal twenty-minute videos—*Multiliteracies in the Early Years*—which explored different aspects of Multiliteracies and *Learning by Design*. Anne recruited four 'well-regarded early years teachers' to see what they would make of these ideas and theories in practice—'staged filming seemed a useful way of harnessing technology to share snippets of the journeys with a wider audience'. The first video explored the question of why the notion of literacy needed to be re-examined and redefined; the second video looked at what was meant by multiliteracies; video three examined ways in which teachers might enact the theory in their classrooms; while the fourth video addressed issues associated with assessment and teacher learning.

The videos provided a broadly accessible means to communicate both theory and practice to others using film to recount 'the story of how a group of primary teachers agreed to explore the theory and make it come to life in their classrooms'. Her co-creators, the four early years teachers who featured in the videos, were seen applying the theory, using the pedagogical framework to guide their practice, and discussing their experiences:

> And so the teachers worked to make connections with children's life-worlds, to engage them in conceptualizing and analysing representations of different kinds and applying this learning in the creation of new representations.

The films were commissioned by the Victorian Education Department as a professional learning resource to be distributed to schools and used by teachers as an introduction to Multiliteracies. Also featured on the videos were the theory-makers Kalantzis and Cope describing and explaining their theories and ideas.

Anne's four videos stimulated a lot of interest in schools.

Following the release of the videos Anne received many calls asking for more information and invitations for her to come and talk about Multiliteracies and *Learning by Design* in person. During one of the conversations the author had with her, she opened her diary of engagements for the following month—the month-per-opening-view was filled with appointments that would take her all over Victoria. Principals and teachers clearly wanted to know more.

The four videos found their way to Queensland and the ACT via the other project-consultants. The videos filled a niche in terms of introducing the theory of Multiliteracies and *Learning by Design* in an easily accessible and inviting way that complemented the more complex and elaborate territories explored via the Queensland professional development package (book and CD-ROM) titled 'The Teaching of Reading in a Multiliterate World'.

Anne Cloonan's videos offered a 'way in' to Multiliteracies and Learning by Design—a way of understanding the basic ideas and how those ideas might be applied—that other modes of communicating could not. This, at least in part, appears to be related to the choice of film as a means of articulating the Learning by Design theory and sharing teacher practice—a medium which documented, recorded, preserved, and communicated that theory using multimodal means: linguistic, visual, audio, gestural and spatial. This medium allowed Anne to capture some of the richness and complexity of the theory and practice, including some of the visual, audio, gestural and spatial nuances that would not have been possible using a traditional text. The videos also introduced and explained the professional language that was at the heart of the project. That is not to say that Anne's videos supplanted the need for a written text—that is the purpose of this book—rather they demonstrated the importance of these other modes of making meaning in a tangible way. The videos were true to the theories of Multiliteracies and Learning by Design and seem particularly apt given the orientation of the project and Anne's focus on engendering a practical understanding of the theory to help teachers better teach.

Anne Cloonan's films are evidence of an accomplished researcher wherein the films are manifestations of, and map her research journey, a journey *alongside* her four teacher-co-researchers. Writing in *Australian Screen Education* Anne makes some observations regarding the outcomes of the research constituted by her year-long *Learning by Design* film project:

> The project has started to suggest a profile of an ongoing learner-teacher, a lifelong and lifewide learner-teacher; a learner-teacher who engages in the complexity of their own and their students' world; who engages with new learning and tolerates the ambivalence of developing understandings and practices; who attempts to 'keep up' with emerging technological developments; who analyses layers of meaning rather than 'skimming across the surface'; who is a knowledge producer writing locally-developed exemplars and sharing practice with colleagues.

Anne's four films are a vehicle for communicating this compelling image of the 'lifelong and lifewide learner-teacher'; her films prompt a series of questions that relate to the future of the project, in particular the diffusion of Multiliteracies and the idea of *Learning by Design*.

How can this work of translating the theory into practice, making the ideas accessible and comprehensible be extended in ways that are consistent with the theory and underlying ideals of that theory? Anne's work suggests that a rich, multimodal internet-enabled collection of resources might be useful in terms of providing a means to share both teachers' work and their experiences with others. This collection could include a wealth of multimodal material—sound recordings; video recordings; clickable images of the teachers that unfold an audio story, supported by digital images with 'details' from the classroom and classroom practice; a 'flash' show or presentation with comments from the teachers in text; a gallery of experiences, including impact stories, stories about practice and engagement; links to the teachers' published Learning Elements; audio interviews with, or conversations between, key figures, theory-makers, policy-makers, academics, the project-consultants; perhaps interviews with children and their parents might also be included.

Such resources might perhaps open the door to many people interested in Multiliteracies and *Learning by Design*, perhaps the same people whose interest has been stimulated by Anne Cloonan's videos and the work of her four teacher-co-researchers.

If researchers and practitioners had a means by which they could contribute to this collection – expanding the body of knowledge – it would remain fresh and interesting, a place to visit and search for resources and inspiration.

Following on from this work Anne, who has subsequently secured a lectureship at Deakin University, decided to use the framework with her third-year student-teachers. Following classroom instruction and discussion about the theory of Multiliteracies she asked the students to use the framework as a form of heuristic during a week-long school placement—the students were asked to observe teachers' classroom practices and to map those practices to the knowledge processes set out in the framework. Students were also asked to write a formally-assessed reflective essay about their experience. Anne indicated that many of the students reported being surprised at how narrowly focused many of the practices were that they observed.

Anne's work with student-teachers is instructive for a number of reasons. The reflective 'double-loop learning' created by the need to write about the experience and to receive considered feedback on that writing could be expected to deepen the students' learning. Also instructive was the inventive use of the pedagogical framework as a heuristic to scaffold student teacher experiences and to further student understanding of the theory of Multiliteracies and *Learning by Design*. This novel repurposing of the framework and the associated reflective essay would seem to offer an excellent model for teaching the theory and application of Multiliteracies and *Learning by Design*. Some variation on this approach could be employed for practicing teachers in peer-based professional learning situations or for mentoring inexperienced teachers.

In the absence of any hard data in relation to the impact of this experience on the student-teachers involved the author can only speculate that they would be well-primed to use the *Learning by Design* pedagogical framework in their practice. It would be both interesting and informative to undertake follow-up research with this group of teachers as they begin their transition to teaching.

Anne Cloonan's interest in teaching teachers extends to considering how the teaching of Multiliteracies and Learning *by Design* might be formalised via inclusion in, or toward, an accredited professional learning program. This, she suggested, could take the form of a subject in a Master's degree. The subject could involve use of the pedagogical framework by the teachers in their respective classrooms; presentation of the completed frameworks as Learning Elements to peers and instructors; and completion of a reflective learning essay. Each of these activities she vouched would offer opportunities for formal, graded assessment with feedback from both peers and instructors.

The completion of an accredited Masters level subject would acknowledge the professional development of the teachers and contribute significantly to that development. Anne could see an opportunity for the extant material created by Kalantzis and Cope to be adapted to support such a subject and existing expertise developed through the *Learning by Design* project, in particular the expertise of the project-consultants, could be deployed to teach the subject and assess and provide feedback on teachers' work.

Such a step would underscore the value of the theory of Multiliteracies and the pedagogies of *Learning by Design* as essential professional competencies for teachers.

THE COMBINED CONTRIBUTION OF THE PROJECT-CONSULTANTS: MORE TO THINK ABOUT

The multifaceted roles played by the project-consultants have been instrumental in the way in which the project has unfolded and their various interventions provide opportunities for further reflection and discussion.

In terms of what this means for the development and dissemination of Multiliteracies theory, *Learning by Design*, and use of the *Learning by Design* pedagogical framework a number of instructive lessons can be drawn from their work:

- Many teachers, particularly in the early stages of their engagement with the theory and concepts associated with Multiliteracies, and with initial uses of the pedagogical framework, *need* hands-on support, feedback and mentoring;
- A potential model for this support, and therefore dissemination of the ideas and practices promoted, can be found in Mary Neville's approach where teachers were selected for involvement in the project, and the professional development associated with that
- project, because of their skills, interests and commitment to 'build capacity' in their schools for 'Multiliteracies pedagogy';

- Multimodal 'texts' of a type that includes the linguistic, visual, audio, gestural and spatial, aspects of which were exemplified in Anne Cloonan's videos, provide a useful and complementary 'way in' for teachers to the theory and practice of Multiliteracies and *Learning by Design*. The potential for such 'texts' to be developed and deployed using the internet, thereby introducing these ideas to a broader constituency need to be explored further.
- Anne Cloonan has provided a useful model for adapting the Kalantzis and Cope pedagogical framework as a heuristic for student teaching, supported by suitable assessments. This prompts thinking about the potential for including a pedagogy-focused subject in a formally accredited professional learning program.
- The project-consultants' engagement with the project led to the development of key pedagogical expertise which directly benefited both themselves and their constituencies.

Each of the project-consultants has contributed something unique to the way in which the *Learning by Design* project has unfolded—the depth and breadth of their contribution can be glimpsed in the preceding account. In the following chapter the various roles played by teachers is explored.

CHAPTER 11

The Role of the Teacher as Theory-enactor and Author-publisher

Peter Burrows

A Canberra-based teacher in the *Learning by Design* project, speaking at a focus group exclaimed 'We can't keep doing the same things we have been doing for the last 50 years'. In this chapter the roles played by teacher-participants as enactors and translators of theory, and as author-publishers are explored.

There are a number of key insights and lessons emerging from this chapter:

- Use of the *Learning by Design* framework has led to expanded pedagogical repertoires;
- *The models of teaching* prompted by the *Learning by Design* framework and the theory of Multiliteracies *were seen to be models of learning,* serving to expand and transform students' conceptions of learning and what it means to learn;
- Where these expansions were most clearly evident they seemed to be inextricably linked and mutually reinforcing;
- There appeared to be an emerging relationship prompted by the framework between teachers exploring ideas more deeply and students responding in-kind;
- Teachers demonstrated a preparedness to adapt the pedagogical framework to their own preferred ways of working;
- Student learning may be manifested in artefacts which only hint at the deep and complex learning process that underlie those artefacts—this is also true of the published Learning Elements which tell only part of the learning story;
- The teaching and learning of new literacies raises questions of how these new literacies are to be assessed;

- There are significant developmental benefits of bringing teachers together in professional forums to share and discuss their teaching practice;
- Documenting and publishing pedagogical knowledge casts teachers in a new and unfamiliar role, that of author-publisher. This new role transforms that which formerly was *individual and private* into that which is *shared and common;*
- The implications and consequences of this new role are not yet clear but the movement of work from individual and private to shared and common is significant;
- Teachers recognised that their published Learning Elements would serve as resources both for themselves and for their peers and that these resources would be judged by those peers – this led to a strong desire for these resources to be of a 'professional standard';
- The Learning Elements make manifest the pedagogical expertise otherwise hidden in the classrooms of experienced teachers;
- The Learning Elements create a pool of resources for use and adaptation by others, in particular they provide a means to induct and support beginning teachers;
- How widely and effectively such resources will be used by others will need to be the focus of future research.

The insights and lessons offered in this chapter are a result of analysing: transcripts of interviews with teacher-participants; impact statements collected by the project-consultants; the material in the teachers' published Learning Elements; data collected via the author's attendance at focus groups and participant-forums in Canberra and Brisbane and via conversations the author had with project-consultants *about* the teachers' work.

Engagement in the *Learning by Design* project, particularly at first, was often described by teachers in terms of being 'difficult', 'a struggle' or 'a challenge'. As mentioned in an earlier chapter one of a pair of Canberra-based teachers who worked on the project together in the same school said, 'when we first saw the document we broke into a sweat…'.

Although initially experience in these terms, eventually teachers almost invariably described their involvement in the project in positive terms. One of the Brisbane-based teachers believed that the project had helped improve her literacy knowledge and practice 'enormously' and that it had taught her 'to reflect and make positive changes to my teaching. Most of the support was practical and not just theoretical so I could take action to get results, not simply make decisions without fully understanding what I was doing'.

A number of focus groups and forums were conducted with teachers involved in the project—in the case of the Brisbane and ACT projects these forums were conducted at the mid-point and at the end of teachers' involvements in the project. The author attended the final forum for the Brisbane group, and both mid and final forums for the ACT group—it is somewhat misleading to talk of the ACT group as having had a 'final' forum because plans for the next meeting were organised – there was a strong sense that the group's involvement in the project and use of the pedagogical framework would continue, regardless of the formal status of the RMIT-funded project. A sustained interest was also manifested in ongoing use of the pedagogical framework with a number of ACT teachers having completed two or more Learning Elements and speaking at the forum in terms of their 'next Elements'.

Although originally constituted to gather data and obtain feedback concerning the teachers' experiences of using the pedagogical framework and their experiences of applying the theory in the classroom these forums became opportunities for teachers to share and discuss their work and experiences *with each other*—often this meant showing their work and the work of the children in their classes, sharing their difficulties and their successes, *telling the story of their involvement*. This inspired further engagement with the theory and practice of Multiliteracies, *Learning by Design* and the pedagogical framework and prompted speculation about what might be possible next time.

Being present at these forums allowed the author to see and experience the multiple ways in which teachers had responded to the pedagogical concepts promoted in the framework and how they had engaged with the theory. As an observer at these forums there was a strong sense of an emerging community of practice with a shared professional language. It became apparent that these forums were a vital aspect of the project as they helped to create the conditions necessary to support the professional learning of the teachers.

In fact, in the case of the Brisbane group, the teachers literally took over the forum so engaged did they become in exploring and discussing each others work. It quickly became apparent that Mary Neville's schedule of what-would-happen-when, including time allotted for peer-facilitated focus groups and interviews would need to be revised as the teachers became engrossed in each others' presentations and the discussions that followed. It became clear that these forums, and the reflection and engagement they promoted, were crucial to the quality of the professional learning of the teachers involved. 'Look, this was terrific, I feel inspired to try some of the things we have been seeing and discussing today' said one teacher. 'We need to do more of this, I just got so much out of the day' said another. 'I feel as though I have been part of something special.'

There was a sustained level of engagement throughout the forum. At one point, the author, having watched and listened to eleven teachers present and discuss their work was suddenly struck by the idea that what appeared to be going on in the classrooms of these teachers was a modelling and transference of what it meant to learn— the students were actually learning how to learn and how to articulate their learning:

> Models of teaching are really models of learning. As students acquire information, ideas, skills, values, ways of thinking, and means of expressing themselves, they are also learning how to learn.

Students were being taught, at the *meta-level* via teacher behaviour and practice, about how to acquire information, the potential variety of *legitimate sources* of information and learning, including one's own personal knowledge and experiences, how to interrogate this material, and how to express themselves via expanded modes of meaning-making—the students' implicit understanding of what constitutes the learning milieu was being radically transformed. It appeared that this was happening at the same time as a shift and expansion was occurring in the teachers' conception of what constitutes a legitimate learning milieu. There appeared to be something of the character of the chicken and the egg in this relationship.

This idea was tested with the teachers present at the forum and, after a brief pause, ten minutes of animated discussion ensued about the ways in which the teachers' conceptions of learning had shifted or, in some cases, been confirmed.

One of the impact statements by a Brisbane-based teacher who participated in this forum revealed the shifts in practice that the development of a project for Year 2 students using the pedagogical framework had prompted. The project involved an investigation of SMS texts, emails, letters, web pages, faxes, computer programs, facial expressions and gestures as ways of communicating messages and meaning. This particular teacher had employed multimodal forms of expression and meaning-making prior to her involvement in the project however she observed:

> What perhaps has intensified in my teaching practice is a sense of equality I now apply to different modes of communication and forms of literacy practice. Whilst previously I would have regarded a child's ability to read the written word as the most essential level of literacy competence, I now regard the ability to use and comprehend visual,

audio, gestural, and spatial texts as equally important for students to become multimodal and multilingual communicators.

This expanded notion of what it means to be literate, and the multimodal learning experiences necessary to become literate, were common themes that emerged from the data.

According to Rita van Haren 'some teachers believed at the beginning that they were already doing what the (pedagogical framework) was asking them to do' but, as she observed, 'when asked to articulate the pedagogy they were using they realised some knowledge processes were favoured over others'. There was a sense for Rita that the pedagogical framework made sure that the teacher 'considered their practice and their teaching methods'.

One of the Canberra-based teachers observed that the framework 'encourages us to go deeper', later this same teacher added '…and the students are taking us deeper, surprising us…surprising us with what they know and what they want to know'. There appears to be an emerging relationship prompted by the framework between teachers exploring ideas more deeply and students responding in-kind.

It seems too that, as the teacher more deeply explores, they become producers and products of more interesting and challenging learning milieus— there is a reciprocal quality to this engagement— this was described by one of the Brisbane-based teachers as 'me learning with the children'.

Another teacher serendipitously broke out of the boundaries created by the A4-size pedagogical framework/Learning Element— drawing on her previous experience of using large-format A2 books in the classroom this teacher adapted the pedagogical framework to this format and involved the students in planning classes. She 'began to play with the other side of the (framework), the student side' and discovered that this helped her 'to clarify the teacher side…further explain the teacher side…' She realised 'that the two could be complementary and inform each other'. The children added cut-out pictures and drawings and wrote some of the text, establishing a sense of collaboration in the planning process between teacher and students, blurring the distinction between planning and doing.

This teacher often used 'big books' as a learner resource and this seemed like a natural extension of this idea. Later she used the big book as a means of sharing with parents what the children had been working on in class. The teacher believed that the dual format of the pedagogical framework, which included a 'teacher resource' on one side of the page and a 'learner resource' on the facing page, to be well-suited to this purpose. The teacher resource was written in the professional language of the teacher while the learner resource was in a plain language intended for the children. As well as engaging the children in planning classes the teacher was able to explain and share her pedagogy with their parents. In telling this story the teacher became excited and exclaimed 'here was a real purpose, I could let parents in on our secrets, explain to them what we were doing and why...the (pedagogical framework) does make planning more time-consuming...the time, ok that's all the time we have...but if I see there is a real use for (the framework) then I will finish it, I will keep going... and I see a real purpose in this, that's why I will continue to use it...'

The Learning Element was no longer just a planning document for this teacher but a means of communicating both with the children and their parents and as a consequence had become for her a fundamental aspect of the teaching and learning process.

Another teacher related the way she and the group of teachers with whom she worked adapted and used the pedagogical framework to suit themselves. She described a process where they used butcher's paper to begin the planning process so that they could more readily collaborate, creating what she called 'a very messy visual diagram, a concept map of where we wanted to go'. She continued, 'at the beginning when ideas are flowing you need to get them down quickly, the butcher's paper helped us to capture these ideas as they spilled out'.

She described the way they then transcribed the *Learning by Design* knowledge processes onto the large sheets so that they could work on them together. They subsequently refined and transferred their plans to the computer-based pedagogical framework. 'That's what seemed to work for us, when you are a teacher something seems to happen when you use big sheets of paper and have a pen in your hand, I guess it's a way of working that we are comfortable with, it's familiar and has a more informal feel than sitting around a computer.'

Another teacher described a different process, an adaptation of the framework where seven teachers from a variety of subject areas including maths, science, food-technology, geography, English and SOSE, worked together sharing their planning and ideas via a data projector. 'We wanted more out of this than just documentation and busy work for kids...we wanted a way to work together across a common theme'.

These various examples demonstrate that teachers are prepared to adapt the *Learning by Design* pedagogical framework to their own preferred ways of working and that the pedagogical framework does not constrain or limit how teachers use it, either alone or together.

Project-consultant Rita van Haren identified a shift in planning prompted by the *Learning by Design* framework (template):

>This is a huge step in terms of planning, because in the past planning has been hit and miss, the template prompts you to plan and think about your practice. Some people relish the opportunity to plan, some people need to be nudged…but once they see a benefit, or a reason for planning the need for nudging people disappears…some teachers in the cluster have already completed three Learning Elements.

The *Learning by Design* project is, in many ways, a tangle of ideas and practices, an imbrication of theory and experience – this means that aspects of the impact on teachers and students of involvement in the project are sometimes difficult to delineate. Student learning may be manifested in artefacts which only hint at the deep and complex learning process that underlie those artefacts. One of the Brisbanebased teachers provides some sense of the complex learning experience engendered by involvement in the *Learning by Design* project for both teacher and students and highlights a number of common themes that emerged from the research.

Her plan, using the *Learning by Design* materials and pedagogical framework, was for the students to make a documentary film. She said that the *Learning by Design* materials had provided her 'with a new way of considering the teaching of literacy'.

Involvement in the project she said had allowed her 'to focus previously disparate competencies' in her teaching, for example she believed her capacity to teach critical and visual literacies had been focused 'into a more unified and purposeful intent.' She said that this meant the learning context felt less contrived and more authentic.

The process of planning and producing a documentary she saw as an extremely complex and demanding task that called upon students to use higher order thinking skills as well as acquire and develop the technical skills necessary to make and edit a film.

Although she saw the film as providing 'concrete evidence of new masteries in literacy' for her the film survived 'as an artefact of the somewhat invisible intellectual process, which culminated in its production'. She then went on to list a series of complex learner outcomes that she saw as a consequence of the students' involvement in the process.

Underscoring her sense that the students' film was an artefact of the somewhat invisible process, she identified the many discussions and conversations she had been privy to throughout the project as 'the most potent evidence of enhanced literacy outcomes'.

Later, when describing the 'world premiere' of the film to a small audience of parents she observed that the students were 'justifiably proud of their film and the parents were vocal in their praise of the kids' efforts'. This had made her feel quite emotional, she said, but it had also caused her to feel a degree of frustration:

> Watching a film is one thing, but the audience doesn't really gain an insight into the students' intellectual growth that I see, and value so much, as their teacher. It's hard to put all that into words – you have to be there and listen to their conversations and appreciate the complexity of how these 11 and 12 year old kids were thinking and behaving.

This account suggests a thoughtful, reflective teacher, someone likely to take their teaching seriously whether or not they were involved in a special project. Nevertheless there is a strong sense of professional learning in this teacher's account which includes 'a new way of considering the teaching of literacy' and a capacity to focus previously disparate competencies in her teaching into 'a more unified and purposeful intent'. This capacity to focus one's skills and to be more purposeful suggests more powerful learning designs.

Beyond the issue of the ephemeral qualities of this type of learning, this teacher's observations raise questions about how these new literacies are to be assessed, suggesting that new ways of 'seeing' students' skills and competencies, new rubrics will be required to capture these potentially more elusive learning outcomes—perhaps assessments that explore and consider the 'process' of learning as well as the retention of knowledge 'content', or the traditional examination of the 'products' of learning. In the ACT for example some teachers have begun to explore the potential of creating 'digital portfolios' to capture and document students' multimodal work, thereby making it available for assessment.

That is not to say that involvement in the *Learning by Design* project has been without measurable outcomes—another teacher from the Brisbane project reported that more than half of her class were caught in the 'Year Two Net with an average reading recovery level of 6'. This teacher reported that by the end of her class's involvement in the project the majority of students were reading over level 20. She also reported that her students received 'over half of the schools' lunch time red cards (for problem behaviours) in Term One and this decreased to only one red card in Term Two'. She said that students wanted to come to school, that they did not want to miss out on the 'interesting and connected work' they were doing.

This teacher's account hints at something crucial in the experience of using the *Learning by Design* framework to design one's teaching the teacher learns through her use of the framework, in fact the teacher *becomes a learner*. This was reiterated by one of the Canberra-based teachers who observed that 'we are all such learners with this', pointing out however that she came to understand the concepts by using the framework, 'you really understand it when you use it...'

This may have implications for the distribution (publication) and use of completed Learning Elements where teachers who use these resources may not have the same level of understanding as the teachers that created them. It remains to be seen whether use of the pedagogical framework in this way will have the same impact as when engaging with the concepts more directly—this is an area for future research.

There is ample evidence that teachers were challenged by their involvement in the project, and that involvement opened up gaps in whether the teacher had the requisite expertise, particularly where the teacher was experimenting with multimodal interventions. For example the teacher who set her students the goal of making a documentary film sought the help and advice of a professional film-maker. This person became involved in her project, conducting workshops with the students—a collaboration ensued where the teacher became a learner alongside the students and film-maker.

The enlistment of expertise-from-elsewhere and the idea of the teacher-as-co-learner were themes that emerged from conversations with a number of teachers as gaps in knowledge or know-how were recognised. In one case this took the form of a collaboration between an English teacher and an Art teacher – the Art teacher was recognised as having more advanced visual literacy skills and 'a better grasp of aesthetics'. A collaboration between an English teacher and a drama teacher came about because the English teacher recognised the drama teacher's better grasp of gestural and spatial modes of expression and meaning-making. A number of teachers mentioned the importance of the assistance provided by specialist ICT support staff or via teachers with more advanced ICT skills. In each of these cases the teachers involved reported learning valuable new competencies or, as offered by one teacher, 'learning a new lingo'.

The teacher who introduced documentary film-making to her students identified having developed skills with both digital and video cameras and as having learned the technical and professional languages associated with the deployment of those technologies.

The previously mentioned collaboration between seven teachers covering maths, science, food-technology, geography, English and SOSE demonstrated that the framework could be used in an integrative way across disciplines—serving to bring teachers together on a shared project. The title of this Learning Element was Global Citizenship and involved the students researching and organising various activities related to travel—the goals for the project were related to the importance of being a lifelong learner; being a member of a local, national and international community; and learning communication and Information Technology skills. The maths teacher for example designed learning experiences related to budgeting, using credit cards and calculating exchange rates while the food-technology teacher explored the role of food in different celebrations around the world and students prepared dishes related to these different cultures. The project culminated in round-table presentations by the students that 'crossed' the various disciplines in which they had been studying.

This project also demonstrated that the framework could be used effectively regardless of the discipline in which it was deployed and highlighted the potential for cross-curricular collaboration using the pedagogical framework as a focus for that collaboration. 'We see a purpose and a value in this (framework), it has created a reason to work as a team... given us things to do, ideas to share and discuss' said one of this team. Later adding that 'in the past I was planning on my own...it's so inspiring to bounce ideas off each other' and went on to describe the process of the team's collaboration and how they used the framework to inspire them.

Such collaborations were roused by teachers grappling with the knowledge processes, how these processes translated to their practice, and as they explored what it meant to be multiliterate—but not everyone used the framework as a prompt.

One teacher for example began to use the *Learning by Design* framework 'retrospectively, to write up each process', mapping what was happening in class to the concepts in the framework. The teacher observed that this was 'not the approach that was intended by the authors but...I feel I learnt more, and in a very valuable way'. The framework became a heuristic for reflective consideration of practice, making explicit and more comprehensible aspects of practice which may formerly have been tacit or not well understood.

A teacher from the Brisbane cohort commented on how engaged the children in her class were in their work 'the noisiest they had ever been', but admitted that she would never have tried such methods in the past—she said she 'had learnt so much from being involved in the project and 'it had forced her to find out more about technology and think hard about my pedagogy'.

When another teacher was asked 'has it changed the way you think and work?' she responded 'Definitely, definitely...and because I am working differently, using different pedagogies and different modes I am getting engagement from children who would not usually engage'.

One teacher talked about the project giving the students 'a sense of purpose and focus' and 'a way of channelling their collaborative (and) intellectual efforts'.

From the responses of teachers explored in this section it is clear that involvement in the project and use of the *Learning by Design* framework has led to more diverse pedagogical practices and greater engagement with children. Moreover, and perhaps more importantly, it appears that the models of teaching prompted by the *Learning by Design* framework and the theory of Multiliteracies are also models of learning influencing students' conceptions of what it means to learn.

In addition the *Learning by Design* framework has provided teachers with a means of sharing their pedagogical practice, casting teachers in a new and unfamiliar role. The notion of teacher-as-author-publisher is explored in the following section.

THE TEACHER AS AUTHOR-PUBLISHER

The *Learning by Design* project has been informed by ideas and practices drawn from electronic publishing and knowledge management—to make explicit and shareable formerly tacit personal knowledge and know-how (Cope & Kalantzis, 2002; Davenport & Prusak, 2000; Scarbrough, 2001; Stewart, 1998). This represents a shift in the character of pedagogical knowledge from *individual and private* to *shared and common* thereby creating a pool of resources—a body of knowledge and practices – for use and adaptation by others. In terms of the project this body of knowledge takes the form of the various published Learning Elements.

The completed Learning Elements were submitted for editing and peer-review then published to a website created for the project so that teachers' plans and practices, their designs for learning, could be shared with others. This process has facilitated access by others to the work of teachers—at the time of writing the website had been operational for less than a month—while also providing a means of ensuring quality.

Teachers' concern for 'quality' was evident in the presentation and articulation of their work. Teachers recognised that they were creating resources both for themselves and for their peers and that these resources would inevitably be 'judged' by those peers—this meant that there was a strong impetus to create work of a professional standard. This also represented a significant shift in cultural practice—the teacher-as-author-publisher making his or her practice public as contrasted with the traditionally private practices associated with the classroom-as-(en)closed-personal-space.

This shift was not without discomfort or anxiety—particularly as teachers came to terms with the implications of sharing their work with others and working with, what for most was a new and unfamiliar language.

The editorial-review process ensured that the content of Learning Elements was consistent in the sense that the various activities planned by teachers were mapped against the knowledge-processes set out in the framework. The editorial-review process also ensured that the Learning Elements were of a professional standard and publishing ready. For the purposes of the project the editorial-reviewers and arbiters of 'quality and consistency' were the project-consultants—Anne Cloonan, Rita van Haren and Mary Neville.

The publishing of Learning Elements authored by teachers is, however, still in its infancy. There is an expectation that the quality and sophistication of these Learning Elements will develop over time as teacher-authors develop acumen with the tools and come to realise the potential of the medium. The promise of future developments, manifested in this initial flurry of publications, is in the creation of a rich and accessible database of vivid examples of teaching and learning interactions, founded on rigorous pedagogical theory.

There remain, however, longer term issues related to quality and how this is to be managed if many teachers begin to use the framework and want to publish and share their work. Just because a teacher can publish their Learning Element does this mean they should? Will there always be a need for an editor or editorial process? Can a way be developed for readers and users to indicate their perceptions of quality or effectiveness of a particular published Learning Element – perhaps providing authors with feedback? Should there be a process of peer-review and critique? Perhaps modelled on the process for peer-reviewed journals? Could such a process be sustained?

The internet-enabled publishing medium employed for the project will accommodate both text-based and multimodal/multimedia examples of teaching practice. In the context of the project teachers have only just begun to explore what might be possible as a consequence. This is important because it will significantly extend what may be documented and shared in the future while offering opportunities for teachers to create learning encounters that are potentially more interesting and engaging. This should make it practical for teachers to connect classroom activities with the technology-rich life-worlds and everyday experiences of students and to document and share these activities with peers.

There is also a strong rationale for creating and sharing such resources—teachers across Australia and in other parts of the world are aging, many of the baby-boomers will soon be retiring. The average age of primary school teachers in Victoria for example is 49 Alan Luke tells us that between 2005 and 2010 in Australia there will be 'a fifty percent turnover of teachers, a seventy percent turnover of principals...and a fifty to seventy percent turnover of teacher educators and academics'. A sea-change in terms of new and beginning practitioners is imminent. Luke prompts us to think about managing this transition; to consider the kinds of systems, plans, strategies and precedents we might want to hand over; and to explore how we might 'mobilise an aging workforce'.

There is likely to be a great deal of knowledge and know-how locked up in the practices of these practitioners; Alan Luke for example believes that significant pedagogical expertise is hidden in the highly isolated and 'privatised' work of teachers, both existing and new. The *Learning by Design* process appears to offer a means of unlocking and sharing this expertise.

The notions of *learning by design* and *designs for learning*, the pedagogical framework that prompts and guides such designs, and the teacher created Learning Elements that are a consequence of the design process offer a means of re-invigorating interest in practice and pedagogy. The published Learning Elements make manifest the pedagogical expertise hidden in the classrooms of experienced teachers, as well as providing a means to induct and support beginning teachers. They also provide a means to manage and make accessible extant knowledge—a process that in other domains is referred to as knowledge management—building up banks of shareable practice and know-how. In this way retiring teachers leave behind a legacy for the burgeoning cohort of beginning teachers both at their own schools and beyond.

So, in the context of considering the prospects of *Learning by Design* and the pedagogical framework that is at its core, we need to know to what extent teachers will be prepared to share their designs for learning and classroom practices. We have seen that in the context of being involved in a special project teachers will author, document and publish their work and there are indications that teachers have continued to use the framework beyond their involvement in the project. But, will teachers more generally, outside the hot-house environment created by the project, be prepared to make explicit and public what formerly has been unvoiced and private? Will some teachers prefer to retain the anonymity of private practice? Will teachers be prepared to invest the thinking, the time and effort, required to use the pedagogical framework as a regular and ongoing part of their practice?

We also need to know to what extent teachers will use or adapt the learning designs and lesson planning of others—this is still very much unknown. Will, for instance, older teachers whose practices may be more settled engage with these ways of working? Will younger teachers prefer to blaze their own trails rather than follow their older peers?

And is an internet-enabled publishing medium necessary or appropriate to support the professional development and pedagogical fluency of teachers? Might some teachers prefer to use a print-based pedagogical framework and use it more informally, with a few rough ideas jotted down in pencil? Or, as noted by one of the Canberra-based school principals perhaps teachers will become so adept with the pedagogies that the *Learning by Design* 'approach will be internalised by teachers and become their own way of teaching whether or not it is documented'.

On the other hand, perhaps the internet-publishing medium and *Learning by Design* framework will prompt the emergence of a new cultural figure—the teacher-practitioner as author-publisher producing work for the use of others—a modern day, but more prolific, more diversely sourced and more context-appropriate equivalent to the textbook authors of the past.

Questions such as these will need to be explored in the next phase of the project as published Learning Elements are made available via the internet and begin to be used by teachers other than their creators.

Conclusion

One of the long-term goals of the *Learning by Design* Project has been fundamental change at the level of cultural practice, in particular, shifts in everyday pedagogical routines with the aim of positively altering learning outcomes for both students and teachers. The evidence suggests that in relation to the teachers involved in the project this goal has been achieved. Principally this goal was achieved by promoting multiple modes of communication and expression; prompting multiple pedagogical processes; and via the provision of a pedagogical framework that prompted both mindful and reflective designs for learning.

In this section the means of achieving this goal are briefly summarised and reiterated, the most influential factors are identified. This is followed by a series of open-ended questions which are left for the reader to consider.

The pedagogical practices of teachers were affected because of the confluence of a number of interdependent factors—these factors were elaborated in this and earlier chapters;

- The existence of a climate for pedagogical renewal at both state/territory and local school-level was important in providing the impetus for initial involvement;
- Participants in the project elected to be involved rather than being co-opted, some via a competitive selection process;

- The leadership and support of school principals was crucial in establishing a beachhead for the project—this leadership and support was communicated via what principals said and did and through funding the provision of relief for teachers attending workshops and when planning and designing Learning Elements;
- The direct, hands-on involvement of theory-makers Kalantzis and Cope provided necessary credibility at the beginning of the project. Their continued involvement, in partnership with the teachers, throughout the research process and in the development of the pedagogical framework and internet publishing medium ensured a strong relationship between theory and practice where each informed the other;
- The professional learning workshops and the printed guide/workbook were crucial in terms of setting the scene and introducing teachers to the theory and the language of Multiliteracies and *Learning by Design*;
- The hands-on support, feedback and mentoring provided by the project-consultants was essential for the professional development of participating teachers;
- The Brisbane Multiliteracies project provides a useful model for diffusion of the *Learning by Design* theory and pedagogical framework—in this context teachers were selected for the professional development offered by the project because of their skills, interests and commitment to 'build capacity' in their schools;
- There was an overarching value in teachers coming together to share, present, demonstrate and discuss aspects of their professional practice—particularly in terms of deepening and intensifying the professional learning and development that occurred.
- The *Learning by Design* framework offers teachers the potential to author and publish multimodal texts—linguistic, visual, audio, gestural and spatial—to support the further diffusion of Multiliteracies and *Learning by Design*;
- The pedagogical framework can readily be adapted as a heuristic for teaching student teachers and for peer-review—Multiliteracies, *Learning by Design* and the pedagogical framework could become part of the curriculum for student-teachers;

The single most important theme to emerge from the research relates to the professional learning and development of the teachers who played such a critical role in transforming the theory of Multiliteracies and *Learning by Design* into practice.

In order for teachers to help children have richer and more engaging learning experiences and to become more multiliterate they had to expand their pedagogical repertoire—often this meant coming to grips with new concepts and new ways of working, *becoming a learner*. The knowledge processes used in the pedagogical framework are quite complex and it proved difficult at first for some teachers to understand and relate these processes to their practice. There was, nonetheless a recognisable value in this struggle for understanding.

However, the research indicates that teachers need to be introduced to the theory and practice of Multiliteracies and *Learning by Design* via a systematic approach that includes some form of professional development and mentoring or support, at least in the initial stages.

In the context of the project there was a perceived need to create feelings of inclusiveness (belonging) and self-worth rather than feelings (for some children) of alienation and disaffection produced by some traditional teaching methods and classroom practices.

The project has attempted to address this issue of a need for more inclusive teaching by expanding the repertoire of teachers' practices— in terms of both 'what' and 'how' teachers teach—while simultaneously working to expand the child's repertoire of how to understand the world and how to communicate in ways that improve the possibility of being understood.

The expansion of repertoires of practice and ways of knowing has been central to *Learning by Design* and is manifested in many of the chapters in this volume.

There is a strong sense emerging from the research that teachers are modelling a process of 'how to learn' and through this are significantly expanding the learning milieu—perhaps the most important 'lessons' being transferred are at the meta-level 'this is how we learn around here' and 'these are legitimate mediums for learning' with the product being both teachers and children who are learning how-to-learn and learning how to communicate that learning in multiple ways.

The process of designing, documenting and applying-in-theclassroom, publishing and sharing, thinking about, talking about Multiliteracies and *Learning by Design* has created the conditions in which 'value' was both created and realised. For example a three minute film created and produced by a group of Year 7 students was an outcome of an intense process of engagement, research, experimentation and application in the space created between the teacher, the students, and the ideas and ways of working that emerged in this space. Highly complex and multi-layered, the film represented the traces left behind by this rich and complex process.

Similarly, the Learning Elements—that which the teachers design and share with others—provide traces of a pedagogical and curricular process, manifestations of learning-in-action, signposts and trails for others that might follow but perhaps these traces need to be supplemented by stories that describe, elaborate and explain *how* teachers arrived at their designs. The teachers that follow might not have the collegial environments that were created around the project.

This opens up the question of how the richness and complexity of such processes can be captured, and captured in ways which can be communicated to others. This represents a significant challenge for teachers as they negotiate the transition from a focus primarily on curriculum and content to more conscious considerations of pedagogy and process.

This is reflected in the focus of the project—*Learning by Design* is primarily about pedagogy—*how* one teaches rather than *what* one teaches: a variety of *hows* is both prompted and promoted. The idea of 'multi' seems to be at the heart of *Learning by Design*—multimodal, multiliteracies, multi-pedagogies—'multi' makes enrichment and enlivenment possible for both teachers and students—at the very least possible for *more* teachers and *more* students.

The following series of open-ended questions are offered to the reader as food for thought.

How will expanded conceptions of learning, and expanded pedagogical practices, affect student outcomes in the long term?

How will shifts in pedagogical practice and modes of meaning-making affect the disposition of the teacher toward individual students, in particular teachers' perceptions of student acumen or engagement?

How will having one's mode of meaning-making recognised or promoted or legitimated and extended in *the context of the classroom,* affect students?

Will broadening the 'domains of literacy' in which it is possible to become *officially adept* increase the probability that more children will be recognised and acknowledged as successful learners?

Will this mean, for example, that less children will be seen as 'deficit' than was previously so?

Will the theories and pedagogical practices promoted by *Learning by Design* provide for a permanent widening of the gateway to learning and admit a more diverse cohort of students?

Earlier in this chapter a line was borrowed from William James which suggested that theories were not destinations but a means of transport. The reader is asked to consider the use practitioners have made of the theories of Multiliteracies and *Learning by Design* as evidenced in the preceding chapters and to think about where these theories have transported these practitioners and their students.

The reader is asked to keep these considerations in mind as they read the chapters authored by the project-consultants that follow.

CHAPTER 12

Professional Learning and Enacting Theory: Or Trying to be a Lifelong/Lifewide Teacher-Learner while Hanging on to Your Sanity

Anne Cloonan

INTRODUCTION

The world is an information-saturated one where 'making-meaning' might relate to various combinations of words, images, sound and data; often on some type of screen; certainly created in all manner of ways; and originating from all manner of sources around the globe.

In this chapter I offer a description of my own professional learning in the area of Multiliteracies theory and my subsequent involvement in the *Learning by Design* project. I draw heavily on the theories of the New London Group and Mary Kalantzis and Bill Cope in describing the pleasure, the pain, the highs and the hurdles in the application of theory into practice. Finally, I reflect on broader issues of professional learning.

FINDING SOME NEW STUFF THAT CAN EVOLVE THE OLD STUFF

There is a wealth of material written on the inability of traditional approaches to language, literacy and pedagogy to prepare young people to thrive in the 'knowledge society' in which:

> Value is increasingly located in the intangibles of human capacity, organisational flexibility, business processes, customer relationships, brand identity, technological know-how, product aesthetics and service values. This represents a shift away from the in the old grounding of value primarily in fixed capital and basic skills (see Chapter 4).

Lankshear and Knobel (2003, p. 55) argue that:

> Knowledge work is now unquestionably regarded as the highest order of productive activity ... and the most potent and valued forms of literacy will be ... those that tend toward the highest order manipulation of symbols to generate ... 'data, words, oral and visual representation' (citing Reich, 1992:177).

But possibly the most potent catalyst for professional learning I found was observation and interaction with the 'digital' generation themselves. Their world and way of interacting with it comprises textual landscapes and literate practices I've rarely seen in a classroom.

Four year olds switching between the use of three different remote controls to watch programs on television, Pay TV, video and DVDs. Five year olds hearing a web address announced at the end of a favourite television program and independently logging into the webpage and interacting. Six year olds navigating through the menu of a DVD to view bonus material, select scenes and enable the showing of subtitles to decipher incoherent dialogue. These to name just a few.

And yet 'digital literacies' have been dismissed or overlooked by many teachers, especially in early childhood classrooms (Durrant & Green, 2000; Healy, 2004). And my anecdotal experiences with many elearning environments was consistent with Cope and Kalantzis's observation that:

> 'elearning' environments replicate and often even accentuate all that was inadequate about the traditional classroom—transmission of received knowledge, individualised learner communication, question and answer routines, narrowly focussed tests and uneven access to learning resources. Despite their aura of newness, they are just as irrelevant to the needs of the knowledge society as the traditional classroom. (see Introduction)

If preschoolers could make such refined selections through knowledge gained informally, what potential was there for students who travelled through an education system which privileges equally new and old technologies? Where the form of ICTs doesn't triumph over the content? Where the dazzlement factor was kept in moderation? And where the classroom and the curriculum gets more than the 'digital makeover' identified by Lankshear, Snyder and Green (2000)in their research into classroom practices of literacy and technology?

What might it look like and result in, this learning that enables describing and critiquing experience? A pedagogical approach that fostered a 'creative capacity in the process of meaning-making (that) implies that new literacies are not simply tools to acquire, but tools to be created'? (Bruce, 2003, p. 331). Learning that addressed making-meaning from print embedded in texts and that integrated all manner of contemporary and traditional designs? And privileged equally with print other modes at work in designed texts?

> The significance of the new technologies is that, as media, they allow for very different ways of engaging, relating and communicating. (see Introduction)

What do we, as teachers of these students, need to know to facilitate such learning? Rather than despair, I took to reading. Some of this reading included, belatedly, *A Pedagogy of Multiliteracies: Designing Social Futures,* (New London Group, 1996). The title intrigued me, each word ringing with relevance and connection. This quote jumped out at me,

> ... (Multiliteracies) will supplement, not critique, existing curricula and pedagogical approaches to the teaching of English language and literacy.

Here was an invitation. Teachers often inhabit a pragmatic ground surrounded by children's diverse orientations; parent, community and government expectations; school traditions; and our own assemblage of professional beliefs and understandings. In the sometimes combative arena of literacy teaching and learning, a theory which didn't require the joining of a particular tribe was welcome.

> Cope and Kalantzis refer to: ... fashions of pedagogy which have at times favoured some knowledge processes over others ... disciplines which relied on some more heavily than others; and the preferences of learners and teachers have also played a role. (see Chapter 5)

Honan (Healy, 2004) and others borrow the French term 'bricoleur', when talking about teachers' practice. She defines a *bricoleur* as 'someone who draws on a variety of resources around them to create a meaningful assemblage of practice'.

The image of teachers selecting and assembling threads of knowledge as different fashions come and go, is, for me, one of practitioners in charge of their own learning. Cope and Kalantzis also say:

> Teachers ... need to be self aware and expert in the range of knowledge processes ... they need to have a wide repertoire and know when to plan,

scaffold and deploy which knowledge processes and for which goal. (see Chapter 5)

In an era of school-based decision-making, one could argue that teacher engagement with theory that supports the evolution of their learning and practice is more important than ever:

> Herein lies an enormous challenge, and an enormous opportunity for education. What education does—building the knowledge capital of a society as well as the sensibilities to navigate ambiguity and complexity—is now fundamental. (see Chapter 1)

This *Learning by Design* project is concerned with what teachers, schools, and the institutions of education uniquely offer: learning *by design*, not the informal learning students do in their lives out of school. It enables the application of Multiliteracies theory-in-action; holding the potential for teachers to enter into the theory via multiple doorways. My entrance was with a distinct interest in the increasing multimodality of texts. But of course it was to be more complex than that

First Engagement with the Pedagogical Template: The Pleasure and the Pain

I undertook a short course and was introduced to the three aspects of the Multiliteracies theory (New London Group: 1996):

- a focus on diversity amongst learners and attention to enabling belonging (the starting point of learner identity and subjectivity) and transformation (as the changes wrought on human capacity and subjectivity through the learning process).
- engagement in meaning-making with multimodal designs of meaning: (combinations of linguistic, visual, audio, gestural and spatial designs)
- deployment of four pedagogical traditions when planning, implementing and reviewing teaching and learning: situated practice; overt instruction; critical framing and transformed practice.

Annah Healy (2000) describes Multiliteracies as a vehicle for travelling the curriculum, in ways that make sense to students, a bridge between community and school text practices.

The 4-6 year olds in my life were obsessed with Hi-5, an Australian group with their own television program (its rumoured that the popularity of this program on the Nine Network prompted the ABC to overhaul the presentation of its classic preschool attraction, *Playschool*). The group also has a series of related merchandising items and promotional activities.

So, when as part of this course I was asked to choose an area of study to write up into a Learning Element, 'something to do with Hi5' sprang to mind. I had some nervousness about debunking the children's heroes. I didn't want to deny them the *pleasure* of being fans (Mission, 2004). Nor did I want to engage in a fun-sapping politically correct exercise. But I wanted them to be in control of the pleasure. A *knowing* pleasure if you like. And I also wanted them to be able to think about questions such as, *Why does playdoh with Hi-5 on the packaging cost more than playdoh in a plain package?*

Cope and Kalantzis later re-named and re-framed the pedagogies from Multiliteracies theory as four ways of knowing:

> Effective pedagogy employs ways of knowing that are capable of drawing the knower closer to the knowable. It also uses learning contents which have purchase on the learners' lifeworlds and educational experience. It is the process of engaging with the stuff of the world which affirms (belonging) and extends (transformation) the learner's framework of knowing. (see Chapter 5)

- Immersion became *experiencing,* be that 'experiencing the known' or 'experiencing the new';
- Overt instruction became *conceptualising,* be that 'conceptualising by naming' or 'Conceptualising with Theory';
- Critical framing became *analysing,* be that 'analysing functionally' or 'analysing critically'; and
- Transformed practice became *applying,* be that 'applying appropriately' or 'applying creatively'.

Within the context of professional learning, I was presented with a Microsoft Word document template to develop my 'Learning Element'. These elements were to be published in an online environment. In the deceptively simple template, pedagogical choices (how I was planning to teach) are presented as knowledge processes, or ways of knowing. Different ways of knowing can be described as different 'movements' or moments in the learning process.

The template has two columns, a *Teacher Resource* and a *Learner Resource*. I had to decide on 'knowledge objectives'. I reflected on why I wanted these students to be engaged in learning about Hi-5.

- Hi-5 is a highly popular feature in the lifeworlds of the children for whom I was planning (local students aged 4-6). The students had experienced much informal learning about Hi5 through watching the television program and through related merchandise such as videos of the program, books, games, jig-saw puzzles and clothing.
- I had witnessed Hi-5's highly charged promotional activities including concerts and guest appearances at shopping malls. I had experienced the persistence of avid collectors of their associated merchandise. I was interested in how young students might explore issues of commodification of entertainment and branding of merchandise.
- The activities and packaging of the group took form in a range of multimodal 'texts'. These offered diverse and popular examples of multimodality (combinations of print with visual, audio, gestural and spatial designs of meaning) direct from the children's lifeworld. I was interested in how children engaged with these texts to make meaning.

The template guided me through the formulation of broad objectives under the headings of knowledge processes. After some reworking, these are as follows:

Experiencing (Or Knowing Things 'By Being'—To Translate Professional Teacher Talk into Learner Talk)

- Watch and relate to a familiar children's television program.
- Watch and relate to an unfamiliar children's television program.

Conceptualising ('By Connecting')

- Articulate concepts of character, puppetry, sound effects, setting, colour, costume, logo.
- Distinguish different visual representations of character: photo, caricature, signature.
- Identify different program themes: summer, treasure, animals etc.
- Distinguish between segments shot in the studio and segments shot on location.
- Identify program segments: drama, stories, song, art/craft, dance, etc.
- Identify associated merchandising: videos, books, games, CDs, clothing.

- Identify merchandise sales points such as stores and the program webpage.

Analysing ('By Thinking About')

- Identify the 'function' of Hi5 (characters/group).
- Identify the appeal of Hi5 (characters/group).
- Identify the target audience of Hi5.
- Applying (by doing)
- Plan a short program segment.
- Present it to an audience.
- Film the segment.

The drafting (and re-drafting) of learning activities was not a simple case of planning a unit of work. This template (call it a framework or a heuristic) was prompting me to consider aspects of pedagogy in a new light. (To access this Learning Element, visit www.L-by-D.com, and take the links Projects -> Early Years Multiliteracies.) I had a sense of being involved in a number of dimensions of professional learning *simultaneously;* a kind of juggling act where I was trying to keep a number of balls aloft.

Ball 1: I was getting my head around the pedagogical tags. I was sorting out what I was currently doing and re-organising these into the (newly named for me) pedagogies or knowledge processes.

Ball 2: I was identifying 'gaps' in my practice as well as 'preferences' or comfort zones. I was dipping down into the definitions of each of the tags as I made fine decisions about the type of experiencing; the type of analysing, etc. This is consuming work/learning and I found it needed much discussion and reflection. I also saw it as the major purpose for my engagement with the template (in the first instance in a self-centered 'me and my class' kind of experience).

Ball 3: I was trying to incorporate the two 'multis' of the 'Multiliteracies' theory into the learning experiences—the multi'lingual' and the multimodal. While the template doesn't overtly encourage this, the training does (the context of me using the template). This involved considering technological co-learning with students that I hadn't yet undertaken but wanted to, such as using PowerPoint; or getting kids going with webpages; or using digital cameras; or some animation software.

Ball 4: I was positioned as a published teacher-author. This raised the bar in terms of the documentation I offered. It included the ponderous, 'who am I to publish this as I don't even know what these pedagogical tags really mean yet?'

Ball 5: The template seemed to be guiding me, by its very layout—a kind of tacit prompt as to what I should be including. For example, if the pedagogies are ordered in a certain way, did I intuitively feel that I should be following that path? And what about the learner resource—what belonged where? Was it a case of using different language (learner and teacher); did all the gaps need to be filled? I discovered I was sometimes more comfortable with 'learner language'. This has issues for being a teacher-author.

Ball 6: I was trying to reconcile planning using the template with other pedagogical frameworks which I may draw on (e.g. Bloom's or Gardner's) and my former methods of planning (e.g. brainstorming, using a concept map and then timetabling).

Ball 7: I was thinking, 'but I'd never do this for everything I plan!' (this is connected to the teachers-as-authors point).

Ball 8: I was involved in technological issues which were outside of my comfort zone, such as importing graphics, particular ways of copying and pasting, the architecture of the template, file sizes which require burning onto CD, not having a CD burner or broadband, to name a few. Well, eight balls is more than anyone outside of *Cirque du Soleil* should have to keep in the air. It was hard work. So what was I getting from it?

While my interest in working more with the multimodal was my entrée to the theory of Multiliteracies and the theorists' subsequent work on pedagogical frameworks/knowledge processes, the framework acted as a prompt for considering all three aspects of the Multiliteracies theory as I asked myself questions such as: What do I want to achieve? How might I do it? Where are my preferences? Where are my gaps? How do I need to 'stretch' my pedagogical comfort zone? What impacts do the specific learners' needs have on my choices? And how does the content I brought to the template (an analysis of a popular, packaged children's phenomenon) impact on my selection of knowledge processes?

Despite all the juggling, I found the professional learning energising and, despite the many questions I still have, satisfied in part my search for a theory which could support the learning of clickeratti students.

SECOND ENGAGEMENT: FILMING AND FRAMEWORKS

I continued to bemoan the dearth of examples of resources and work which took what might broadly be called a Multiliteracies approach in the early years. I was keen to see what a group of well-regarded early years teachers (teachers of students aged 5-9) would make of the Multiliteracies manifesto. So as a way of developing some shareable 'Multiliteracies influenced' early years examples, the

Department of Education and Training in Victoria funded a series of videos, which I produced.

Over the course of 2003, four teachers and I met with Bill Cope and Mary Kalantzis, with a view to engaging with the theory and enacting it in practice. Staged filming was utilised in an effort to capture the reflective learning journeys—rather than a single moment in time.

The result was *Multiliteracies in the Early Years*, a series of four videos which explores various issues: *why* a re-think of definitions of literacy is timely; *what* is meant by Multiliteracies and *how* this group of teachers approached enactment of the theory in their classrooms.

The content of the classroom segments, which was threaded through all four programs, developed organically as the teachers developed their practice as influenced by the theory. Another thread was the teacher reflection on their learning. And a third thread was input from New London Group members.

These videos have become a professional learning resource for Victorian teachers and their showing has stimulated a great deal of interest in the theory and practice of Multiliteracies. However, while the videos did capture shareable classroom examples of Multiliteracies theory-in-practice, and did stimulate engagement with the theory there was a concern raised by the teachers that it was more a taste of their developing programs, rather than the richness of what was happening in the classrooms. So we decided to use Cope and Kalantzis *Learning by Design* template (pedagogical framework) to document more fully—as Learning Elements—the happenings in their classrooms. These Learning Elements are published under at www.Lby-D.com, and can be found by taking the link to 'Projects', then 'Early Years Multiliteracies'.

MORE ENGAGEMENT: BYO CONTENT TO THE PEDAGOGICAL FRAMEWORK

They say that you never really learn something until you have to teach it to someone else. Or have to apply your learning in some way. I was reminded of this when I read that adding a second metacognitive loop to single loop learning adds to epistemological depth (Argyris & Schon, 1978; Schon, 1983).

I was invited to come on board the RMIT *Learning by Design* Project as research assistant. In this role I worked with other teachers engaged in developing Learning Elements:

- reading other teachers' curricula designs (Learning Elements) and reflectively critiquing their use of the pedagogical tags

- providing feedback to support curricula development and gleaning implications for professional learning.
- This involved me in considering uses of the template in a range of contexts, well beyond my own use of it. In addition to the Early Years project, diverse groups were trialing the use of the template.

SEAMLESS PEDAGOGICAL SEGUES/DISQUIETING DISEQUILIBRIUM

While providing support, guidance and a means for self-evaluation, the template is content free. Waiting, if you like, for teachers to clarify an enactment of their own purposes. The template is not looking to prescribe curriculum, and the four knowledge processes are not necessarily sequential. Rather, the framework is a means of mapping a range of pedagogies, which will be determined by the requirements of a specific area of learning content, or the preferred learning style of an individual or group. So each teacher/author (or group of teacher/authors) is involved in designing context-specific curriculum.

Reading through other teachers' Learning Elements and 'quality assuring' their use of the pedagogical tags involved some slippery issues. As had been the case in my own use of the template, each teacher clearly came to the task with their own purposes. Some brought a disciplinary orientation (such as bridge design) while others brought a personal orientation (being an active citizen). Most (perhaps all) brought more than one focus.

Interpretations of the knowledge processes in the template are, to a large extent, context bound. For example, it is usually at the local level that differentiation can be made between *experiencing the known* or *experiencing the new*. This requires an intimate knowledge of a community—a classroom community. Of course, within each classroom community, experiences will differ. But the teacher's knowledge (both in terms of student abilities and interests) is critical here in designing learning that is appropriate to students' zone of proximal development (L. S. Vygotsky, 1978); where students can achieve with support, what they may not be able to without.

Which ten year olds already know how to independently work on PowerPoint presentations; or have knowledge of worm castings; know how to insert hyperlinks; know about tectonic plates; or have proficiency in visual/print procedural texts; or have been to an aquatic park? And for which is this new? This is local knowledge best described by the teacher/author to alert other teachers to their own contexts.

Experiencing the new and *conceptualising naming* posed strong resemblances which are sometimes difficult to separate.

> *Experiencing the new* is a process in which the learner is immersed in an unfamiliar domain of experience, either real (places, communities, situations) or virtual (texts, images, data and other representational meanings). *Conceptualising by Naming* is a process involving the development of abstract, generalising terms.

But when involving students in *experiencing the new*, be it information about types of bridges or keeping worms, or analysing documentaries, teachers tend to introduce and use the language of the discipline or area of study in question. Because it's something new, it needs scaffolding.

I came to see that while *experiencing the new*, the language is slipped in or summoned up carefully by the knowing teacher. It generally involves a placing of the terms into the students' textual environment, using the terms in a number of different ways; possibly giving them special emphasis.

When *conceptualising by naming*, the language is far more formally articulated. Teachers often write or record the language in the form of a glossary or poster of some kind; the language is isolated from the everyday use, drawn out and precisely defined. And definitions may surprise. Whether it be the word 'credit' in accounting; or the multi-definitional language of ICT such as hacking, virus, Word, Access, etc.

Another slippery area of categorisation is that of Conceptualising with Theory and *analysing functionally*.

> *Conceptualising with Theory* is a process by means of which concept names are linked into a language of generalisation; while *Analysing functionally* is a process involving the examination of the function of a piece of knowledge, action, object or represented meaning.

The fine differentiation here seems to be that conceptualising *with* theory involves describing or learning about theory itself. For example, in a Learning Element investigating global citizenship, students taking an imaginary trip use knowledge of credit cards and travellers cheques to theorise what they might require. They consider how many transactions they will expect to have and what fees this will attract if using credit cards; or how many travellers cheques they might need and what commission they would pay.

Moving into *analysing functionally*, students might write an explanation of when and why they would choose to use credit cards or travellers cheques.

Or in another unit involving an analysis of Reality TV, students would be involved in *conceptualising with theory* by making inferences about what morals and values Reality TV promotes and by identifying particular actions as representations of morals and values. Moving into *analysing functionally,* they may analyse the morals and ethics that are promoted by Reality TV.

Maybe it's more a case of describing theory when *conceptualising with theory* and analysing the function of the theory when *analysing functionally*. In any case, I found this a challenging differentiation for teachers to make.

Looking for evidence of learners *applying* knowledge is, like experiencing, a somewhat contextualised endeavour. In any case, designing opportunities for students to apply newly acquired knowledge requires a deep and close knowledge of students' learning trajectories.

> *Applying appropriately* is a process by means of which knowledge is acted upon or realised in a predictable or typical way in a specific context. *Applying creatively* a process which takes knowledge and capabilities from one setting and adapts them to quite a different setting.

It was interesting to note was that all teachers took their students into *applying appropriately*. And since application is never mere replication, all application is in some way original (and so contains some degree of creativity). However, many teachers, no doubt for a range of reasons, did not take their students to *applying creatively*. Dependent on the content and the objectives of the learning, there are valid reasons why appropriate application is as far as you would want to take students. Cope and Kalantzis (see Chapter 4) suggest, for example, that creative application of elementary particle physics; or Koran learning of devout Muslims, would be highly inappropriate.

However, in many cases, some lateral thinking by teachers could extend application of learning into the creative realm.

In one example, a teacher had planned a Marine Studies unit purchasing a tank to support students in establishing a business enterprise through breeding fish. The fish tank accidentally broke; the students expressing great disappointment *(experiencing)*.They problematised the loss of the fish tank studying similar losses in a small business *(conceptualising)*. They compared and contrasted at a range of business plans, speculating on their purposes and audiences *(analysing)*.

The students went on to create a business plan for a business that could conceivably run successfully at a school level for a profit *(applying appropriately)*. The teacher then had the students use their business plans as the basis for a sales pitch in which they tried to persuade the class to adopt their business concept for a whole class business enterprise. Students selected various means to promote their business concept—persuasive speech, role-play, PowerPoint presentation, etc. *(applying creatively)*.

When talking about the processes for making meaning in a changed world, (Bruce, 2003, p. 331) says that the 'creative capacity in the processes of meaning making implies that new literacies are not simply tools to acquire, but tools to be created.' He goes on to say that 'We need to ask both what is and what can be?'

Many of the Learning Elements proved to be authentically interdisciplinary, not in a merely thematic way, asking questions such as 'how can I do some maths while teaching about recycling?' Rather the teacher/authors had asked and answered questions which crossed disciplinary/domain areas, such as:

- what knowledge do I want my students to learn?
- why do I want them to learn this? *(knowledge objectives)*
- how do I want them to learn this? *(knowledge processes)*
- in what ways will they be transformed? *(knowledge outcomes)*

TEACHERS AS REFLECTIVE DESIGNERS OF LEARNING

Darling-Hammond (Darling-Hammond, 1998, 1999), builds on the work of Shulman (1987) in identifying the sorts of things teachers need to know to educate 'the most diverse student body in our history to higher academic standards than ever before'.

Recognition of the subject-specific nature of 'pedagogical content knowledge' and of the heavy influence it has on teachers means that our learning needs to be cognisant of knowledge 'encoded' in different subject matter. Darling-Hammond (1998) suggests that teachers need to understand subject matter deeply and flexibly; they need to help students build cognitive maps; they need to cross different disciplinary traditions; they need to connect disciplinary knowledge to everyday life.

Researchers have found that the students' context is what is most immediately important to teachers (Cohen, McLaughlin, & Talbert, 1993; Darling-Hammond, 1999). Effective teachers develop 'pedagogical learner knowledge' through which they can link into and support each child's emotional and identity development; and they need to be able to reflect on their teaching practice and act reflexively on the basis of good professional judgment (Darling-Hammond, 1998).

Luke believes that considerable pedagogical expertise is hidden in the highly isolated and 'privatised' work of teachers. As teachers we walk out of our highly privatised work world (usually the classroom), amble along the corridor then poke our nose in someone else's classroom. And here we get into it. The door frame reflection. Our bags at our feet, we lean against the door frame; and first two, three, maybe more teachers debrief about their students; their practice. This is the stuff theorists call 'personal knowledge' (Polanyi, 1962). And which theorists wonder how to capture.

Teacher developed and shared Learning Elements, are a way of capturing teacher practice and teacher thinking. Much more than planning documents, they provide the individual with a means for mapping, reflecting and evaluating pedagogical practices. From a profession-wide perspective, they offer exemplars on which to focus teacher dialogue and critique, and a knowledge bank from which the profession can borrow or contribute to and in so doing, learn.

In pursuing the *Learning by Design* framework, we can thus build our professional capacity which current research indicates has more influence on the learning outcomes of children than other variables such as socio-economic background or the curriculum .

Acknowledgement

I would like to extend specials thanks to my co-learners, Mary Dowling, Fiona Knight, Ruth Moodie and Monica Taylor and our students for their gracious forbearance. I also extend warm thanks to the Footscray North and Rosedale Primary School communities for their continued support.

CHAPTER 13

Innovation in Queensland Education: Multiliteracies in Action

Mary Neville

INTRODUCTION

Following recent reforms in Queensland education, the theory and practice of Multiliteracies is emerging as a fundamental aspect of the learning process and as an important indicator of learning outcomes in all areas of curriculum. The term is incorporated into the *New Basics* Project, a Queensland Education initiative to identify and teach the building blocks for learning in the twenty-first century. Multiliteracies is also integral to the *Literate Futures* state literacy strategy. A concern with Multiliteracies is also reflected in a suite of professional learning materials developed for by the Department of Education for Queensland teachers. However, the meaning many teachers make of Multiliteracies depends largely on their previous professional learning experiences, the reflective connections they make with the theory and with how they have taught literacy, or how they have been taught to teach literacy, in the past.

Multiliteracies theory incorporates a particular approach to teaching literacy— representing a way of thinking about diversity, multimodality and pedagogy. Because it is relatively new, teachers' grasp of the meaning and application of the approach may vary in emphasis from classroom to classroom and from school to school. However, teachers' practices have been to varying degrees influenced by the theory and the approach to teaching and learning which it represents.

Opportunities for professional development that relate to the teaching of reading in a multiliterate world, have been made widely available in Queensland, and many schools and districts have action learning projects for teachers underway. The Learning by Design project, which is the subject of this chapter, was initiated as a part of this professional development emphasis, with the specific aim of translating state literacy priorities and Multiliteracies theory into everyday classroom practices. Whilst Learning by Design is an approach to pedagogy applicable right across the curriculum, the focal point for using the Learning by Design approach in this project was specifically in the area of literacy, and in particular to bring the broader view of literacy to classrooms that Multiliteracies embodies. This main innovation in this project has been the Learning by Design pedagogical framework, as described by Kalantzis and Cope earlier in the first part of this book.

This chapter describes the *Learning by Design* project in Queensland and the impact of the pedagogical framework on teachers' practice. It has been written for practitioners and educators interested in learning more about how the *Learning by Design* framework can be used to translate Multiliteracies theory into practice, as well as relating to other educational priorities such as the balanced literacy programs using the Four Resources Model (Luke & Freebody, 1999) and the Productive Pedagogies (Queensland Government, 2003) initiatives. While many practices associated with Multiliteracies theory are common in schools in Queensland, until recently the specific work of teachers translating theory into practice—making it real in classrooms—has not been widely documented or readily available to others. This chapter begins to addresses this gap.

A CLIMATE FOR PEDAGOGICAL RENEWAL—LITERACY STRATEGY IN QUEENSLAND

The climate for pedagogical renewal in Queensland has been fuelled by the strategic curriculum reform agenda spearheaded by the state education document 'QSE 2010' (Education Queensland, 2000). Objectives included in this document include 'Multiliteracies for learning' and 'developing pedagogy for the post-industrial environment'. Aspects of the reform agenda are also evident in the *Literate Futures: Report of the Review of Literacy in Queensland Schools* (Luke & Freebody, 2000) through priorities that include addressing student diversity, developing whole school programs and community partnerships, the teaching of reading, and the idea of 'future literacies' (Education Queensland, 2002).

The release of the Queensland Schools Reform Longitudinal Study (Lingard & Ladwig, 2001) prompted Education Queensland to recognise that improved teaching practices were required to raise the bar on the intellectual substance of classroom lessons —the term coined was 'Productive Pedagogies'. The authors of this study suggested that 'Productive Pedagogies' should be an integral feature of all schools' curriculum planning.

The twenty elements detailed in the Productive Pedagogies supported intellectually challenging learning experiences that incorporated recognition of difference, connectedness to the world, and a focus on collaborative learning in supportive classrooms. Consequently, Productive Pedagogies have been picked up by schools involved in the New Basics Project (Queensland Government, 2003) and adopted by the majority of Queensland schools guided by the Years 1-10 Curriculum Framework (Queensland Government, 2001)—another statewide initiative aimed at improving educational outcomes.

These various policy initiatives, Literate Futures, Productive Pedagogies and the New Basics project, have provided Queensland Education with foundational points of reference for change and a rich climate for pedagogical renewal. Together these initiatives have prompted a sustained interest in developing appropriate and effective approaches to teaching literacy and creating curriculum suitable for 'new times' across year levels and discipline areas in this state.

This climate for renewal has provided conditions ripe for the theories and practices engendered by the *Learning by Design* pedagogical framework. The following section briefly outlines the background to this project is briefly outlined, followed by a sketch of the teaching context.

PROJECT BACKGROUND

Twenty primary and secondary teachers joined the Queensland Department of Education's Learning by Design project over a period of two years, 2003-2004. The Learning by Design project was a part of The Gap Cluster Learning and Development Centre's major focus area of literacy (The Gap is a suburb of Brisbane, Queensland). At the time the centre was about to embark on deeper and more sustained professional learning pathways about literacy for schools with diverse student populations in the Stafford and Geebung Districts. My work as Coordinator of the Learning and Development Centre focused on teachers' professional knowledge about the implementation of Multiliteracies in classrooms. By linking the Learning and Development Centre into the Learning by Design Project, I was able to improve the depth of professional learning opportunities and experiences in literacy and pedagogy for the teachers and schools involved.

Teachers whoparticipatedinthe *Learning by Design* Project varied in age and had a wide range of teaching experience, as well as teaching right across the year levels, from Years 1 to 12. Many of the teachers became involved because they saw this project as a professional learning opportunity to expand their knowledge of Multiliteracies and as a means to apply this new knowledge. They knew that there was a strong commitment to Multiliteracies led by the executive directors of schools and the teachers' principals. In addition, some teachers commented on the connection between the project and the need to match teaching practices with the everyday lives of today's children. One teacher, working in a hospital school, was particularly articulate about meeting this need:

> ... certainly, working more on hybrid texts as opposed to the traditional genre structure, I mean that's the real world, that's where kids are livingthese days. Sotheyneedtobeable todecode that, access the meaning and deconstruct it, and they need the skills and the strategies to do that. I mean even living within the hospital environment; it is a multi-modal environment. Living in the school environment is a multi-modal environment so they need to be able to access that and get meaning from it. *Meredith, Mater Hospital Special School, Ward Teacher.*

Others pointed out that their professional learning from involvement in the project might also help them to support other teachers in their schools through the additional roles they held— enrichment coordinators, Middle Schooling Head of Department, literacy and curriculum coordinators and membership on literacy and IT committees.

THE CONTEXT OF TEACHERS' WORK

The profiles of teachers' work contexts were substantially different, spanning three districts with culturally diverse student populations— one school had students from 48 different cultural backgrounds. While just over a quarter of the schools were situated in highly affluent suburbs, the remainder of schools were in mid to low socio-economic locations. The research findings outlined in this chapter are drawn from structured interviews with teachers and an analysis of many of the teachers' previous curriculum planning artefacts.

Primary classes that were taught during this project covered Years 1-7. There was evidence that prior to the *Learning by Design* project teachers planned their curriculum and classroom activities drawing on a wide range of theories and frameworks. Outcomes-based education with an emphasis on the integration of Key Learning Areas was a common element of teachers' curriculum designs. The way teachers chose to document units of work, the pedagogy and the planning templates or tools they used to plan curriculum were distinctly varied and not necessarily well focused on the new kinds of text and textual practice identified by the concept of Multiliteracies.

The seven secondary teachers taught English, SOSE, LOTE, Information Technology and Visual Art to Years 8-12 students, or combinations of these subjects. Two secondary teachers were working in a New Basics trial school which meant that subject boundaries were already blurred, while the other secondary teachers were planning to or had experienced the idea of combining knowledge from multiple disciplines knowledge in curriculum delivery for middle schooling students.

Teachers' previous planning artefacts adopted different formats, layouts and terminology. Some teachers previously planned in table format with headings for the curriculum intent of the Key Learning Areas, Core Learning Outcomes, a task statement or context question, objectives, content, resources and assessment. Some reference was made to the elements of Productive Pedagogies at a macro level, either highlighted or circled at the beginning of a planning document or in a separate column within the learning experiences sections. Apart from sections in the planning documents which outlined the content of learning activities, there was little explicit indication of deliberate and sequential pedagogical processes. The exception was when the planning artefacts had been originally created for two or more teachers to use, hence the need to include pedagogical detail. This is very revealing in the light of the intention of *Learning by Design* project to establish a framework for professional and curriculum knowledge sharing.

The Learning by Design pedagogical framework was used as a heuristic to analyse these previous planning formats. Through this analysis, it was evident that teachers previously made reference to experiential knowledge (experiencing the new) and applied knowledge (applying appropriately and creatively) in sections of their documentation that outlined what students would know and do. This was often written out in terms of what students would experience and gain knowledge about in the objectives section—mostly new rather than known experiences. Instances of conceptual and analytical knowledge to be taught and learned were hardly in evidence at all. All documentation made reference to how students would apply new knowledge, mostly appropriately, although in some cases some innovation in applied knowledge was noted.

The popular planning framework of *Orienting, Enhancing and Synthesising* using a genre approach from the 1994 English syllabus was prevalent in some of these previous planning artefacts. When teachers used this genre approach framework, they generally outlined the integrating device or task statement, the prior knowledge to be foregrounded (orienting) the new knowledge to be taught (enhancing) and the assessment task statement detailing how new knowledge would be applied (synthesising). References in the enhancing phase were made to the concepts students would be taught rather than how students would be taught to conceptualise (concept naming and theorising) and analyse (functions and interests) the new information. Most synthesising activities were concerned with students applying knowledge appropriately—replicating a generic structure in spoken, written or multimedia mode.

The two main differences between previous planning documents and the planning evidenced in the Learning by Design Learning Elements that teachers produced during the project relate to the questions of audience and pedagogy. First, in writing the Learning Elements, teachers were authoring curriculum designs for a wider online audience including students and were aware that greater attention to detail was required. Second, the Learning Elements themselves explicitly detailed pedagogy at a micro level because teachers had an in-depth planning template and resource book to guide them. Using the pedagogical description of alternative knowledge processes provided by the Learning by Design framework, teachers specifically tagged their learning elements to show which knowledge processes were being used to support students' learning at a particular phase. As a consequence, the newly created Learning Elements were mindfully detailed and sequenced to capture different ways of knowing. These Learning Elements explicitly outlined micro teaching, learning and assessment of experiential, conceptual, analytical and applied knowledge. Project teachers specified how new knowledge could be acquired through specific pedagogy in teacher and student language using the four knowledge processes existing in the Learning by Design pedagogical framework.

The teachers were also mindful of much broader pedagogcial objectives, so that students using the learning designs would not only be able to belong to the curriculum (engagement with their interests and identities) but also, through connecting new knowledge to known knowledge, gradually be transformed by the curriculum. It could be argued that the previous curriculum planning approaches used by many of the project teachers reflected only a macro overview of a curriculum framework or unit for a term—what students will know and do. However, while the newly authored Learning Elements were also able to state what students would know and do, the teachers found that they were in fact creating another layer of curriculum design which detailed how students *would* learn and be transformed.

Before the project began, the teachers' perceptions of the specific needs of their learners and what they wanted to achieve with their students could be grouped into three categories. The first detailed the range of learning needs that were presenting themselves from gifted children, and children who were very keen to learn, to those requiring varying degrees of extra support. The second related to motivating students, with some teachers expressing a need to make learning more engaging for students in their classes who were having difficulties with learning and literacy—students who, for a number of reasons, were disengaged and lacked confidence in themselves as learners. The third point teachers made revealed the fact that they wanted the students in their classes to become confident, tolerant, creative thinkers, also problems solvers who questioned things and who knew different ways of finding out and producing answers to problems.

At the initial Learning by Design professional development days, teachers were also asked to reflect on their views about the future of schooling. A common response was that education is constantly changing, becoming more student-centred, problem-based and creative. A focus of this reflection on being a teacher these days was that it required a considerable amount of self-transformation—they referred to changing teaching styles, having to keep up to date with ICTs, as well as the new texts of the new communications media. The teachers agreed that today's children and the environments they grow up in are worlds apart from their own childhood experiences. The changing nature of the way children spend their leisure time often involves the use of new technologies which are superceded very quickly. They play online games with global friends, use online chat rooms, text message, view global multimedia productions and have access to instant global news, information, movies and music via the Internet and television. Many children today are motivated by the need to acquire new skills and knowledge as they negotiate different and sometimes virtual social situations and new, constantly advancing technological experiences with their friends. This means that traditional, teacher-directed pedagogy and a generic content approach to learning are having less and less traction on them. This, in part, is what drew these teachers to the notion of Multiliteracies project and the expectation that Multiliteracies theory and practice would help them to be able to cater for the individual needs of the diverse students in their classrooms.

MULTILITERACIES PROJECT IMPLEMENTATION—ENGAGING WITH THE LEARNING BY DESIGN PEDAGOGICAL FRAMEWORK

This section provides a brief outline of how the project evolved. A number of key terms such as *Multiliteracies, pedagogical framework, knowledge processes, template,* and *Learning Element* will be introduced and briefly explained. An understanding of the terminology of the *Learning by Design* project is important because these terms form part of an emerging professional language that centres on pedagogical knowledge and practice.

Kalantzis and Cope, along with other members of the New London Group (Cope & Kalantzis, 2000b; New London Group, 1996), developed the theory of

Multiliteracies to highlight two essential forces that were impacting on the generally accepted meaning of literacy and being literate. One force was associated with the significant presence of multimodal texts (combinations of linguistic, audio, visual, gestural and spatial modes of communication) in our personal, public, work and educational environments and the consequences of a lack of attention to the development of literacies in these texts, or understanding and using such texts. The other force was related to a new 'globalised' world in which cultural and linguistic diversity (technical and social languages, diverse uses of English and other languages) had produced a multiplicity of ways of communicating that, predictably, would have an increasing impact on meaning making.

In essence, the theory of Multiliteracies put the case that although mastery of oral and written language remained essential, it was only one aspect of what it meant to be literate. A new and expanded meaning of literacy and being literate was emerging—it was no longer enough to be literate in the narrower, traditional sense; one needed to be multiliterate. Being *multi*literate meant that one could make meaning from, and express oneself in a range of different modes and combinations of modes of meaning—linguistic, audio, visual, gestural and spatial.

Queensland Education, through involvement of key figures such as Luke and Freebody (Luke & Freebody, 1999) translated the theory into strategic imperatives and Multiliteracies became a central concern in published strategic plans, professional learning publications and in local school initiatives.

Kalantzis and Cope developed the *Learning by Design* approach as an extension of the pedagogy of Multiliteracies and as a means of applying the theory via the design of a 'pedagogical framework'. They used the framework to set out major aspects of the theory, including pedagogical techniques that they identified as 'knowledge processes'—situated practice (learning through experiencing the known or experiencing the new); overt instruction (learning by conceptualising); critical framing (learning by analysing and critiquing); and transformed practice (learning by applying).

Using the ideas developed for the pedagogical framework, Kalantzis and Cope, created a 'template' using the ubiquitously available Microsoft Word—the choice of this particular program was driven by a concern for access and a need for teacher familiarity. Teachers who used the template were prompted to consider mindfully and document their teaching practices using the 'knowledge processes' as a guide, first as a means of classroom planning, later as a means of reflecting on their practice and writing up what they had taught in a way that could be shared with other teachers. The template also acted as a heuristic—a way of asking more questions—in that it allowed teachers to discover 'gaps' or 'narrowness' in their practices for themselves.

In the language of the Learning by Design Project, the teacher-completed templates are called 'Learning Elements'. Completed Learning Elements are peer-reviewed and later published via the Internet so that successful classroom strategies and activities can be shared with other teachers. Examples of the Queensland State Education Learning Elements can be found at www.L-by-D.com

The Queensland *Learning by Design* project aims were to:

- Train a group of teachers to adopt pedagogical practices based on the theory of Multiliteracies.
- Offer and encourage multimodal expressions of meaning and communication in the learning process: linguistic, visual, audio, gestural and spatial.
- Experiment with the *Learning by Design* curriculum documentation and pedagogical template.
- Develop exemplars of the Multiliteracies approach for primary and secondary classes to support wider use in schools.

Teachers came to the initial professional development days with ideas about what the aims of their individual Multiliteracies projects would be. There were school and system curriculum expectations to consider, as well as the project's expectation that a strong emphasis on the use of Multiliteracies requires an understanding of the cultural and linguistic diversity of the class as well as a working knowledge of multimodal literacy. Dr Annah Healy of the Queensland University of Technology was invited to support the teachers and help them make links between state literacy and curriculum priorities and the use of the theory of Multiliteracies as a means of addressing these priorities.

It would not be correct to say that the teachers were completely comfortable with the way of documenting and planning their practice suggested by the *Learning by Design* approach, and particularly at the initial stages of the project. There was a new terminology to grapple with, an online planning and publication site to learn how to use, and an atmosphere of anticipation about what this project would mean to them in terms of extra time commitment and all the challenges of professional learning. However, while all teachers were a little hesitant and unsure about using the pedagogical framework at first, they persisted and committed themselves fully to authoring curriculum that they knew was part of a trial involving dozens of teachers from both Australia and Malaysia.

CREATING THE LEARNING ELEMENTS

Over the next six weeks, the teachers threw themselves into the task of collaboratively planning classroom modules, online and face to face, using the Learning by Design Guide (Kalantzis & Cope, 2004b), with the aim of completing their Learning Element so it was ready to be taught in the following term. They wanted clarification at different times during this planning stage as they were coming to terms with their understanding of the Learning by Design approach and what this would mean for their teaching practice. The issues that came up not only concerned the use of the template—writing and categorising activities under 'knowledge processes' in both teacher and student language—but of the meaning of Multiliteracies, the ICT skills they may require, the publishing website they would need to use during the collaboration process, and what all this entailed in terms of their professional knowledge.

Mid-way through the project, a point where teachers had already begun to develop their teaching and learning plans, they were asked about their experiences of using the pedagogical framework, and the Microsoft World template in which the Learning Element scaffold had been presented to them:

> A lot of the teaching is not that different from what I would do normally; the only difference is that it is of a different order and I am giving things different names, making my teaching tighter. I feel that the way it {the Learning Element template} is organised is quite logical and it's interesting to be bringing in the two perspectives—the teacher and student side—as well. *Melissa.*

> I think it is extremely useful to have a framework to bring the many facets together and to work out where they all fit. I find it difficult at times to remember the big picture when immersed in a small part of the learning and vice versa. *Alison.*

> Well to me it's a natural progression; it's a sensible framework it could be applied in any sort of knowledge base or learning situation. *Meredith.*

In other words, teachers found that the Learning Element template reflected the way they worked already, adding at times some new insights—situating specific learning activities into a larger learning plan, introducing some pedagogical concepts identifying the components of the learning process, prompting them to tighten up that learning process, and highlighting the contrasts and crossovers between the professional discourse of teaching, and classroom or learner discourse.

Next, by teaching the activities documented in the Learning Elements the teachers were able to find out whether the designs they had created would work. Along the way they also added more to, rearranged or deleted some aspects of the teaching plan as documented in the Learning Elements—those aspects that didn't seem to work as well as they thought at the time of planning, and new ideas that came up during the teaching process. In this way, the final, published Learning Element went through a planning phase, and then a redrafting phase following teaching which reflected the experience of interacting with the learners.

The following two examples of completed Learning Elements provide an overview of some of the major learning experiences that were derived from their use. Key state priorities—Multiliteracies for Learning and Productive Pedagogies—are evident in these works. For the purposes of summary exposition here, the knowledge processes are listed here sequentially, something which is rarely the case, and certainly did not happen in these cases. However, the full Learning Elements, published at www.L-by-D.com, more closely reflect the complex weave of the actual Learning Elements, as taught.

This first example of a Learning Element demonstrates how the learning process had a transformative effect on students from diverse cultural and linguistic backgrounds. Teresa Anderson, the teacher who developed, taught and wrote up this Learning Element, spoke on several occasions throughout the project about how many of these students were at risk of falling behind state and national literacy benchmarks and had difficulty relating to the formalities of school life. As a result of her reflective curriculum design and as a consequence in part of her professional learning in the *Learning by Design* project, the young students in her class began to emerge as engaged and committed learners. They tackled a real life problem in the Brisbane environment—the problem of children being bitten by insects in the playground at lunchtime and sightings of (potentially deadly) red-back and white tail spiders and wasp nests. Some insects looked large and threatening, but were harmless; others seemed small and inoffensive, but in fact were quite dangerous. In the children's minds, these insects posed a potential threat to their safety at school.

This Learning Element began with the student's experiential knowledge—the apparent problem of insects at their school—and proceeded toward improving the level of all students' literacy, with a focus on Multiliteracies.

EXAMPLE 1

Is There a Problem Insect Population in our School Grounds?

Based on the Learning Element, 'Insects: Friend or Foe?' By Teresa Anderson for a Year 2 class at Stafford State Primary School, Brisbane.

Some Intended Literacy Learning Outcomes:

Having undertaken this unit of work, students will be able to:
- Create a multimedia information expo including clay animations to inform the school community of the dangerous and friendly insects that live in the school grounds.
- Identify the codes and conventions of report genre.
- Identify the ways in which linguistic, audio, visual and gestural meanings are interconnected in the design of clay animations and PowerPoint presentations.

Knowledge Processes

Experiencing the Known

- Discussion of the problem of children being bitten by insects in playground, sightings of red-back and white-tail spiders.

Experiencing the New

- Visit insect 'hotspots' in school grounds and at local creek.
- Read and view print and multimedia texts and listen to guest speaker presentation (a local pest control worker) on insects and spiders.
- View clay animations on the Internet produced by another school.

Conceptualising by Naming

- Features of a clay animation: writing a script, backdrop, creating plasticine characters (gestures and facial expressions).
- Using a digital camera: colour, lighting, movement, angle, sound effects, design, background, foreground.

- Generic features of an information report.
- Features of an insect, habitat, eating habits.
- Life cycles of insects being researched.

Conceptualising with Theory
- Categorise the insects in the school environment.
- Discuss how the various design features of a clay animation work together to create a message about insects.
- Create a storyboard for the clay animation.

Analysing Functionally
- Analyse information sources: multimedia, written language, guest speaker. What genre is the information presented in? Why do we need to know about insects?

Analysing Critically
- Who created the texts? For what reasons? Whose interests are represented when insects are described as pests?

Applying Appropriately
- ☐ Write an information report about an insect in the local environment.

Applying Creatively
- Produce a clay animation and PowerPoint presentation to inform the school community of local insect population.
- Present answers to the problem "Is there a problem insect population in our school ground?" at a school multimedia expo.

This summary shows how the teacher mindfully considered the variety of 'knowledge processes' that would create an engaging and effective learning environment, as well as introducing key Multiliteracies concepts and practices. The class decided the best way to tackle this insect problem was to find out more about them and then to present their new knowledge to the school community. They also decided that the presentation about the school insect population would take the form of a multimedia information exhibition. The class then had to work together cooperatively to achieve this goal through a variety and range of texts and old and new technologies.

The teacher used the knowledge processes to harness the diverse life experiences of students in her class. This was achieved by affording students opportunities to experience, conceptualise, analyse and apply knowledge of insects while using multimodal texts that were appropriate to the discipline of science and, in the case of a formally written report about insects, also to meet traditional literacy goals. She achieved this because the learning was closely connected to her students' everyday lifeworlds, interests and concerns. For instance, all children were given choices about the insect they would research and how they would share information with the school community. Some took the opportunity to speak and present PowerPoint at the school assembly; others made safety instruction cards for teachers' playground duty bags detailing what to do if a child was bitten by a dangerous insect; still others recorded their information report on cassette and designed the cassette title covers. Another group of students became engaged in designing posters with flaps that required readers to lift them in order to locate the insect information underneath. Digital photos were taken by the children of the school insect species and cross-checked insect identification in science books before inserting the photos in to PowerPoint presentations. All children (and many of their parents) were interested in making a clay animation movie about an insect fact. This major activity brought children and their parents together as many children pleaded with parents to come to the classroom on a regular basis to see the work evolve. The final community insect exhibition—attended by well over one hundred people—was planned and organised by the class. Children self-identified their roles in this exhibition which included presenters, caterers, hosts, invitation and program designers and those children who were willing to use their design skills to set up the display. Comments from parents and other community members who attended the exhibition were glowing. One community member said he had never seen anything like this event and was amazed at the confidence and engagement of the young students and academic standard of the work produced.

The intellectual depth in the Learning Element for this group of young learners is a tangible example of Productive Pedagogies and clearly addresses aspects of the Literate Futures agenda in relation to balanced literacy practices. Using Luke and Freebody's Four Resources Model (Luke & Freebody, 1999)—*code breaker, meaning maker, text user* and *text analyst*—as a lens, we can see that students are *breaking the codes* of clay animations, information sources and the specific 'report' genre, and not in isolation but at the same time as they are *making meaning* from texts about insects, and *using texts* in their broader sense for real purposes of communicating information and understanding their functions. And finally, the students are *analysing* information in *texts* to determine whose scientific interests are foregrounded.

After project completion, Teresa Anderson wrote and shared an impact statement about how the professional learning about Multiliteracies she received as a part of the *Learning by Design* project helped her professional work:

> Enormously! I have received excellent professional development through being part of the project and it has taught me to reflect and make positive changes to my teaching. Most of the support was practical and not just theory so I could take action to get results, not simply make decisions. ... I now understand more clearly the focus for literacy in the future and how it will complement my teaching.
>
> This professional learning came at a wonderful time for me because I have quite a challenging Year Two class this year both academically and behaviourally. The Learning and Development Centre support helped guide me to make huge impacts in my classroom ... . My own planning is now more thorough as I am thinking through my teaching steps and strategies. This in turn is reflected in my teaching and ultimately improved outcomes from the students.

Teresa also discussed the impact the *Learning by Design* pedagogical framework and extended knowledge about Multiliteracies and ICTs had on her students' basic literacy outcomes:

> The improvement in interest, writing and reading ability in my class has been astounding. Half of my class was caught in the Year Two Net {the state diagnostic assessment of literacy and numeracy in the second year of school} with an average reading recovery level of 6. The majority of them are now reading over level 20. My Year Two class also received over half of the school's lunch time red cards {breaking school rules} in Term One and this decreased to only one red card in Term Two, and very few for the rest of the year. The students wanted to come to school and not miss out on the interesting and connected work they were doing.

In presentations to other teachers after this project was completed, Teresa confirmed the impact her *Learning by Design* project had on student literacy and behaviour. She said that students felt they had control of where their learning was headed, that they had made decisions to control their behaviour because they didn't want to be excluded from learning activities that interested them. As a consequence their engagement in all the multimodal literacy practices and knowledge processes associated with this Learning Element, steady progress in reading skills was achieved.

This case study indicates that the approach taken had the capacity to support improvements in basic literacy skills of a diverse range of students as well as developing new capabilities and sensibilities—real life problem solving, collaborative group work and improvements in multimodal literacy.

The second Learning Element began as a real life social and environmental investigation into the creek that ran alongside the school.

EXAMPLE 2

Is Kedron Brook a Creek or Is It Really a Drain?'

Based on the Learning Element 'Kedron Brook: The Past, the Present and the Future' by Alison Kilpatrick for a Year 4/5 class at Grovely State Primary School,

Some Intended Literacy Learning Outcomes:

Having undertaken this unit of work, students will be able to:
- Create a collage to depict a scene showing what Kedron Brook was like before settlement.
- Create a historical character and give an oral presentation about how and why they used the Kedron Brook. Write an explanation.
- Take photographs of the Kedron Brook demonstrating the use of the rule of thirds and specific camera shots.
- Cooperatively make a group model of a river catchment. Plan together in groups, share jobs and materials and solve problems cooperatively.

Knowledge Processes

Experiencing the Known

- The Kedron Brook runs along our school boundary. Do you think it is a creek or is it really just a drain?
- What do you already know about the use of digital cameras?

Experiencing the New

- Visit the Kedron Brook and take photographs.
- Explore the interactive river systems on the National Geographic website.
- View and read information about the Kedron Brook in the past.

Conceptualising by Naming

- Name the parts of a river.
- Name the features of life near the Kedron Brook in the past.
- Name the parts of still photography, camera shots, the 'rule of thirds'.
- What are the features of a written explanation?
- What are the parts of a collage?

Conceptualising with Theory

- A river is….
- Describe a historical character's lifestyle who may have used the Kedron Brook in the past.
- Plan a model of a river.

Analysing Functionally

- What are the functions of a creek?
- Categorise photographs that use the rule of thirds and those that don't.
- What are the functions of the explanation genre?

Analysing Critically

- Who benefited from Kedron Brook in the past?
- Who benefits from the Kedron Brook now? Who will benefit from Kedron Brook in the future?
- Image-makers can create a photograph that presents a particular point of view or benefits some people over others: how do they do this?

Applying Appropriately

- Write an explanation of your historical character's life near Kedron Brook.
- Give an oral presentation of your historical character.
- Apply the rule of thirds to take photographs of the Kedron Brook.

Applying Creatively

- Create a group collage of the Kedron Brook before settlement.
- Make a group model of a river catchment.

This summary of Alison's Learning Element for 9 and 10 year olds suggests that she is using a rich combination of knowledge processes to support the development of deep knowledge and deep understanding (Productive Pedagogies). Students learnt more about of the uses and appearances of Kedron Brook as it flowed through the area over a couple of centuries. They used and produced a variety of multimodal texts to facilitate learning. The local creek and a preplanned excursion to Bunyaville State Forest Education Unit linked well with the Key Learning Areas that Alison needed to cover during the semester.

Also, we can overlay the Four Resources Model (Luke & Freebody, 1999) onto this example to discover the balance of literacy practices being offered. For example, there is *meaning making* from past information about Kedron Brook, online interactive river systems and viewing the creek on several occasions. Students are also *breaking the codes* of still images (camera shots and the rule of thirds) and the specific parts of a written explanation. They are also *using and analysing texts* to describe their functions and to discuss the gaps and silences in texts about the Kedron Brook.

The following summaries in Tables 1 and 2 show how Queensland education priorities can be mapped against the *Learning by Design* pedagogical framework. The also illustrate the concrete and practical ways in which the state's refocus on pedagogy can be accomplished by teachers in individual classrooms. The example of the pedagogical framework-in-use in Table 1 presents us with ways to implement Productive Pedagogies with a futures perspective— putting the pedagogies into action through authentic learning. Here the *Learning by Design* pedagogical framework is not seen as an add-on to Education Queensland priorities; rather, it represents an anchor for innovative curriculum development and delivery.

Table 1: Cross-Link of Queensland State Priorities to *Learning by Design* Pedagogical Framework

Education Queensland Priorities	Queensland *Learning by Design* Project
QSE 2010: Developing pedagogy for the post industrial environment	Teachers reflect upon existing practices and consider new pedagogical frame for designing learning: www.L-by-D.com
A refocus on pedagogy: • Queensland Schools Reform Longitudinal	*A Pedagogy of Multiliteracies* (Cope & Kalantzis, 2000b; New London Group, 1996)

Study	*Learning by Design* (Kalantzis & Cope 2002-4, this volume)
• Years 1-10 Curriculum Framework • New Basics	• **Experiencing—the known and the new** (Connectedness, Recognition of Difference, Supportive Classroom Environment) • **Conceptualising—naming parts and theorising** (Intellectual Quality) • **Analysing—functions and interests** (Intellectual Quality) • **Applying—appropriately and creatively** (Connectedness, Recognition of Difference, Supportive Classroom Environment Intellectual Quality) • Interconnecting discipline knowledge (Connectedness) SOSE, English, the Arts, Science.
Productive Pedagogies INTELLECTUAL QUALITY • Higher-order thinking • Deep Knowledge • Deep Understanding • Substantive Conversation • Knowledge as problematic • Metalanguage CONNECTEDNESS • Knowledge integration • Background knowledge • Connectedness to the world • Problem based curriculum RECOGNITION OF DIFFERENCE • Cultural knowledge • Inclusivity • Narrative • Group identity • Active citizenship SUPPORTIVE CLASSROOM ENVIRONMENT • Student direction • Social support • Academic engagement • Explicit quality performance criteria	Through mindful considerations of the knowledge processes: Students develop their **experiential knowledge**—what they know and how that relates to new experiences outside their lifeworlds. For instance, the experiential knowledge in some of the teachers' learning designs included: *insects in the playground, the creek that borders the school, popular culture texts of teenagers' everyday lives, images of Australians, popular children's' games, how rules dictate the outcomes of a game.* Teachers design learning activities that take students from their lifeworlds into new worlds. Students begin to develop deeper knowledge as they are supported to **conceptualise knowledge—naming and defining** particular concepts and **theorising** or connecting these concepts. This is where metalanguages and specific discipline concepts are explicitly taught. Concepts are taken apart to name their features or properties. The parts then can be put together to theorise about the concept and to demonstrate conceptual knowledge. For example, conceptual learning in the Queensland Learning Elements included: *the parts of insects, life cycles, river systems, Australian national identity, events leading up to the Redfern Riots, autobiography, marine parks, sports day, a video documentary, a clay animation, a web page, report genre.* Students **analyse the knowledge** sources to determine their purposes and **functions** and treat knowledge as problematic as they determine the **interests** of the producers of the knowledge. Examples of this type of knowledge process in the Queensland project included: *The functions of specific genres, how the choice of elements*

• Self-regulation	*of design combine to make meaning in particular multimodal texts, comparing information sources to analyse underlying interests.* Transformation, as newly acquired knowledge is **applied** by students as individuals and in-group projects, both **appropriately and creatively** thus demonstrating a deep understanding of the discipline knowledge and the modes of communication at the core of the Learning Element. Application of knowledge in the Queensland Learning Elements is illustrated in the following examples: *Writing an information report, an autobiography, interviewing and videotaping a migrant, undertaking a web quest, producing clay animations of facts about insects, filming, editing and producing video documentaries about specific issues related to the core discipline knowledge, creating collages, creating puppet shows.*

Table 2 helps to explain the literacy practices in which students were engaged throughout the *Learning by Design* project and how they are cross linked to Literate Futures State Literacy Strategy priority action areas and Luke and Freebody's Four Resources Model. Thus, Table 2 describes the implementation of Queensland educational innovations through the project and reinforces the fact that the teachers did not teach the basics and new basics in isolation from each other or in superficial ways, but in ways which are holistic and involve authentic learning experiences, connected to real life.

Table 2: The Translation of aspects of Literate Futures Priority Action areas into the Queensland *Learning by Design* Project

Education Queensland Priorities	**Queensland *Learning by Design* Project**
QSE 2010: Multiliteracies for Learning (Education Queensland, 2000) *Literate Futures:* State Literacy Strategy – priority action areas (Luke & Freebody, 2000)	Project Emphases: • Diversity. • Multimodality: Multiliteracies in • action. • Pedagogy. • Knowledge producing-schools: • creating and publishing 'Learning • Elements'.
1. Student diversity The challenges raised by diverse students and school communities, and young people's increasingly diverse life experiences and pathways.	Engagement of learners in familiar social and cultural experiences. Engagement of learners and families who are culturally and socially diverse who may have previously been disengaged with the school or the 'business' of school.

2. Whole school programs and community partnerships The challenges of renewal, integration and balance of literacy programs within schools conducted in partnership with parents, other educational service providers and community organisations.	Many project teachers planning cooperatively with colleagues many using community knowledge and partnerships to achieve desired outcomes; partnership of teachers, district consultants, university.
3. The Teaching of Reading The challenge of a shared, understandable professional dialogue around the teaching of reading.	Balanced range of literacy practices included in the project. The Four Resources model (Luke & Freebody, 1999) used as a lens by teachers to check balance and ranges of literacy practices in the Learning Elements. • Code breaker. • Meaning maker. • Text user. • Text analyst.
4. Future Literacies Future Literacies Goal Statement: Curriculum plans to be redeveloped to demonstrate blends and balances between traditional and emergent modes of communication.	Designing texts using new technologies in familiar and unfamiliar contexts; Multimodality, or drawing on linguistic, audio, visual, spatial, gestural and integrated digital textual designs for meaning: • Clay animations. • Video documentaries. • Still photography. • Web quests. • Web pages. • PowerPoint. • Online collaborative work. • Broad repertoire of digital and • traditional literacy practices.

THE IMPACT OF THE PROJECT ON TEACHERS' PROFESSIONAL LEARNING

During the collaborative planning and teaching stages of this project, teachers used the *Learning by Design* pedagogical framework to provide students with rich, multi-layered experiences, offering many opportunities for the mobilisation of Education Queensland's literacy and pedagogical reform priorities. The Learning Elements which are now published on the www.L-by-D.com website provided a kaleidoscope of meaningful experiences for students. At the final project review, all teachers made comment about the high levels of student engagement, including collaborative engagement in each other's work. A revealing and common response by teachers to the question 'In what ways did this project have an impact on student learning?' was increased student engagement and higher quality knowledge outputs.

> One day my principal was visiting my classroom and she was overwhelmed at the students' standard of work and their ability to explain how they were tackling their group tasks. She was astounded—actually in tears because she was so used to dealing with the constant behaviour issues of certain children and wasn't expecting to find these same children so engaged and working cooperatively in groups to apply their new knowledge. *Alison, during the presentation of her Learning Element at the final project review.*

> All students belonged in this lesson today—especially the walk around the school to observe the native flora which has existed in the local area long before settlement. In the group work you could see the engagement of learners and listen to their talk. It was all about their learning. *Researcher's observations of Alison's class in her reflective journal.*

Other teachers also commented that skills improved all round, such as cooperative learning, group work, metalanguages for reading and skills associated with producing multimodal texts and the use of ICTs. A group of teachers in a focus group discussion also noted that through engaging with the activities in the Learning Elements students learned that there were many ways to communicate their ideas.

> Your Learning Element picked up a wide variety of literacies and modes of communications—this was a rich task in so many ways. *Peer review feedback to Rachel about her Learning Element presentation.*

All projects initially supported familiar contexts and content for student learning. All project teachers shared their observations about the level of student engagement in the work presented. Teachers claimed that students had been very well engaged because there was evidence being presented from classroom group activities, discussions and from individual and group multimodal work samples. Teachers used these classroom artefacts to demonstrate high student engagement and increased knowledge output. All teachers provided feedback to one another about their learning elements on a peer review form. The following comments relate to how individual teachers catered for their student's diversity and learning.

Responses are to questions: 'How well has the teacher built on the diverse life experiences to create improved student learning outcomes?' and 'How well have the learning experiences been designed and selected?'

> "This was superb at catering for diversity."

> "You involved the school community to 'hook' students into the work— gave them an authentic context."

> "High student engagement. You found out where students were. Use of what was happening in the world around the students led to obviously highly intense discussions as a good base to the development of a take-home message for the student's documentary."

> "Students well engaged through knowledge that relates closely to their experience."

> "Students obviously loved it!"

> "A strong sense of design and design sensibility that has engaged with the kids in a powerful way." *Project teachers at project review.*

Reflecting at the end of the project, teachers' thoughts about what sort of learners they wanted their students to become, remained consistent with their responses to the same question when it had been put to them at the beginning of the journey. During the project review, teachers cited ideal learners as being confident, independent but cooperative, having an understanding of how to learn, analytical, and lifewide/lifelong and problem solvers. In response to the curriculum planning and pedagogical design challenges of the Learning Elements, teachers believed that the keys were understanding the students' needs, linked with purpose and relevance of the topic in terms of prior knowledge.

Evidence in teachers' impact statements and from the researcher's field observations indicated that during the teaching of the Learning Elements many of these attributes of the ideal learner were emerging and developing for the diverse range of students in the project.

> The project has involved many problem solving tasks and oral interactions as well as advancing the students' repertoire of computer skills. They have used print, visual and multimedia resources to gather

> information. Work done on a class and group basis fostered co-operative reading, viewing, speaking, writing and thinking skills. *Marg, in her project impact statement.*

Statements and observations recorded high levels of engagement, substantive group discussion, sophisticated metalanguages and explanations of ideas, finding solutions to real-life problems and rich project work involving application of knowledge for authentic purposes.

While the *Learning by Design* framework affirmed the teachers' existing effective teaching practices and helped them to see that Multiliteracies theory was intrinsically linked to the Literate Futures and Productive Pedagogies initiatives, it also challenged them to consider a number of issues. The first was the need to acknowledge the interests and prior life experiences of their students. Second, teachers mentioned that there was a need to analyse the types and ranges of multimodal texts students were using. The third challenge was to reflect consciously upon their teaching practices to ensure that a wider range of knowledge processes were being covered over an extended period of time, instead of running the risk of favouring a few.

> I think one of the best things to come out of the project is the knowledge processes and getting teachers to evaluate what they do against those knowledge processes. It's making sure that they cover those knowledge processes in a variety of different tasks using a variety of different multimodal texts. This should be a major consideration for teachers. *Melissa*

> I have learnt so much from being involved in this project. It forced me to find out more about technology and think hard about the pedagogy I was using. *Jodie.*

Any reservations teachers might have had during the *Learning by Design* project had more to do with understanding the meaning of the knowledge processes and the amount of detail required to write up a Learning Element. Many teachers constantly referred to the *Learning by Design* Guide (Kalantzis & Cope, 2004b) for reference to examples of the knowledge processes in use. However, during the planning stage a few teachers found that in some situations it was difficult to discern the difference between two knowledge processes—some activities could be classified as centrally involving more than one knowledge process simultaneously. In addition, a concern was expressed that teachers might not view themselves as authors of curriculum, and that the template demands significantly more detail than the more familiar planning documents.

The teachers' advice to other teachers wishing to apply the Multiliteracies and *Learning by Design* theories was to be prepared to become familiar with a new professional language. They agreed that teachers should be willing to step outside their comfort zones, seek the resources (professional learning and materials) they require and have a critical approach to their teaching. Two teachers offered the following advice:

> ... realise that we all have to be lifelong learners. Being in this project makes you realise how fast education is moving. It made me think about what I'm doing and I'm analysing now what I'm doing so that I can improve how I deliver and plan lessons so that children are getting the best—and even though I've been teaching for over thirtyyears, we're learningsomuchfaster now andwe really have to keep up with things. *Alison Kilpatrick Year 4/5 teacher, Grovely State School.*

> For me it's been a really worthwhile project. I want to take my work in the project further, use the same Learning Element, improve it and take it to an extra stage. This is because my involvement in the project provided me with validation that I was 'on the right track' in delivering a curriculum, and engaging in pedagogical practices that were appropriate for students in the 'here and now'. What perhaps has intensified in my teaching practice is a sense of equality I now place on all forms of literacy practice. Whilst previously I would have regarded a child's ability to read the written word as their most essential level of literacy competence, I now regard the ability to use and comprehend visual, audio, gestural, and spatial texts as equally important for students to become multimodal and multilingual communicators. As a result {of using a variety of knowledge processes} to question and discuss with students the multi-modal aspects of all texts, this has become a natural part the of the interaction between students and texts in my classroom. To complement these curriculum and pedagogical changes, I have made the move to incorporate rich tasks into my pedagogy. *Melissa Burke, Year 7 teacher, West End State School.*

Conclusion

The Queensland *Learning by Design* Project aimed to provide in-depth professional learning for teachers in order for them to translate aspects of the state literacy strategy and Productive Pedagogies into authentic practice—Multiliteracies in action. Teachers' exploration with the *Learning by Design* pedagogical framework provided them with a way to consider their existing teaching practices, engage with the various knowledge processes and mindfully design learning experiences for a diverse range of students, incorporate multimodal texts and document all this using the Learning Element template. The trial of the *Learning by Design* project promoted reflective pedagogical practices and provided teachers with self-generated feedback on how they were implementing Education Queensland's state literacy and pedagogical reform agenda.

The outcomes of the teaching of the Learning Elements indicate there is a compelling rationale for other teachers to explore Multiliteracies learning experiences for themselves. The concept of Multiliteracies was used to facilitate the learning process for both teachers and students while providing opportunities to confirm that learning had occurred. Equipped with an emerging Multiliteracies professional language, the Queensland Learning by Design project teachers have authored Learning Elements that emphasise the knowledge processes students in their classes require if they are to belong to and to be transformed by the curriculum.

Acknowledgement

The twenty teachers who participated in this project have a strong commitment to education and the students in their care. They have been an inspiration to work with and continually strive to be innovative and conversant with education initiatives in this state.

Alison Kilpatrick, Grovely State School
Terri Barker, Grovely State School
Lillian Oh, Wavell State High School
Meredith Bubb, Mater Hospital Special School
Teresa Anderson, Stafford State School
Jenny Green, Hilder Road State School
Rachel Hodgson, Ithaca Creek State School
Mary Campanella, Everton Park State High School

Damien Klarwein Brisbane School of Distance education
Brenda Milinovich, Hendra Secondary College
Susan Smith, Hendra Secondary College
Melissa Burke, West End State School
Marg Macginley, Ashgrove State School
Pip Sturgeon, Wavell Heights and Mitchelton State Schools
Jodie Armstrong, Ascot State School
Kristine Atkins, Ascot State School
Patrick Went, Kenmore State High School
Heather Henderson, Kelvin Grove State College
Linda Crane, Mitchelton State School
Deborah Carter, Everton Park State School

CHAPTER 14

Effective Teaching and Learning: Pedagogy and Multiliteracies

Rita van Haren

Every teacher will tell you about the range of interests, backgrounds, needs, resources, potentials and abilities of students in their classes and the challenges of addressing this diversity. Successful teachers understand their responsibility to all students rather than just to the students who want to learn and they develop strategies to engage students and ensure learning occurs. Emphasising effective teaching and learning rather than socio-cultural and socio-economic factors affecting learning outcomes represents a fundamental change in educational thinking. It does not negate the influence of background, learning styles and attitudes and behaviours; rather it foregrounds pedagogy.

Teachers make a difference—the significant impact individual teachers can make is a common theme in national and international research. Teachers have been identified as having a greater influence on the learning outcomes of students than factors such as peer group, gender, cultural and socio-economic background or than school and classroom-related issues such as school culture and organisation, resources, curriculum and assessment practices (Lovat, 2003; Rowe, 2004). Teaching has also been identified as the central profession of the knowledge economy as it is critical to economic prosperity, social cohesion and the promise of democracy (Australian Council of Deans of Education, 2004).

Darling-Hammond (1998) argues that skilful teaching is required to achieve high levels of student understanding while Newmann (1996) emphasises the importance of teacher pedagogy and in particular how teachers address and implement intellectual quality. Not only is intellectual quality a key factor in improving overall student academic performance, he argues, it is also important in diminishing equity gaps. Comber and Kamler (2005) and Thomson (2002) also focus on equity issues, emphasising the need for teachers to develop rich repertoires of practice to address the diverse learning needs of students. They argue that non-deficit approaches to students by teachers are essential, approaches which recognise and affirm the resources students bring to classroom as well as being designed to meet their needs and engage them.

THE ACT MULTILITERACIES PROJECT

The focus on pedagogy and diversity were the two key ideas which drew us in the Australian Capital Territory (ACT) to Multiliteracies and then to *Learning by Design*. In 2002-2003 I worked in the Student Support Services Section of the ACT Department of Education (ACTDET). My role involved supporting schools and teachers to develop more inclusive practices in literacy so that all students, particularly underperforming students, could be successful in their learning. This was reinforced by a system-wide professional learning focus on inclusivity in ACT government schools in 2002 and 2003. Inclusivity is defined as understanding and catering for the different potentials, needs and resources of students through effective learning and teaching and starts with a recognition of diversity (ACTDET 2002).

The initial Multiliteracies project in the ACT in 2003 was based on this system focus. After hearing initial presentations by Bill Cope and Mary Kalantzis on the importance of diversity and pedagogy, we were motivated to explore further. The *Learning by Design* framework (Cope & Kalantzis, 2003) offered us a possibility of exploring the 'how' of inclusivity in regular classrooms. With the support of my manager and a small amount of funding from the ACT DET professional learning fund, we implemented a project.

The project involved 40 teachers, K-12, in professional learning led by Mary Kalantzis and Bill Cope. In this project, teachers took units of work that they were currently teaching or planning to teach and documented them using the Learning by Design framework, making sure they included multimodal means of making meaning including print, visual, auditory, spatial and gestural. This was very difficult work as we were all learners and there were at this time few documented exemplars of the Learning by Design Learning Elements that teachers could use. Teachers found the language to be very complex and the process of documenting very time consuming. My role to support teachers was also very challenging as I was a learner too. It was important to be positive and affirming of the work of teachers, many of whom were adding this project to an already demanding workload.

Nevertheless, teachers collaborated to produce rich and innovative Learning Elements. These covered a range of learning areas. For example in the Maths, Science and Technology areas, the teachers developed *Building Better Bridges, Magnets: Stuck On You, Picking the Padlock on the Periodic Table,* and *Just an*

Average Year 8 Student. In the Arts area teachers developed *Being an Animator* and in English and Social Science they developed *How do World Issues Affect Us?, Fantasy in Literature, Bertie Botts Flavoured Beans and Other Magical Treats* and *What do we do in Emergencies?* These Learning Elements have been published on the www.L-by-D website.

THE LANYON CLUSTER LITERACY AND NUMERACY PROJECT

In 2004, I moved to a new role in the Lanyon Cluster of Schools in which I introduced the *Learning by Design* framework. Pedagogy has been central to work in the Lanyon Cluster. This has involved professional learning about the Multiliteracies ideas with 160 teachers in four primary schools and one high school. Of these, 80 teachers have begun to use the *Learning by Design* framework and some have developed up to three Learning Elements.

This initiative has been part of the Lanyon Cluster Literacy and Numeracy Project. This is a cluster-initiated project focused on improving literacy and numeracy outcomes for students in four primary schools and one high school in the Tuggeranong region of the ACT. The schools include Bonython Primary School, Charles Conder Primary School, Gordon Primary School, Tharwa Primary School and Lanyon High School. The Birrigai Outdoor Education Centre is also part of the Lanyon Cluster of Schools.

Tharwa was opened in 1899 and has a very long tradition as a country school. However, the other schools are very new, all opened since 1992. Structures range in the school from traditional age/grade classes to K-6 sub-schools, early (K-2), and middle (2-4) and upper (4-6) teams in the primary schools and three curriculum banks in the high school. These curriculum banks are Arts/Design and Technology; English/Studies of Society and the Environment /Languages Other Than English; and Maths/Science/Physical Education.

Lanyon is in the far south of Canberra and because of the mobility rules of the ACT Department of Education, there is a high turnover of staff, with many beginning teachers employed. With this level of staff turnover, a high level of school based support and professional development are necessary. Also performance by students from cluster schools in the ACT Assessment Program, a territory wide assessment program, demonstrates uneven patterns of success, with many students performing below the ACT mean in literacy and numeracy.

In 2002, the executive of the five schools in the cluster formalised the Lanyon Cluster Literacy and Numeracy Project. Drawing on current research related to teacher effectiveness, this initiative aimed to establish a model of effective teaching and learning practice focused on improving student learning outcomes. Principals, deputy principals and literacy and numeracy coordinators attended initial workshops where we looked at current trends in pedagogy and in particular, literacy and numeracy. From the outset, the commitment of the various school leaders, and their support to build capacity in pedagogical leadership, were evident. We looked at Productive Pedagogies (Education Queensland, 2003) (Education Queensland 2001, 2003) and decided on using this as our overarching framework for the project. We saw it as a powerful tool to evaluate our curriculum, pedagogy and assessment practices. See Table 1, Chapter 11.

Early in 2003, teachers in the cluster began to look at the Productive Pedagogies framework through professional learning sessions led by Dr Martin Mills, one of the researchers in the Queensland Schools Research and Longitudinal Study (Education Queensland 2001). We complemented this with readings and discussions at staff meetings. The richness of the framework with its many components and language that was new to teachers, made us realise that we needed to narrow our focus. So we decided to look primarily at the area of 'intellectual quality'.

The Productive Pedagogies framework identifies components of intellectual quality and by looking at videos of classrooms in action we were able to identify problem solving, teachers problematising knowledge and students using metalanguage. Identifying deep knowledge and deep understanding were more difficult but sometimes evident in student discussions and more commonly in assessment tasks. In two schools, teachers formalised the process by visiting each other's classrooms, observing and identifying aspects of intellectual quality, and giving feedback about the lessons. In many cases the task was to identify the opposite of intellectual quality; activity driven worksheets and blackline masters headed this list. Teachers also commented on students not being engaged and 'doing school'— carrying out teacher directions because they knew that was what they were expected to do at school, not because they saw the learning as valuable or engaging.

While most teachers became more comfortable with the language of the Productive Pedagogies, transfer to classroom practice was limited. It was through the involvement of seven teachers from the Lanyon Cluster of Schools in the initial 2003 Multiliteracies project that we began to see the potential of the *Learning by Design* framework to address the intellectual quality component of Productive Pedagogies in classroom practice.

So in 2004 we began the year with professional learning on Multiliteracies and the *Learning by Design* framework led by Bill Cope and Mary Kalantzis with all teachers in the cluster. Soon after, I was appointed to a position as a cluster deputy principal focused on working with teachers on pedagogy. It was an ideal opportunity to use the *Learning by Design* framework across the cluster schools as a tool to achieve some of the goals of the Lanyon Cluster Literacy and Numeracy Project. These included building coherent and cumulative practice across the cluster using a balanced framework to guide whole school approaches to literacy and numeracy, supporting more professional collaboration through teacher professional learning communities, integrating ICTs more effectively in classrooms, and applying research to practice in literacy and numeracy education and to addressing student needs.

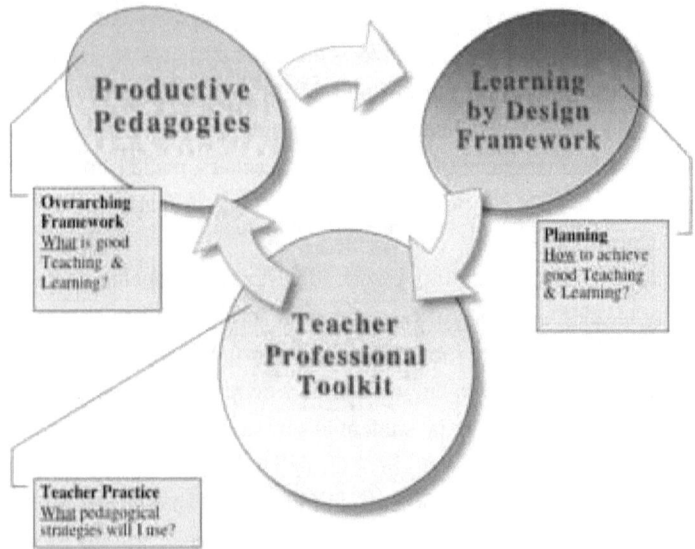

Figure 12.1: The Lanyon Cluster Literacy and Numeracy Project

So while Productive Pedagogies was our overarching framework for the cluster, it did not provide teachers with the strategies they could use in the classroom. We recognised the importance of teachers having a range of strategies that they could draw from to build their repertoires of practice, strategies using, for example, First Steps (Education Department of Western Australia, 1998), the Four Resources model (Freebody & Luke, 1990), Cooperative Reading in My Read (Australian & (ALEA), 2003), Count Me In Too and Counting On (Curriculum K-12 Directorate, 2004; Professional Support and Curriculum Directorate, 2003), Language for Understanding across the Curriculum (ACT Department of Education and Training, 2004), and generic strategies addressing multiple intelligences, thinking skills and cooperative learning. These strategies were still very important and also required ongoing support. The Learning by Design framework was the 'how' of Productive Pedagogies as well as a pedagogical framework for what the cluster executive called the teacher 'professional toolkit' of classroom based strategies. The framework ensured teachers planned and designed learning experiences collaboratively, incorporating the strategies from the toolkit in mindful ways so that they were not just a 'grab bag' of strategies.

LEARNING BY DESIGN AND PRODUCTIVE PEDAGOGIES

The connections between Productive Pedagogies and *Learning by Design* are best exemplified through examining a section from a Learning Element developed for a year 9 English class on reality television, Popcorn for the Hungry, by Ed Cuthbertson and Rebecca Cusick from Lanyon High School.

Figure 12.2: Title page of Popcorn for the Hungry

Table 2: *Popcorn for the Hungry*: Learn Activity 1

Knowledge Processes **Learning Activity 1: What does our TV say about us?**	*Knowing Things* **Learning Activity 1: What does our TV say about us?**
• Discuss students' favourite reality television shows and why they like them. Create a list of the most popular reality television shows and discuss using a Tournament Prioritising activity (Frangenheim, 2002)	• Who regularly watches reality television? What are your favourite shows? In groups discuss the best show by creating two lists which 'play off'. The winner advances to the next round and eventually to the final.
• Data Set: Students create a data set of what elements are common in a reality television program. From this data set students define reality television.	• Create a list of the similarities of a variety of different reality television shows and identify reality television's typical qualities. Now define reality television and what factors make reality television.
• Visual Literacy: Students form groups to analyse one minute of a reality television show. They identify long shots, close ups, panning, group shots and individual shots.	• In groups look at 10 minutes of one reality television program. Focus on one minute and record the number of different shots that are used. Look for long shots, panning shots, close ups, group shots, individual shots.
• Students make inferences about what morals and values are promoted in reality television through a Y chart under the headings 'looks like', 'sounds like' and 'acts like'.	• Describe the ways people act towards each other on reality television. What values and morals are represented by these actions? How do the types of shots make the audience focus on particular actions?

• Use De Bono's Six Thinking Hats (Frangenheim, 2002) to analyse the morals and ethics that are promoted by reality television.	• Thinking from different perspectives discuss why these moral and values would be promoted by reality television.
1. Using the text analyst role of the Four Resources model, students explore how reality television reflects upon society and how the viewer, the contestant and the producer are positioned by a particular reality television program Students can develop their own questions or use learning role cards (Classroom Organisation in ww.myread.org) to select text analyst questions they could ask about reality television.	1. In groups devise questions you can ask about reality television. • How does reality television make its viewers feel about certain characters? • What emotions it is trying to evoke? Why it would do this? • What would change/stay the same if reality television was set in the 1970s? 1870s? • What would reality television look like if people were always kind, polite, cooperative, thoughtful and friendly to one another? Would it be successful? • Who would gain/lose? Have society's values and morals changed?
2. Use a Socratic Dialogue strategy to analyse why people go on reality television. http://set.lanl.gov/programs/cif/CTCM/EdComp.htm	2. Why do people go on reality television? Brainstorm a list of motivations and then rank them in order of importance. In groups explain your top motivation.
3. Use the Five Whys strategy to evaluate the success of reality television. http://www.aea267.k12.ia.us/cia/framework/strategies/	3. Ask a partner why reality television is successful. After their first response ask why and continue asking after each answer until you have asked five times. Reverse roles.
4. Use a Placemat strategy (Classroom Organisation in www.myread.org) to record ideas about the success of reality television and identify what the group considers to be the most important reason for its success.	4. In a group of four each person takes a corner of A3 paper and records reasons that make a reality television program successful. Then discuss the most successful factors of a reality television show and record it in the centre circle of the placemat.
5. In groups, use a PMI (Frangenheim, 2002) to analyse the reasons for reality television's production.	5. Draw up a PMI chart and in groups discuss the reasons for reality television production.

• Write a reflection or an argumentative essay about what reality television says about popular culture.	• Write a reflection or an argumentative essay entitled 'What do television programs say about the society who watches them?'
• In groups, students negotiate a creative response related to reality television. Respond in a variety of multimodal ways to the topic.	• In groups, negotiate a creative response about reality television, e.g. an interview, radio play, PowerPoint or oral presentation, survey, biography, story, poetry, rap, song, video, readers theatre, role play, quiz show, soundscape, board game, poster, etc.

In this Learning Element, the teachers focused on developing critical literacy skills through identifying the elements of reality television, analysing its ethics and morals, and examining how it positions its audience and participants. The Learning Element format used to document the learning activities created by these teachers is the product of the Learning by Design framework and contains a teacher resource side and a learner resource side. The teacher resource is in teacher language and identifies pedagogical strategies as well as content. The leaner side is in student friendly language and focused more on content. Parents and the wider community also find this side more accessible.

In a Learning Element teachers document learning objectives; learning activities to meet these objectives under the headings of the knowledge processes; and assessment of the knowledge objectives. The following section contains an outline summary of the learning activities created for this learning Element. The full Learning Element can be found at the www.L-byD.com website.

Through the experiential knowledge process of 'experiencing the known' teachers built on student background knowledge of reality television. Because reality television is such a popular phenomenon, the discussion of students' favourite reality television shows engaged them, tapped into their knowledge of popular culture and connected to their lifeworlds. The tournament prioritising activity meant students had to go beyond listing to discussing, thinking, problem solving and ranking the shows mentioned on their list. The group activity was inclusive as all students could be involved and could feel they belonged to the group.

Conceptualising

In the knowledge processes of 'conceptualising by naming' and 'conceptualising with theory', students identified the main elements of reality television and developed a metalanguage for the visual conventions of reality television. They discovered that close ups were more commonly used than long shots or mid range shots and that these were deliberately used to play on the emotions of the viewer more. Students were able to come to these deep understandings about reality television by working in groups to problem solve and engage in substantive conversation about their observations. Through the inclusive Y-Chart cooperative learning strategy, students identified the morals and values represented in reality television.

Analysing

Deep understanding and deep knowledge were developed and embedded through the analytical knowledge process of 'analysing functionally' and 'analysing critically'. Using a range of cooperative learning strategies such as De Bono's thinking hats, Five Ys, Placemat and a PMI (Plus, Minus, Interesting), all students were included in the higher order thinking around the morals and ethics of Reality Television. Reading role cards based on the Four Resources model (Freebody & Luke, 1990) enabled all students not just to answer questions but to ask questions which problematised the text, e.g. what would reality television look like if people were always kind, polite, cooperative, thoughtful and friendly to one another? The critical literacy focus connects the learning to students as they explore what reality television says about society and ask questions of a text that is very much part of their lifeworlds.

Applying

In 'applying appropriately', students draw all their learning together into an expository text and a negotiated creative response about reality television. The scaffolding of ideas through discussion throughout the Learning Element enables students to use the tasks to demonstrate their deep understanding and deep knowledge.

While intellectual quality was our focus in the Lanyon Cluster, we soon began to realise that the *Learning by Design* framework enabled us to address the other components of Productive Pedagogies: relevance, supportive classroom environment and recognition of difference.

Table 3: Links between Productive Pedagogies and Learning By Design in the *Popcorn for the Hungry* Learning Element

***Learning by Design* Knowledge Processes**	**Components of Productive Pedagogies evident in Popcorn for the Hungry**
Experiencing ... *The Known:* personal knowledge, evidence from students' everyday lives ... *The New:* immersion in new information and experiences	• Engagement • Background Knowledge • Cultural Knowledges • Connectedness • Problem Solving • Group Identity • Inclusivity
Conceptualising ... *By Naming:* defining and applying concepts ... *With Theory:* by putting the concepts together that make discipline knowledge	• Metalanguage • Problem solving • Deep Understanding • Engagement • Substantive Conversation • Inclusivity
Analysing ... *Functionally:* cause and effect, what things are for ... *Critically:* human purposes, motives, intentions, points of view	• Higher Order Thinking • Knowledge Problematic • Problem-Based Curriculum • Connectedness • Inclusivity
Applying ... *Appropriately:* 'correct' application of knowledge in a typical situation ... *Creatively:* innovative application of knowledge, or transfer to a different situation	• Deep Knowledge • Deep Understanding

ALIGNING PEDAGOGY, CONTENT AND ASSESSMENT

As teachers record the learning activities on the Learning Element, they identify the pedagogical strategies, including the assessment strategies, they will use to cover the content and learning outcomes. *My Wonderful World*, a Learning Element designed by Sheryl Harris, Chris Waslin, Jacqui Williams, Nassim Rezakhani and Keiju Suominen from Bonython Primary School, exemplifies how the content, pedagogy and assessment are aligned. This Learning Element focuses on Studies of Society and the Environment and was designed for Year 3 and 4 students. In it students explore the Earth's natural features and how they are created and changed including weather and climate, vegetation, volcanoes, earthquakes and ice.

Throughout the Learning Element, pedagogical strategies are used to enable students to develop and demonstrate their understandings of how landforms change and to identify and analyse the impact of natural forces on people. The pedagogical strategies include scaffolding group discussions and sharing of ideas through a structured overview, concept maps, and a PMI analysis (Frangenheim, 2002). Building a plasticine model of a volcano provides a hands on activity through which students problem solve and hypothesise about the possible paths of lava flows and the effects on the landscape. Through the PMI activity they discuss more deeply the effects of volcanoes on people and the landscape, drawing on the knowledge they gained in the 'experiential' and 'conceptual' learning activities.

The assessment tasks are aligned with the pedagogical strategies and the content. As well as the ongoing assessment of learning outcomes during group activities, students demonstrate their understandings further through writing an exposition about whether people should be allowed to live near a volcano. The whole Learning Element is linked to the culminating assessment task of designing and making a model of an imaginary country, identifying how the features of the environment affect the country and the people.

Once completed, the Learning Element becomes a real working document. One teacher commented, 'Once it is done, it's so easy to write up my day book and it takes off the day-to-day pressure'. The teachers who designed the M*y* Wonderfu*l* Worl*d* Learning Element also turned the learner side of the resource into a big book. This enabled the teachers to share goals and reflect on their progress with their Year 3 and Year 4 students. In terms of assessment, the students 'know what we are doing and where we are going'. Teachers found that it was not long before the students were using the language of the knowledge processes but more importantly the big book made teacher and student reflection a part of everyday practice.

Effective Teaching and Learning 249

Figure 12.3 Chris Waslin uses the big book she created with students of Bonython Primary School to discuss what they will be doing next in the Our Wonderful World learning element.

Table 4: Our Wonderful World: Learning Activity 4

Knowledge Processes	*Knowledge Things*
Learning Activity 4: Volcanoes	**Learning Activity 4: Fire Show**
Big books about volcanoes, eg Heinemann Turbulent Planet Series. (2004). *Earth Erupts: Volcanoes*. Websites: eg www.volcano.und.nodak.edu Documentaries: eg Jacques Durieux . (2002) *The Lava Hunters*. ABC TV. *Built For Destruction: Volcano*. National Geographic Channel. • In groups, children brainstorm what they know about volcanoes. Groups come together to share their ideas which are categorised under headings in a *Structured Overview*. (www.decs.act.gov.au/ schools/pdf/LUAChandbook.pdf). • View and discuss a documentary about volcanoes. • Read and discuss big books about volcanoes. • Using images of mountains and extinct/active volcanoes, students identify and name aspects of a volcano such as vent, crater, lava, and plume of ash, record them on a concept map. • Identify and discuss 'active', 'dormant' and 'extinct' volcanoes.	Big books about volcanoes, eg Heinemann Turbulent Planet Series. (2004). *Earth Erupts: Volcanoes*. Websites: eg www.volcano.und.nodak.edu Documentaries: eg Jacques Durieux . (2002) *The Lava Hunters*. ABC TV. *Built For Destruction: Volcano*. National Geographic Channel. • Brainstorm what you know about volcanoes. Share your ideas and categorise the information under headings. • Look at and talk about a documentary and some big books about volcanoes. • How are mountains and volcanoes similar and different? • What are the features of a volcano? • What is the meaning of 'active', 'dormant' and 'extinct' volcanoes?

The Multiliteracies Ideas: Pedagogy, Diversity and Technology

Pedagogy

Pedagogy is central to the *Learning by Design* framework and is included in our work at two levels. The first level is through the knowledge processes of 'experiencing', 'conceptualising', 'analysing' and 'applying'. All are important in a teaching and learning cycle. If teachers move directly from 'experiential' to 'applying' then they are in fact testing rather than teaching. All students and in particular, underperforming students, need explicit teaching and scaffolding to ensure learning occurs and these are addressed mainly through 'conceptualising' and 'analysing'. Similarly, if teachers start with 'conceptualising' and move directly to 'applying' then students do not make connections to their own experiences and lifeworlds or build on their own knowledge.

This does not mean that each knowledge process is addressed in each lesson. Sometimes more than one is included. For example, a teacher may address 'experiencing the new' in viewing a documentary about volcanoes and then move on to 'concept naming' by identifying the aspects of a volcano such as vent, crater and lava. Other times there is an overlap between two knowledge processes. For example the teacher may be addressing 'experiencing the known' in asking students to reflect on what they know about volcanoes but at the same time including 'analysing critically' by asking students to reflect on the effects on peoples' lives. The knowledge processes are so open ended that they can match the many different styles and approaches of teachers.

The second level of pedagogy that we have focused on in our work in the Lanyon Cluster is identifying the strategies teachers use to scaffold learning. In the Fireshow example, the teachers used a plasticine model so students could reinforce their knowledge of the aspects of a volcano as well as theorise about how the lava might affect landforms. Cooperative learning and scaffolding strategies are another level of pedagogy which teachers are including in the learning activities of the Learning Element. They provide detail about how to teach rather than just including content. They support colleagues by providing this detail so day-to-day lesson planning time is minimised.

This is particularly useful for new and beginning teachers and a necessary level of support for teachers in the Lanyon Cluster.

Diversity

When I worked with teachers in designing Learning Elements we often had wonderful discussions about successful lessons. These inspired us with great ideas to include in the Learning Elements as well as being an effective way of evaluating and reflecting on lessons. One question we often explored was who was engaged in the learning, particularly which students are engaged most typically in whole class discussions. Teachers generally agreed that many class discussions would only involve half or even a few students but as teachers we often felt these lessons were successful because of the quality of responses we received from those few students. Ensuring that all students are contributing to the discussion rather than having three of four students engage in a discussion with the teacher is one of the challenges of inclusivity.

The knowledge processes of the *Learning by Design* framework support teachers to address diversity and inclusivity. For example, the 'experiential' and 'analysing' knowledge processes enable us to be inclusive and connect the learning to students' lifeworlds. 'Conceptualising' enables us to scaffold student learning and ensure all students are able to access the learning. Teachers using the *Learning by Design* framework have found that it does support them to include more students in the classroom learning. One teacher commented that 'it helped me to provide rich, meaningful and engaging activities where all students experience success.'

Technology and Multimodal Texts

Using multimodal texts is a very important aspect of the Multiliteracies work. While in the Lanyon Cluster work we have foregrounded pedagogy, we have also encouraged teachers to use more multimodal texts. This has enabled teachers to work in their comfort zones of technological expertise. Some teachers have embraced the technology more, using websites, CD ROMs, PowerPoint and SMS messaging. Others have tried to incorporate more visual texts through digital photography and more commonly through using texts from film and television. Nevertheless teachers have still continued to privilege print texts.

The focus on reading multimodal texts means technology becomes the tool rather than the content of the learning. Teachers have used a range of multimodal texts mainly as an effective way of engaging students with material which is more linked to student lifeworlds. What is now emerging in our cluster is the need to explicitly teach students how to read these multimodal texts through a visual grammar. Across the cluster, performance on outcomes such as interpreting information from websites, brochures and other visual texts in the ACT Assessment program has shown that our students are performing well below the system average score. Visual literacy is one of our future directions in professional learning for teachers in the cluster and we will support them to include more multimodal texts in their Learning Elements.

LEARNING BY DESIGN AND SCHOOL-BASED CURRICULUM

We are currently undergoing a curriculum review in the ACT and it has been heartening to see that school based curriculum has been maintained as central to the work of ACT teachers. This principle values teacher professionalism as it is essential that teachers are entrusted with the autonomy to design educational programs and curriculum according to their own professional judgement and based on the resources, needs and interests of their students.

This provides a strong sense of ownership for ACT teachers and places teachers alongside other professions like medicine, dentistry, engineering and law where they are decision-makers about teaching and learning rather than mechanics implementing a standard curriculum or syllabus. School-based curriculum is also essential to avoid the commodification of education—seeing education as a package which standardises teacher behaviour, takes little or no account of teacher and student diversity, and tries to regulate and control the teaching and learning that occur in schools. Prior to the current curriculum review the most common planning tools used by ACT teachers included the ACT Curriculum Frameworks and the National Profile Statements, First Steps and various state maths syllabi. Many primary schools are also using the Inquiry model developed by Kath Murdoch.

The Learning by Design framework supports us in our work in school based curriculum in K-10 and across the curriculum. Firstly, it supports teachers to plan collaboratively and document curriculum. The framework fosters mindfulness and consideration of the knowledge processes which in turn address diversity and pedagogy. At first teachers found it easier to take something they already teach and document it using the Learning Element template. The real transformation in classroom practice occurs when teachers move beyond this 'tagging' process to using the knowledge processes of experiencing, conceptualising, analysing and applying to design new teaching and learning experiences.

The *Learning by Design* framework also provides us with a detailed guide for the teaching and learning that occurs in classrooms. Through the framework, teachers select from a rich range of pedagogical strategies. It is not prescriptive, but it does makes certain that any activities are part of a deliberate and planned teaching and learning cycle.

Collaboration is central to the planning and designing process. The level of support required in this planning process varies from group to group but initially is quite high as teachers grapple with understanding the knowledge processes. Working collaboratively is a necessity but generally teachers find that their understandings are limited until they commence actually documenting, using the Learning Element template. Nevertheless, teachers support each other and through combining many creative ideas the quality of the Learning Element increases.

The discussion of ideas and where to place them in the Learning Element introduces quality assurance. The framework itself produces another level of quality assurance as teachers check that the Learning Element does include all of the knowledge processes and so pedagogy and diversity are addressed as well as ensuring that student learning has occurred. In a school-based curriculum context we must still maintain high levels of accountability to our students and our community. The collaboration and sharing of practice in the Lanyon Cluster has been significant in deprivatising practice and raising the accountability of teachers to each other in a highly professional way rather than just responding to system accountability structures.

THE IMPACT OF LEARNING BY DESIGN ON TEACHER PRACTICE

Teachers in the cluster have responded in a variety of ways to the Learning by Design framework. Some have taken up the framework because they see its potential to transform their teaching and are excited by the innovation and change. Others are much more sceptical and even cynical and are yet to engage with it. One teacher surveyed commented, 'I think that some teachers were sceptical of the framework only because it was new and I think that experienced classroom teachers sometimes feel threatened when asked to change or examine their practices.'

Fifteen teachers in the cluster were surveyed about the impact of the Leaning by Design framework on their work. These teachers included three high school teachers and twelve primary teachers. The range of teaching experience is from one year to more than twenty-five years. Eight of the teachers were in their first five years of teaching. Four teachers have used the framework to document at least one Learning Element. Seven teachers have developed two Learning Elements and four teachers have developed three Learning Elements.

Teachers had many reasons for using the framework. These included seeing the potential of the framework to engage students, cater for diversity, create 'a truly inclusive environment where all students are valued and accepted', promote intellectual quality, and expose students to a greater range of learning opportunities. One said, 'I wanted to transform my pedagogical practices and enhance my understanding of how students learn'. Others felt obliged to engage with it as they saw the school executive had made it a whole school and cluster priority.

All teachers commented on the diversity of learner needs in their classrooms. They identified factors such as socio-economic status, rural background, English as a second language background, Indigenous background, special learning needs and disabilities, and different abilities and interests. They were very professional and had high aspirations for their students which included lifelong learning skills, positive attitudes, an inquiring mind, self confidence, resilience, and the ability to take risks and work independently and cooperatively in partnerships with others. Critical thinking skills were also identified by some teachers: 'The type of learner that I wish to produce in my classroom is willing to engage in deep thinking and has the skills to critically appreciate and understand the world around them. This involves immersing them in rich and relevant tasks.'

These teachers also identified the effective citizen/learner/worker of the future as one who is multi-skilled, and able to apply their skills in a rapidly changing world. They will need to be able to think laterally and reflectively and have critical literacy skills so they are able to challenge ideas and become discerning users of multimodal texts and information communication technologies. They will also need to be flexible, persistent, resilient, determined and have good communication skills.

The importance of schools was identified too: 'Schools contribute to this by making their curriculum relevant, enriched and a microcosm of this future world'; 'Schools need to be progressive and ever-changing in response to their communities' changing needs'.

Teachers surveyed used a variety of planning tools including the ACT Curriculum Frameworks and the National Profile Statements, First Steps and various state maths syllabi. Teachers who participated in the survey saw a great need to document curriculum to ensure there were not 'gaps in students' skills and to maintain accurate curriculum documentation'. Other expectations of the framework included 'a framework to guide pedagogy for our times' and 'a structure in a logical sequence that takes into account the way students learn'.

Four teachers who felt success in using the framework commented they would like to continue in the work without major changes.

In reflecting on the usefulness of the Multiliteracies ideas of diversity, multimodality and pedagogy, teachers liked the way 'it makes you more conscious of including multimodal texts and learning' and 'it has given me an opportunity to improve on a positive classroom environment and engage more students'.

The usefulness of the *Learning by Design* framework included providing structure for the teacher and reinforcing quality teaching. It supports the development of interesting lessons and ensures 'you do extend students' learning and not do what you have always done'. It 'showed students, particularly older students, where they were heading and what to expect'. Beginning teachers commented that they enjoyed a more detailed approach to planning and the extra effort was 'an investment, as the end product was worth the work'. Teachers liked the consistent approach and the opportunities for professional dialogue and sharing of ideas and practical strategies. They felt the framework was sequential but allowed 'a certain amount of flexibility and individual interpretation', and once teachers were comfortable with the language the framework does become user-friendly and 'a good motivator for teachers and students'. Some teachers also felt a completed element was visually attractive and well organised and the published document provided a 'professional edge' which valued teacher work.

Where teachers have understood the complex ideas that the framework is addressing there has been a much greater influence on their pedagogy. Instead of 'teaching students the things they already know, this model ensures you are challenging both their thinking and understanding'.

> The framework allows the teacher to crystallise classroom practice and to examine the journey they have planned for their students. I think more than anything teachers extend themselves in a variety of different areas and to not always play to their strengths. This can be threatening and a lot of work but it also ensures that students are engaged and exploring many facets of literacy. In terms of pedagogy, it is not asking teachers to teach in a different way but more to reflect on their skills and examine how best they can convey a concept or theme. When this happens the framework becomes very useful as it has changed theory into reality. It has become a guide that enables students and makes them active and valued participants in their learning journeys.

The main problems included inaccessibility of the language and making enough time to document collaboratively. Teachers found it wasn't a format that 'you could just pick up and use' and 'you needed a lot of background information and support'. Teachers often needed to refer to the 'learner' side of the framework template for the 'plain English' version. One teacher commented that the change to using more open ended tasks was challenging for students while another commented, 'students took time to adjust to the analysis and creative aspect of the framework'. Some teachers found that the style of the framework template 'has encouraged us often to include too much content,' providing difficulties in documenting and delivering a Learning Element to students within a specific timeframe. Some teachers also found that, once documented, that the Learning Element is too prescriptive. However, another teacher commented, 'you have the power to change it'.

Overall, teachers were very positive about the professional learning experience. They felt the Learning by Design framework gave them a new way of planning and thinking and catering for a range of learning styles. One teacher commented, 'I now think in terms of the knowledge processes' and recognised that they had gained 'improved understandings of pedagogy, learning outcomes for students and more skills in my teacher toolkit'. They learned many new 'hands-on critical thinking strategies' and they saw the value of rich, integrated learning and assessment strategies rather than using standardised testing. A group of early years teachers felt they had developed new understandings about how intellectual quality was possible in the early years.

All encouraged other teachers to have a go and 'give it time; once you tackle the language, it makes sense and you surprise yourself how much does make sense. The structure is fantastic'. Also it is important to 'challenge yourself to allow the students to apply their learning in interesting and challenging ways'. They advised starting with small units and 'write less but ensure the quality is good'. They felt it was difficult to work collaboratively with negative people so their advice was to try to find someone who is motivated in the same way. They universally enjoyed 'sharing work and ideas with other professionals'. One teacher commented that 'it has allowed me to work collaboratively with great teachers who willingly share ideas and knowledge'. Some felt more confident about mentoring and leading others in this work but recognised the importance of the whole cluster approach and the support offered through the leadership of the cluster executive.

BEYOND THE CLUSTER

While the Lanyon Cluster continues to lead the way in the ACT in the Multiliteracies and *Learning by Design* work, a number of other teachers, schools and organisations are also engaging with this work. Some of the teachers who were involved in the 2003 project are continuing to use and promote the framework in their schools. They have formed a focus group to meet each term to share their journeys, support each other in their work and plan for further dissemination across the ACT.

The Learning by Design framework is the pedagogical framework underpinning the ACT Student Pathways Planning project. This project supports students to explore their personal strengths, interests and goals as they plan their potential pathways through school to further study, training and/or work. To implement the project a guide was developed which included lesson plans using the Multiliteracies ideas of pedagogy, diversity and multimodal resources to design learning. Models of lessons using the Learning by Design framework include student identity in English, reflection across all learning areas, planning and goal setting in Maths and PE, and decision making in vocational learning programs. This approach has raised teacher awareness about the importance of planned and designed learning to address the Multiliteracies ideas and the two conditions of learning, belonging and transformation.

ACT teachers have also presented workshops using the *Learning by Design* framework at local, state and national conferences, creating interest in this innovative work. For example, a group of teachers from the ACT Association for the Teaching of English have developed a presentation called *Right Here, Right Now: Exploring Identity in a Multimodal World*. The teachers used the framework to examine the immediacy of our multimodal environment and its impact on the multilayered identities of students. Multimodal texts included reality TV, sitcoms, print media, music lyrics and poetry, and examined themes such as tribalism, extreme popular culture, relationships and personal identity.

CONCLUSION

As our society becomes more globalised and linguistically and culturally diverse, and our students become more immersed in digital technologies, the challenges for teachers will continue to increase. Meeting these challenges through effective and skilful teaching acknowledges the professionalism of teachers who are critical to student performance. It recognises that teacher pedagogy is central to preparing students for life in the twenty-first century 'knowledge society'.

As we continue our pedagogical journey in the Lanyon Cluster of Schools, we will need to build the capacity of teachers not only to participate in the *Learning by Design* project but also to lead others. This work is not about short term goals or quick fixes to improve the performance of our students on system testing. Our ongoing, long term goal is to develop teacher pedagogy so that teachers, like their students, are lifelong learners, reflective about their practice, and designing and achieving positive learning experiences and outcomes for all of their students.

ACKNOWLEDGEMENTS

I'd like to acknowledge all of the teachers in the Lanyon Cluster of Schools who have trialled the development of learning elements of the Learning by Design framework. Firstly I'd like to recognize the work of the teachers and executive staff of Charles Conder and Bonython Primary Schools. In these two schools all teachers have joined the adventure of trialling the framework. I'd also like to acknowledge the teams of teachers and executive staff at Lanyon High School, Tharwa Primary School and Gordon Primary School, who are trialling the framework.

In particular I'd like to acknowledge the teachers who have been key people in the development and the evaluation of our work to date. All of these teachers are innovative and committed teachers and learners who are looking for ways of engaging their students and improving student learning outcomes.

Bonython Primary School: Chris Waslin , Sheryl Harris, Jacqui Williams, Nassim Rezakhani, Keiju Suominen, Bianca Parkin, Kaylene Eichner, Tracey Elliott, Margaret Pyke and Peter Henry

Charles Conder Primary School: Julie Dixon, Elizabeth Pothan, Ally Hodgson, Luke Marsden, Murray Bruce and Liz Tidey

Tharwa Primary School: Sue Gorman and Jane Irving

Lanyon High School: Ed Cuthbertson, Rebecca Cusick, Audra Mckeller, Merle Cohen, Chris Melican, John Mantinaos, Anne Dunn, Michael Hall and Glenys Patulny

Gordon Primary School: Alli Sheedy, Lisa Kalma, Kim Dawson and Liz Bujaroski.

CHAPTER 15

Approaching Learning by Design as an Agenda for Malaysian Schools

Ambigapathy Pandian and Shanthi Balraj

INTRODUCTION

The past few years have witnessed the school system in Malaysia being in constant controversy. Issues on schooling, the teaching vocation and the process of learning have been at the heart of forceful and fiery discussion in the media, in the teaching profession and amongst political groups. There has been a proliferation of books on educational matters and on the role and place of the school in society. The discontent with the learning system in schools have raised numerous issues like the role of the school in the construction of national identity, the emphasis of an examination oriented curriculum, the integration of information and communication skills, the place of the Malay language as the national language and the place of English as a global language, the teaching of Science and Mathematics in English, the implementation of smart schools, the school as an instrument for ethnic integration and social cohesion as well as the increasing homework for school students.

The varied controversies linked to the school system in the present times have sparked the need for Malaysian educators to think about the school system in a rapidly changing social, economic and cultural environment. The International Literacy and Research Unit (ILRU) housed at the School of Humanities, Universiti Sains Malaysia (USM), allied with Royal Melbourne Institute for Technology (RMIT), Australia is concerned with the above stated issues and works to assess the curricula and teaching methods and the ways to make the school system a relevant one for the future betterment of contemporary societies. Members of the Unit are actively engaged in research that covers Multiliteracies, Workplace Literacy; ICT and Language Learning; Issues on Gender and Ethnicity in Education, English and Malay Language Learning and Teachers' Education.

Like Australia, Malaysia is confronting changes in the world order, specifically through developments in globalization and new technologies. The need to provide for the literacy needs of individuals and communities in multilingual, multicultural and multimodal environments to enable them to respond to real conflicts and problems is a significant interest to the Unit. The educational alliance established between USM and RMIT saw the sharing of concerns in refining and developing a critical pedagogy attentive to the changing face of social, political, economical and technological dimensions of contemporary societies. Cope and Kalanztis's (2001b) works on Multiliteracies and the project, *'Learning by Design'* advance profound thinking based on the conviction that every learner is capable of engaging the world in a meaningful manner with others. Their intellectual contribution is an important one as it intends to transform conventional learning settings present in our communities to more relevant learning environments that are more appropriate to the changing world. Underlying this framework is a conscious struggle for the social transformation of our modern and postcolonial world in the interests of granting legitimate space for subordinate populations and cultures from the structures and ideologies that dominate them.

This chapter centers on the social pedagogy advanced by Cope & Kalantzis, which invites teachers to engage in critical problems surrounding their students so that the teachers and learners can participate actively in creative thought and action that makes learning meaningful. The focus on teachers is therefore an important one as it is linked directly to dramatic transformations and if they are to contribute meaningfully to the making of knowledge constructors in the ICT times.

MULTILTERACIES

Noting that the world is changing in startling ways and urging for a change in the ways we make meaning, the New London Group developed an innovative discussion, focusing on the concept Multiliteracies (New London Group, 1996). Giving attention to the bigger picture, the changing world and the new challenges confronting present day communities, the New London Group deliberated on an appropriate framework for literacy pedagogy in an emerging setting of diversities and global connectedness. The concept of Multiliteracies is concerned with two related changes. Firstly, the increasing significance of cultural and linguistic diversities mean that students need knowledge and skills to engage in a variety of dialects, semiotic differences, cross-cultural discourses to ensure that space is available for different lifeworlds to flourish (Kalantzis & Cope, 2001b).

The second change is in the nature of new communication technologies where meanings are made in multimodal ways – the written and print word is intertwined with visual, audio, gestural and spatial patterns of meaning. Students need to understand that distinct modes of representation and communication can be used using different media of dissemination. The new communication landscape of multimodality, specifically in multimedia environments opens potentials for interaction. It is important to deal with various visual, audio, print and dynamic texts. There is much to assess and understand in the multimodal ways in which meanings are made on the World Wide Web, or in video captioning, or in interactive multimedia, or in desktop publishing, or in the use of written texts, in still and moving graphics, images in colour posters and billboards in a shopping mall (Hodge & Kress, 1996; Kalantzis & Cope, 2001b). To make sense of the different forms of communication, messages and meanings surrounding us, we require a new, multimodal literacy which gives attention to recording language, image, space, movements or animation and sounds in reading and writing texts and in creating knowledge and meanings.

Multiliteracies and the Learning by Design project is given substantial attention in the first part of this book. The Multiliteracies framework is strong on design where a combination of knowledge processes, encompassing the four elements—experiencing, conceptualizing, analyzing and applying. The teacher role becomes critical as she or he assesses the knowledge and skills of his or her students and works to design learning and teaching materials according to the diversities and needs of the learners in the class and the wider community. The teacher is committed and attentive to experiences, tensions and power issues faced by their students. The teacher is not only preparing curriculum materials but also documenting observations, teaching practice and understandings of the social dynamics that operates in the classroom. The teacher must also have the necessary ICT skills to engage in conversations and the obligation for professional enhancement. Evidently the agency of the teacher is of paramount importance in ensuring that the learning activities become meaningful and relevant to their daily lives. The Multiliteracies framework underpinning the Learning by Design project also works on the assumption that facilities like computer access, Internet and connectivity and electronic publishing tools are available to enhance collaboration and sharing of ideas among teachers, learners and the surrounding communities. The following section looks at some of the early attempts of appropriating the Learning by Design project in Malaysia.

ADDRESSING LEARNING BY DESIGN IN MALAYSIA

Malaysia is in the midst of a series of dramatic and closely interconnected transformations. It is widely propounded that Malaysia aims to leap into the Information age, driven by private capital and independent agencies embracing foreign companies and skills. The information superhighway is touted as the basis for a new economic and social background. Information technologies are not just mediums of networking that can create new business opportunities; they are also powerful educational tools carrying messages and ideas. To date, the ruling government continues to prioritise the implementation of the Multimedia Super Corridor to propel Malaysia as a knowledge-based economy.

In this vein, Malaysia has taken the lead in articulating the importance of information and communication technologies, science and technology in the school curriculum. This is seen as essential for the creation of workers who are versatile, multi-skilled and able to operate new businesses and management practices in a high-technology environment at both local and global domains as well as enhancing the living quality of the people (Kalantzis & Pandian, 2001).

In Malaysia, the past two decades have witnessed major changes in the living and learning environment confronting learners. Educational institutions have to respond to the radical changes that are currently underway in our lifeworlds and at the same time tread a careful path that will not only focus on the workplace but also have the capacity for other domains of our lifeworlds like the spiritual, family and cultural.

The Education Ministry has produced guidelines to be used as a reference by the various institutions conducting formal education throughout the country. The development of study programmes is linked to several major policies that include Malaysian Multimedia Super Corridor, Vision 2020, 8th Malaysia Plan 2001-2005, Smart Schools and the National Education Philosophy. These policies aim to develop programs that are innovative and relevant to the needs of a changing society and global order as well as the creation of an environment conducive to scholarly pursuit, cultural development, lifelong learning and the development of the individual. In essence, they aim to produce students with broad based knowledge, thinking skills and innovativeness to contribute to the knowledge based economy. At the same time, there is a focus to also emphasize harmonious family and ethnic relations, as well as devotion to God.

The learning settings in Malaysia are set to undergo major alterations—changing the culture and practices of Malaysia's school programmes, moving away from memory-based learning designed for the average learner to an education that stimulates thinking, creativity, and caring in all learners.

As noted in the blueprint on Smart Schools Programme (Ministry of Education (Malaysia), 1997), the roles of teachers have to be systemically reinvented in terms of teaching-learning practices and management in order to prepare learners for the Information Age. The new learning setting in the ICT era marks the need for dynamic interaction with ICT as a means of communication and a source of access to information in the task of knowledge creation and dissemination.

The ICT era has also granted English as the eminent language in almost all forms of global interactions. The Malaysia that advanced the Malay language as part of its nation-building and racial integration strategy is now compelled to accept English as the language for participating in ICT and the global knowledge economy. There is however some resistance to this effort as learning English is commonly perceived as succumbing to postcolonial interests that serve to reinforce the subordinate status of third world countries in the arena of international power. Nonetheless, as argued by Singh et al (2002), banking on the pessimistic perspective will only entrench the people in economic and cultural passivity and there is also a need to be more forthcoming to the opportunities presented by globalisation and ICT so that Malaysia can re-construct its economic, social and educational agenda to enable its people to cross disciplines and cultures in an increasingly borderless economy. The challenges are profound and the first step has to begin with the putting together of new learning settings.

In driving these new learning settings, it is important to recognize that the focus on teachers is crucial as they will play a major role in changing the culture and practices of Malaysian students. Interest in the capacity building of teachers in confronting the contemporary classroom led to the encounter with Multiliteracies and the *Learning by Design* project. The project aims to explore the potentials of new pedagogic approaches as advanced by their transformative curriculum, assisted by digital technologies.

TEACHING ENGLISH: A CASE-STUDY FROM PROJECT PARTICIPANTS

This project involves a team of researchers from the International Literacy and Research Unit, Universiti Sains Malaysia working with teachers to create and reflect upon the new emerging learning environments. Several researchers and teachers have come together to contribute to this ongoing project: Salasiah Che Lah, Gitu Chakravarthy, Sarjit Kaur, Sacitnathan Tachinamoorthy, Alias Abdul Ghani, Parameswari Sarathee and Lee Bee Yong. Both Cope and Kalantzis briefed the teachers on the theoretical underpinnings of the Multiliteracies framework and the *Learning by Design* project. The first workshop was attended by about fifty teachers from the northern region of Malaysia, including states like Penang, Kedah and Perak. There were teachers who were teaching English, Mathematics and Science. While the Multiliteracies approach was welcomed with much enthusiasm from a majority of the teachers, many of them opted not to participate in the project given the administrative and academic demands of teachers in an examination-oriented curriculum. Given that the teaching of Mathematics and Science in English was a very recent development, a large number of teachers who had originally been trained to teach the subjects in the Malay language felt rather uncomfortable about documenting their work in the English language. Nevertheless, there were several teachers who were totally excited and painstakingly followed through the different phases of the project.

Parameswari Sarathee and Lee Bee Yong are two teachers from Perak who are teaching English to 14 year olds in a secondary school. Just like many public secondary schools that adhere to a centralized curriculum, they noted that their English class had specific dominant characteristics. There was a lot of learning by rote where students were required to memorise many facts, sentences structures and model answers. Both teachers and students were focused on scoring high marks for the examinations. The teacher-centered classroom did not provide much room for students' voices. The teacher was the authoritative figure and spoke while the students listened. There was hierarchy in the classroom and the teacher was seen as the powerful figure with the knowledge and skills. Learning refers to a quantity of information that has to be channeled from the teacher to the students and learning was based mainly on textbooks and workbooks. The teachers noted that their students had low levels of English proficiency especially those coming from the rural areas. Many of the students learning English had negative attitudes towards the language.

The project participants, that is the teachers teaching English, on the other hand, were highly motivated and they were bent on making their English lessons more meaningful. Parameswari and Lee were interested in the Multiliteracies framework and they were looking forward to re-inventing the English curriculum in the classroom. They were very enthusiastic about the whole project and were keen to explore if the learning theory can be applied in the Malaysian context.

Parameswari and Lee designed learning materials about their town and village for their English class. Their collaborative work was important as they were constantly sharing ideas and encouraging one another to deliberate on the knowledge processes and the supporting learning elements and materials. In this case, they were interested in getting their students to learn more about their town, Teluk Intan and a nearby fishing village, Kampung Sg. Liang. They were interested in highlighting the diversities in their living areas and wanted to promote understandings of the facilities and differences between the town and village. The students were asked to locate information from books, actual real-life experience, photographs and the Internet and they were to make power-point presentations. This enabled students to engage with the diversities present in their communities and to deliver their thoughts and expressions using new communications technologies.

They found out that the Learning theory and its pedagogical approach was most helpful and that the students were very excited that they could learn English in very interesting ways. The students worked collaboratively and were proud that the works were being published in international websites. The *Learning by Design* model was put to practice in their classes and the following are sample resource material for English lessons developed by the school teachers.

TEACHER RESOURCE **LEARNER RESOURCE**

English Lesson - Form Two

PARAMASWA P SARATHEE
LEE YONG

Contents Page—List of Activites and Topics To Be Covered

TEACHER RESOURCE	LEARNER RESOURCE
Content	Contents
Learning Objectives	
	What You'll be Learning
Learning Activity 1: Discussion about our town i.e. Teluk Intan	Learning Activity 1: Our Town
Learning Activity 2: A visit to an unfamiliar place i.e. Fishing Village	Learning Activity 2: Let's visit a fishing village
Learning Activity 3: Writing a glossary	Learning Activity 3: Listing & writing meanings of words
Learning Activity 4: Mind Mapping	Learning Activity 4: Create a Mind map
Learning Activity 5: Making a comparison between a town and a fishing village	Learning Activity 5: Compare our town to a fishing village
Learning Activity 6: Expressing opinions and preferences	Learning Activity 6: Where would you rather live?
Learning Activity 7: Drafting a plan of a dream town	Learning Activity 7: Planning our dream town
Learning Activity 8: Create a model of a dream town	Learning Activity 8: My Ideal Town
Learning Activity 9: Create a power point presentation-From a town to municipality	Learning Activity 9: Creating a power point- From a town to a municipality
Learning Activity 10: Bring it all together – burning work on CD-ROM, digital pictures, power point and model display for library, exhibition and school magazine	Learning Activity 10 Presenting our work - Burning work on CD-ROM, digital pictures, photographs, power point and model display for library, exhibition and school magazine.
Assessment	How Well Have You Learnt?
Learning Pathways	Moving On

KNOWLEDGE OBJECTIVES	FINDING OUT
To Experience	**By Being**
As a result of completing this Learning Element, students will be able to: • Talk and exchange information about their town, obtain information about an unfamiliar environment and municipality. • Locate information from books, public library and the Internet.	By doing this work you will learn about: • Your town and the village. • The facilities and differences between the town and the village. • Locate information from books, actual real-life experience, photographs and the Internet.
To Conceptualise	**By Connecting**
• Be able to use different sources to take notes: books, photographs, Internet, questionnaires and interviewing people. • Be able to use the power point. • Be able to use digital photographs as a source of teaching.	By doing this work you will learn about: • The town and the village. • The facilities and differences between the town and the village.
To Analyse	**By Thinking About**
- Expressing opinions – Power point	- The advantages and disadvantages of living in a town/village. - The differences between the town and the village.
To Apply	**By Doing Things**
Draw plan of a dream town. • Create a model.	By creating our library display, we will be able to : • Do research by taking notes and writing essays. • Use a digital camera. • Create a dream town.

The first activity involved students talking about Teluk Intan, the town setting that was familiar to the students. The teachers and the students worked together to examine some of the main landmarks and buildings, people and their jobs as well as studies the pictures and photographs that were present in the magazines books, and the Internet. Following this, the students made a visit to a fishing village, Sg. Liang and explored the differences in its physical and cultural living settings of the people. They explored the kinds of jobs and lifestyles of the people in the village. The third activity was constructed where a glossary was prepared—students had to make a list of words and write meanings. Below are the samples of students' works.

LEARNING ACTIVITY 3–WRITING A GLOSSARY

Exhibit A

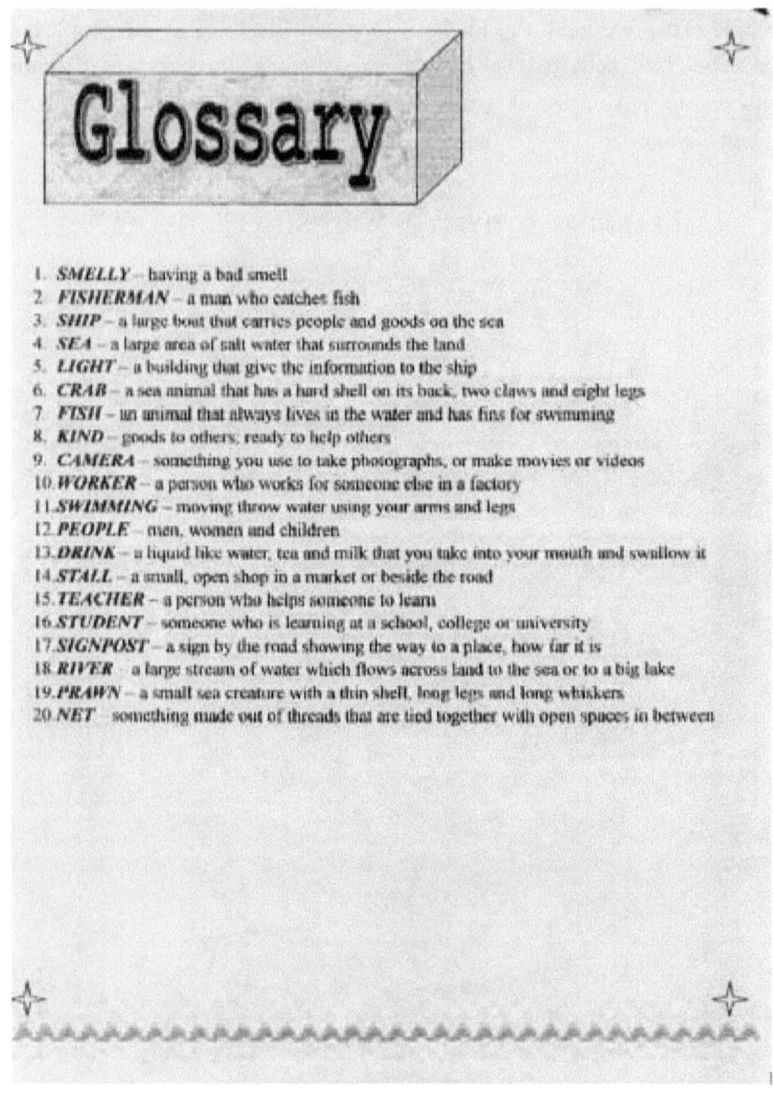

Exhibit B

As can be seen above, the students had made good observations and had captured some of the experiences and the meanings associated with the first two activities. The students had also lots of fun as they prepared their exercises in very attractive and creative ways and these materials were displayed in the classroom.

The teachers then encouraged their students to study the public amenities available in both the town and the fishing village. The students identified facilities like the bank, post office, public telephones, hospitals, schools, modes of transport, places of worship like the mosque and the temple, which played an important role in the growth of communities. The students then presented these exercises in the form of mind maps as seen below.

LEARNING ACTIVITY 4–MIND MAPPING

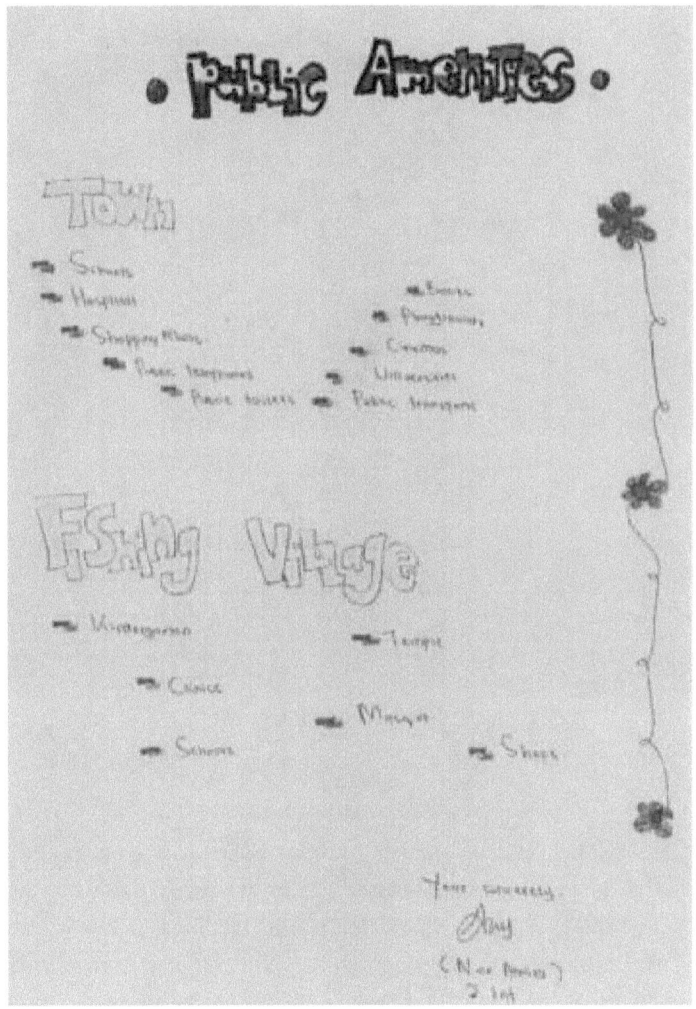

Exhibit C

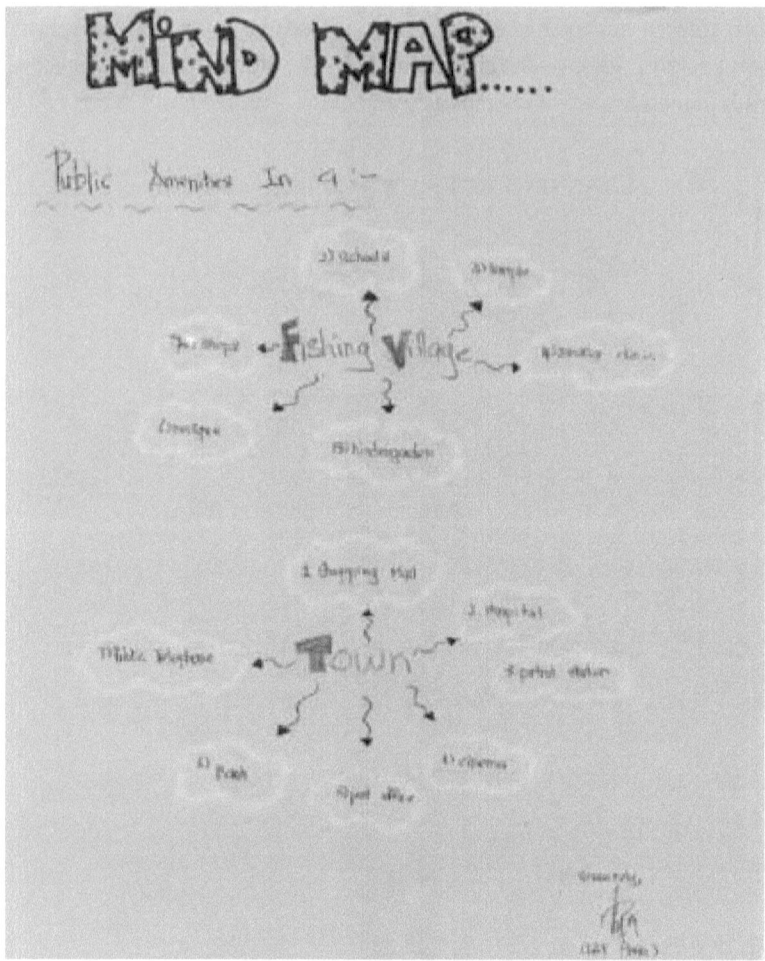

Exhibit D

The next activity involved the students writing short essays on the differences between living in the city and the village. The essays reveal that the students had engaged with some interesting issues like public facilities, places of recreation, pollution, traffic difficulties, job opportunities and modern conveniences. One child also noted that she felt sad that some children in the fishing village did not go to school and worked with parents. In her essay (see Exhibit E), the student writes about a more interesting life in the city with its shopping centres, cinema and other recreation places. She also writes about pollution problems on the city. Some students highlight job opportunities in the city and thought that there were many educational opportunities available as there were more institutions of higher learning in towns.

Learning by Design as an Agenda for Malaysian Schools 273

LEARNING ACTIVITY 5: MAKING COMPARISONS BETWEEN A TOWN AND A VILLAGE

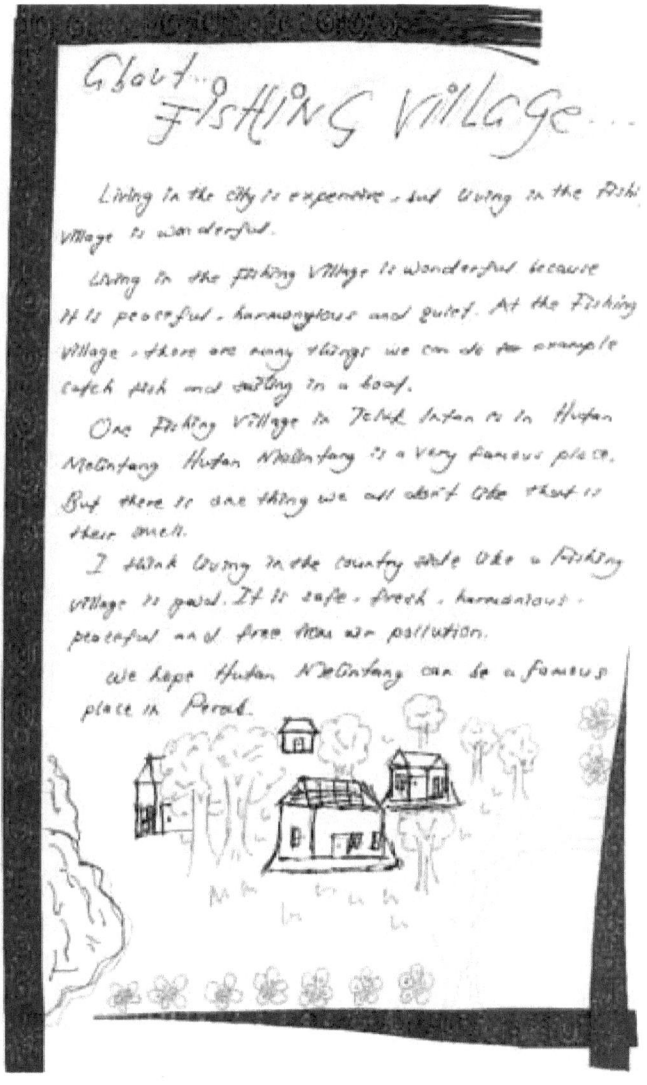

Exhibit E

Exhibit F

The teachers tried to use a variety of approaches to enable their students to express their views. Below are some examples in the form of dialogues and songs.

The students also used a lively mix of visuals, colours and print forms in their exercises.

LEARNING ACTIVITY 6: EXPRESSING OPINION AND PREFERENCE

Exhibit G

Exhibit H

Exhibit I

Exhibit J

Learning by Design as an Agenda for Malaysian Schools 279

Exhibit K

As seen in the above, the songs have interesting lines,

> I love to live in the countryside
> With friendly chat and beautiful scenery
> Peaceful as a cemetery
> Pretty girls are everywhere
> Giving smiles to everyone (see Exhibit K)

After the discussion of the student views on the differences in living in the city and living in the village, the teachers then asked the students to draft their plan of a dream town. Working in groups, the students shared their ideas and worked collaboratively to plan their dream towns. The exhibits below show the students' model towns and it is evident this activity drew on various skills and knowledge processes.

LEARNING ACTIVITY 7: PLANNING A DRAFT TOWN

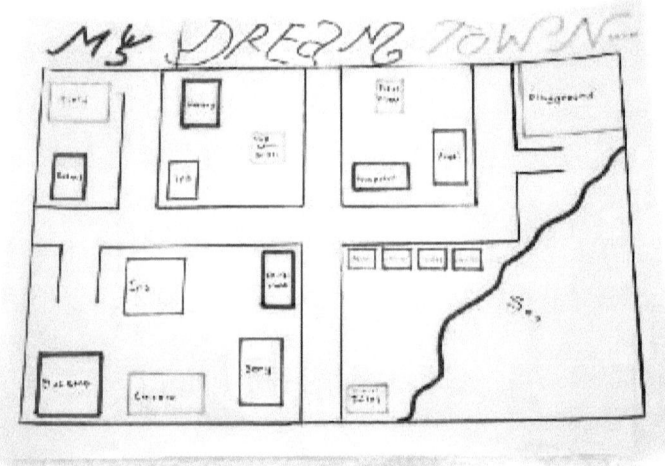

Exhibit L

Exhibit M

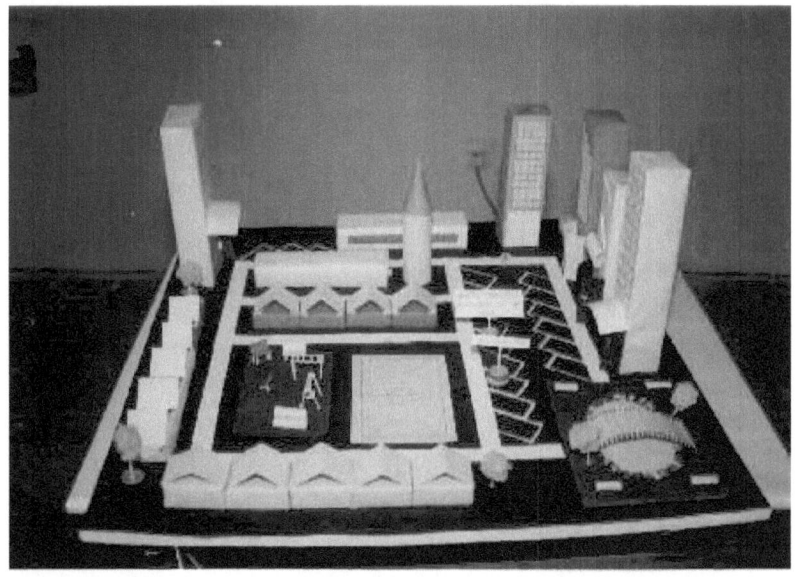

Exhibit N

At the end of this study unit, both the teachers and students felt that so much was accomplished and that the *Learning by Design* approach brought rich and meaningful teaching and learning experiences for them. They found out that the Learning theory and its pedagogical approach was most helpful and that the students were very excited that they could learn English in very interesting ways. The students worked collaboratively and were proud that the works were being published in international websites. The *Learning by Design* model was put to practice in their classes and the following is a sample resource material for English lessons developed by the school teachers.

Discussion—Issues for A Working Agenda for Multiliteracies

The Multiliteracies framework and the *Learning by Design* approach can be relevant when situated accordingly in the local context. The teaching and learning activities that have been generated by the two teachers, Parameswary and Lee Bee Yong indicate an important juncture in innovating educational approaches in the Malaysian learning setting. Indeed it marks a shift from the conventional approaches of grammar drills; classroom confined settings, teacher and textbook-centered methods as well as passive students' voices to a platform where there are more active voices of students and teachers engaged in designing knowledge in critical and creative ways. These innovative approaches inculcate the students' want to learn and to attempt to fight boredom in school. Implementation of the *Learning by Design* idea has raised a number of issues for the project researchers and teachers.

Diversities

Cope & Kalantzis (2001b) note that transformations in language and learning are linked to the decline of monoculturalism, globalisation, immigration and global economic integration. The emergence of new times with new communities and living experiences emphasises the need to negotiate dialects and semiotic differences, hybrid cross-cultural differences and cultural identities. Interestingly, Malaysia has been characterized by the dimensions of multiculturalism and multilingualism even before the colonial administration. Cultural identities are not new and Malaysia has been grappling with negotiation on hybrid cross cultural differences, class, geographic and lingual differences.

The focus on diversities in this project gives the *Learning by Design* a critical edge and makes it a very relevant one for Malaysia. When the teachers and their students embarked on the visit to the fishing village, the students were able to make sense of the differences of living in the town and in the village. They looked at educational and employment opportunities, facilities like banking, telephone and the post office, traffic and transport services as well as environment issues. Some students also noted the ethnic groups and the kinds of work they do in the fishing village. But it was an observation that will not be taken for further discussion in the Malaysian classroom.

Ethnicity and economic imbalances is a challenging issue but is not adequately addressed and discussed in the classrooms as it is considered a highly-charged political issue. The Malaysian school plays a major role in nation-building and as such, issues that may bring uncertainties in the classroom are avoided. It is also possible to suggest that the teachers will feel uncomfortable handling these controversial realities given the lack of knowledge, training and skills in this area. Worse, as the teachers in this case-study asserted:

> We may be seen as anti-establishment and the objectives underlying the teaching activities may be misappropriated and misconstrued.

In order to handle the negotiation of cross-cultural differences, the teachers require a sound understanding of sociological and political issues that ground the Malaysian experiences. For example, a teacher sensitized to gender conflicts and the rule of patriarchy in the local cultural setting may want to provoke the students' views on gender roles in the fishing village. The teacher may also want to connect the school books and media as important shapers of our perceptions and ideas which do not provide simple information about the world, but designed ways of seeing and understanding. It seems important to point out that the pluralistic composition of the students who may make sense of their surroundings in different ways. Students of different ethnic, class, geographical and biological groups may have different perceptions and experiences and may find that the classroom does not open up spaces in learning about their world. How will the Chinese girl sitting at the fourth row negotiate with the views of the Indian boy sitting in the second row with regard to gender roles in the fishing village? What kinds of knowledge and skills will the teacher need in order to enhance negotiation in implementing ideas on Multiliteracies and Learning by Design in a meaningful way?

A major task for the teacher implementing *Learning by Design* is to utilise as fully as possible the perceptions and the insights of the students. The students will have a wider range of perceptions, experiences and cultural reference points. The teacher plays an important role in advancing the denotative investigation to an exploration of connotative and ideological meanings. These are crucial issues for teachers embarking on this Multiliteracies journey.

Multimodality

The written text still forms the dominant form of communication mode in Malaysian classrooms today. Yet, outside of school, the most influential and widely disseminated modes of communication are visual (Masterman, 1985). Today, we are bombarded by colours, layout design, animation and many other visual symbols. Schools will have to recognize the importance of developing in their pupils the ability to examine visual images critically. The works of the student in generating essays, songs, mapping maps and other articles show that the students use pictures, colours, symbols and other visuals.

For example, Learning Activity 6 on 'Expressing views and opinion' produced dialogues and song pieces (see Exhibit H, I, J and K). The student works was composed of the print texts, pictures and other visuals. However, the visuals were not related to the main texts as there were pictures of Mickey Mouse, Winnie the Pooh, Power Puff girls, Kitty Kat and other characters. While the nature of communication has increasingly become multimodal, there has seems to be a missing gap in making sense of the pictures that shaped the text. Interestingly, the teachers did not find this problematic given that the curriculum provided very little space for discussion on visual representation, stereotypical images and building visuals. Given that many messages are communicated through visuals, this is an area that needs urgent attention. The Multiliteracies approach with an emphasis on multimodality provides opportunities for making sense of images; however teachers must also have the necessary knowledge and skills to facilitate this discussion.

Producing Work for Learning Activities

One of the strengths of the Learning by Design project is that it allows room for critical inquiry and allows students to produce practical work in a variety of forms. For example, for the lesson on Changing Scenes, the students had opportunities to work on books, magazines, multimedia and even modeling a dream town. There were about ten learning activities where students were searching, retrieving, managing and understanding information from a variety of sources. They wrote essays, dialogues, the lyrics of song, mind maps and even constructed model towns. As noted earlier, while writing dialogues, essays and songs, the attention given to the visual design emerged as a critical issue where the learning activity in the class lesson did not open spaces for visual critical inquiry. Students also drafted maps of the town and designed dream towns. In this case, some students had discussed traffic and environmental problems and envisioned a green town as a dream town. There was a conscious attempt to identify the town as problematic and the students then worked to improving the structure of the town in a more environmentally friendly way. Not all groups were able to do this as some of them reproduced models without any critical inquiry. A meaningful learning activity will encourage learners not to simply record life events and experiences, but to critically assess the works that have been produced to get something done in their environment.

The link between practical work and analytical activities needs to be consciously forged by the teacher. Practical work will become less meaningful if the students do not employ critical inquiry and understand the underlying values, assumptions and knowledge that ground the designed texts. Without this informing purpose, most of the works produced for the learning activities becomes 'busy work'. Worse, it may also lead to cultural reproduction in which dominant practices may be naturalized rather than deconstructed and transformed. It is therefore essential for teachers to re-assess the objectivities and the design of the learning elements to enhance cultural criticism over cultural reproduction.

Teacher Dilemma

The Multiliteracies pedagogy tries to develop critical consciousness and gives voice to students. It creates opportunities for students to do a lot of discussing and writing instead of listening to teacher talk. As asserted in the discussion on Multiliteracies, this pedagogy works on a number of assumptions. The teacher has an important role here and their task is to help the students make problematic what they think they know. The teacher is committed and attentive to experiences, tensions and power issues faced by his or her students. The teacher makes a conscious effort to recognize ethnic, regional, age-based and sexual cultures in society to examine the structures and processes of dominant and non-dominant values, beliefs that lead to discrimination and inequality. She or he must also have the necessary ICT skills to facilitate student discussions. Facilities like computer access, Internet and connectivity and electronic publishing tools should be available to enhance collaboration and sharing of ideas among teachers, learners and the surrounding communities.

All these features of the Multiliteracies pedagogy invite teachers to become change agents in school and society. The Malaysian learning setting however is one that is examination driven and highly charged with political and cultural sensitivits. The development of critical inquiry is associated with complicated risks and the uncertainties in the political landscape induce reluctance to engage in critical discussions and learning activities. As highlighted, contradictions between curricular reforms based on innovative approaches and an examination anchored regime frustrate the already over-worked teachers.

The teachers who participated in this project were committed, courageous and had done remarkable work in their learning settings. Many more who were attracted to the *Learning by Design* Project, were unable to continue, given the huge demands of the project in the controversial, examination and textbook based curriculum of the Malaysian educational scenario.

Both Parameswari and Lee Bee Yong stressed that they were overwhelmed by the opportunities it created for learning. The students were extremely excited about the project and demonstrated that they could be very creative and the project also enhanced collaborative work among the learners and a delightful partnership between the teachers and students. They, however, maintained that such a project will be fraught with difficulties like time constraints, support from the school and state education ministries, physical facilities and lifelong-learning capacities of the teachers. The agency of teachers is a critical issue as teachers should be convinced of the potential benefits of bringing critical or sociological perspectives to the classroom to the learning contexts. This is a challenging task as the present teacher training programmes make very little attempt to include sociological perspectives. And as asserted earlier, many teachers may lack the knowledge and skills in discussing about cultural and social in a climate shrouded with risks and uncertainties.

CONCLUSION

Malaysia is witnessing major shifts in the literacy arena and there are many theoretical frameworks and practical strategies that will steer our learning experiences in distinctive ways. Like many other countries in the world, Malaysia is working towards a multilingual and multiethnic complex community engaging with information and communications technology as the new global currency.

In this turbulent global transformation phase, the spread of the Multiliteracies pedagogy is essential if all citizens are to wield power, make rational decisions, become effective change-agents and have a lifelong active involvement with learning processes. The transformative feature of their curriculum model and the moral content of Cope and Kalantzis's work is a groundbreaking event for researchers, teachers, practitioners and policy-makers in search of new ways of linking social theory to the citizenry narratives of human experiences. The *Learning by Design* project is an innovative approach that can be appropriated to the Malaysian context. The Multiliteracies theory and the project cast an important undertaking in the present times. It will, however, need greater linkages and networking with the Malaysian educational authorities in terms of sharing of ideas, materials, information, training and human resources. Only through this, will it mark the beginning of a lifelong learning process that will enable learners in our communities to become not just passive and docile spectators and consumers, but reflective and active citizens of the world.

References

ACT Department of Education and Training. (2004). Language for Understanding Across the Curriculum: Literacy and Diversity in the Middle School 2004-2006 Workshop booklets 1-5: Australian Capital Territory Government.

Anderson, L. W., & Krathwohl, D. R. (2001). A Taxonomy for Learning, Teaching and Assessing: A Revision of Bloom's Taxonomy of Educational Objectives. New York: Longman.

Argyris, C., & Schon, D. (1978). Organisational Learning: A Theory of Action Perspective. San Francisco: Jossey-Bass.

Australian, A. A. f. t. T. o. E. A., & (ALEA), L. E. A. (2003). MyRead: Strategies for Teaching Reading in the Middle Years. Canberra: Department of Education, Science and Training.

Australian Council of Deans of Education. (2004). New Teaching, New Learning: A Vision for Australian Education.

Australian Government. (2003). Australia's Teachers: Australia's Future, Volume 1. Canberra: Department of Education, Science and Training.

Bell, D. (1973). The Coming of Post-Industrial Society. New York: Basic Books.

Bereiter, C. (1994). Constructivism, Socioculturalism, and Popper's World. Educational Researcher, 23(3), 21-23.

Bernstein, B. (1971). Class, Codes and Control. London: Routledge & Kegan Paul.

Bruce, B. C. (2003). Literacy in the Information Age. Delaware: International Reading Association.

Bruner, J. (1977). The Process of Education. Cambridge MA: Harvard University Press.

C-2-C Project. (2001-2003). Creator to Consumer in a Digital Age: Book Production in Transition: A Research Project Investigating Future Technologies, Future Markets and Future Skills in the Book Production and Publishing Supply Chain, from http://www.C-2-CProject.com

Castells, M. (2000). The Rise of the Network Society (2 ed.). Malden MA: Blackwell.

Castells, M. (2001). The Internet Galaxy: Reflections on the Internet, Business, and Society. Oxford: Oxford University Press.

Cazden, C. (2001). Classroom Discourse: The Language of Teaching and Learning (Second Edition ed.). Portsmouth, NH: Heinemann.

Chandler-Olcott, K., & Mahar, D. (2003). 'Tech-Saviness' Meets Multiliteracies: Exploring Adolescent Girls' Technology-Mediated Literacy Practices. Reading Research Quarlterly, 38(3), 356-385.

Chartier, R. (1998). The Transformation of Written Culture. Retrieved 9 Oct 2002, 2002, from http://www.honco.net/archive/rt-1.html

Chartier, R. (2001). Readers and Readings in the Electronic Age. Retrieved 17 October, 2001, from www.text-e.org/conf

Cherednichenko, B., Davies, A., Kruger, T., & O'Rourke, M. (2001). Collaborative Practices: From Description to Theory. Paper delivered at the AARE Conference, Fremantle.

Cohen, D. K., McLaughlin, M. W., & Talbert, J. E. (Eds.). (1993). Teaching for Understanding : Challenges for Policy and Practice. San Francisco: Jossey-Bass.

Comber, B., & Kamler, B. (2005). Turn-around Pedagogies : Literacy Interventions for At-risk Students. Newtown, N.S.W.: Primary English Teaching Association.

Common Ground. (2003-2005a). CGPublisher, from http://www.CGPublisher.com

Common Ground. (2003-2005b). Common Ground Markup Language, from http://www.CommonGroundSoftware.com

Cope, B., & Kalantzis, M. (1993a). The Power of Literacy and the Literacy of Power. In

B. Cope & M. Kalantzis (Eds.), The Powers of Literacy: A Genre Approach to Teaching Writing (pp. 63-89). London: Falmer Press.

Cope, B., & Kalantzis, M. (1997a). "Multiliteracies", Education and the New Communications Environment. Discourse: Studies in the Cultural Politics of Education, 18(3), 469-478.

Cope, B., & Kalantzis, M. (1997b). Productive Diversity: A New Approach to Work and Management. Sydney: Pluto Press.

Cope, B., & Kalantzis, M. (1998). Multicultural Education: Transforming the Mainstream. In S. May (Ed.), Critical Multiculturalism. London: Falmer Press.

Cope, B., & Kalantzis, M. (2000a). Designs for Social Futures. In B. Cope & K. Mary (Eds.), Multiliteracies: Literacy Learning and the Design of Social Futures (pp. 203-234). London: Routledge.

Cope, B., & Kalantzis, M. (2001). e-Learning in Higher Education. In M. Kalantzis &

A. Pandian (Eds.), Literacy Matters: Issues for New Times (pp. pp.193-217). Penang: Universiti Sains Malaysia.

Cope, B., & Kalantzis, M. (2002). Manageable Knowledge: Communication, Learning and Organisational Change. In B. Cope & R. Freeman (Eds.), Developing Knowledge Workers in the Printing and Publishing Industries: Education, Training and Knowledge Management in the Publishing Supply Chain, from Creator to Consumer (Vol. 4, pp. 1-15). Melbourne: Common Ground.

Cope, B., & Kalantzis, M. (2003). Digital Meaning and the Case for a Pedagogy of Multiliteracies. In A. Pandian, G. Chakravarthy & P. Kell (Eds.), New Literacies, New Practices, New Times (pp. 26-52). Serdang, Malaysia: Universiti Putra Malaysia Press.

Cope, B., & Kalantzis, M. (2004a). Significado digital y defensa de una pedagogía de los multialfabetismos (Digital Meaning and the Case for a Pedagogy of Multiliteracies). In M. A. Pereyra (Ed.), Multiliteracies in the Digital Space. Granada: Consorcio "Fernando de los Ríos".

Cope, B., & Kalantzis, M. (2004b). Text-Made Text. E-Learning, 1(2), 198-282.

Cope, B., & Kalantzis, M. (Eds.). (1993b). The Powers of Literacy: Genre Approaches to Teaching Writing. London and Pittsburgh: Falmer Press (UK edition) and University of Pennsylvania Press (US edition).

Cope, B., & Kalantzis, M. (Eds.). (2000b). Multiliteracies: Literacy Learning and the Design of Social Futures. London: Routledge. Cuban, L. (2001). Oversold and Underused: Computers in the Classroom. Cambridge, MA: Harvard University Press. Curriculum K-12 Directorate. (2004). Counting On. Ryde, NSW: NSW Department of Education and Training. Darling-Hammond, L. (1997). The Right to Learn : A Blueprint for Creating Schools that Work. San Franciso: Jossey-Bass. Darling-Hammond, L. (1998). Teacher Learning That Supports Student Learning. Educational Leadership, 55(55), 6-11. Darling-Hammond, L. (1999). Teaching as the Learning Profession. San Francisco: Jossey-Bass. Darling-Hammond, L. (2001). The Right to Learn: A Blueprint for

Creating Schools that Work. San Francisco: Jossey-Bass. Davenport, T. H., & Prusak, L. (2000). Working Knowledge: How Organisations Manage What They Know. Cambridge MA: Harvard Business School Press. Delpit, L. D. (1988). The Silenced Dialogue: Power and Pedagogy in Educating Other People's Children. Harvard Educational Review, Vol. 58(No. 3), 280-298. Dewey, J. (1966 (1916)). Democracy and Education. New York: Free Press.

Drucker, P. (1998). From Capitalism to Knowledge Society. In D. Neef (Ed.), The Knowledge Economy (pp. 15-34). Woburn U.S.A: Butterworth - Heinemann.

Drucker, P. (2001). A century of Social Transformations: Emergence of Knowledge Society. In The Essential Drucker: Selections from the Management Works of Peter F. Drucker (pp. 299-320). New York: Harper Collins.

Drucker, P. F. (1993). Post-capitalist Society. Oxford: Butterworth Heinemann.

Durrant, C., & Green, B. (2000). Literacy and the New Technologies in Schools Education: Meeting the L(IT)eracy Challenge? The Australian Journal of Language and Literacy, 23(2), 89-108.

Education Department of Western Australia. (1998). First Steps Developmental Continua and Resource Books. Melbourne: Rigby Heinemann.

Education Queensland. (2000). Queensland State Education 2010. Brisbane: State of Queensland Department of Education.

Education Queensland. (2002). Literate Futures: Reading. Brisbane: State of Queensland Department of Education.

Education Queensland. (2003). New Basics Project: Productive Pedagogies.

Eisenstein, E. L. (1979). The Printing Press as an Agent of Change: Communications and Cultural Transformation in Early-Modern Europe. Cambridge: Cambridge University Press.

Ferguson, D. (2001). Technology in a Constructivist Classroom. Information Technology in Childhood Education Annual, 45-55.

Frangenheim, E. (2002). Reflections on classroom thinking strategies. Loganhome, QLD: Rodin Educational Publishing.

Freebody, P., & Luke, A. (1990). Literacies programs: Debates and demands in cultural context. Prospect: Australian Journal of TESOL, 5(7), 7-16.

Gardner, H. (2002). Who Owns Intelligence? In M. Singh (Ed.), Global Learning (pp. 181-196). Melbourne: Common Ground.

Gee, J. P. (1997). Two Kinds of Teenagers: Language, Identity, and Social Class. In D. Alverman (Ed.), Secondary Literacy. Hillsdale, New Jersey: Lawrence Erlbaum.

Gee, J. P. (2003). What Video Games Have to Teach Us about Learning and Literacy. New York: Palgrave Macmillan.

Gilster, P. (1997). Digital Literacy. New York: John Wiley and Sons.

Halliday, M. A. K. (1994). An Introduction to Functional Grammar (2nd ed.): Edward Arnold.

Hatie, J. (2003). Distinguishing Expert Teachers from Novice and Experienced Teachers. Melbourne: ACER.

Healy, A. (2000). Teaching Reading and Writing in a Multiliteracies Context : Classroom Practice. Flaxton, Qld: Post Pressed.

Healy, A. (2004). Text Next, New Resources for Literacy Learning. Newtown, N.S.W.: Primary English Teachers Association.

Hodge, R., & Kress, G. (1996). Language as Ideology. London: Routledge.

Husserl, E. (1970). The Crisis of European Sciences and Transcendental Phenomenology. Evanston: Northwestern University Press.

Kalantzis, M. (2000). Multicultural Citizenship. In W. Hudson & J. Kane (Eds.), Rethinking Australian Citizenship (pp. 99-110). Melbourne: Cambridge University Press.

Kalantzis, M., & Cope, B. (1989). Social Literacy: An Overview. Sydney: Common Ground.

Kalantzis, M., & Cope, B. (1993). Histories of Pedagogy, Cultures of Schooling. In B. Cope & M. Kalantzis (Eds.), The Powers of Literacy: A Genre Approach to Teaching Literacy (pp. 38-62). London: Falmer Press.

Kalantzis, M., & Cope, B. (1999). Multicultural Education: Transforming the Mainstream. In S. May (Ed.), Critical Multiculturalism: Rethinking Multicultural and Anti-Racist Education (pp. 245-276). London: Falmer/Taylor and Francis.

Kalantzis, M., & Cope, B. (2001a). New Learning: A Charter for Australian Education. Canberra: Australian Council of Deans of Education.

Kalantzis, M., & Cope, B. (2004a). Designs For Learning. E-Learning, 1(1), 38-92.

Kalantzis, M., & Cope, B. (2004b). Learning by Design. Melbourne: RMIT University.

Kalantzis, M., & Cope, B. (2005). The Learning by Design Guide. Melbourne: Common Ground.
Kalantzis, M., & Cope, B. (Eds.). (2001b). Transformations in Language and Learning: Perspectives on Multiliteracies. Melbourne: Common Ground.
Kalantzis, M., Cope, B., & Harvey, A. (2003). Assessing Multiliteracies and the New Basics. Assessment in Education, 10(1).
Kalantzis, M., Cope, B., Noble, G., & Poynting, S. (1991). Cultures of Schooling: Pedagogies for Cultural Difference and Social Access. London: Falmer Press.
Kalantzis, M., & Pandian, A. (Eds.). (2001). Literacy Matters: Issues for New Times. Penang: Universiti Sains Malaysia.
Kolb, D. A. (1984). Experiential Learning: Experience as the Source of Learning and Development. Englewood Cliffs NJ: Prentice Hall.
Kress, G. (1990). Linguistic Process and Sociocultural Change. Oxford, Eng.: Oxford University Press.
Lankshear, C., & Knobel, M. (2003). New Literacies. London: Open University Press.
Lankshear, C., Snynder, I., & Green, B. (2000). Teachers and Technoliteracy: Literacy, Technology and Learning in Schools. Sydney: Allen and Unwin.
Lash, S. (1994). Reflexivity and its Doubles: Structure, Aesthetics, Community. In U. Beck, A. Giddens & S. Lash (Eds.), Reflexive Modernization: Politics, Tradition and Aesthetics in the Modern Social Order (pp. 110-173). London: Polity Press.
Light, J. S. (2001). Rethinking the Digital Divide. Harvard Educational Review(Winter), 710-734.
Lingard, B., & Ladwig, J. (2001). School Reform Longitudinal Study: Final Report. Brisbane: Education Queensland.
Lovat, T. J. (2003). The Role of the Teacher: Coming of Age. Canberra: Australian Council of Deans of Education.
Luke, A., & Freebody, P. (1999). A Map of Possible Practices: Further Notes on the Four Resources Model. Practically Primary, 4(2), 5-8.
Luke, A., & Freebody, P. (2000). Literate Futures: Report of the Literacy Review for Queensland State Schools. Brisbane: Education Queensland.
Luria, A. R. (Ed.). (1976). Cognitive Development: Its Cultural and Social Foundations. Cambridge, MA: Harvard University Press.

Martin, B. (2002). Knowledge and Learning as Drivers of Change in the Organisation. In B. Cope & R. Freeman (Eds.), Developing Knowledge Workers in the Printing and Publishing Industries: Education, Training and Knowledge Management in the Publishing Supply Chain, from Creator to Consumer (pp. 17-33). Melbourne: Common Ground.

Martin, J. R. (1992). English Text: System and Structure. Philadelphia: John Benjamins.

Masterman, L. (1985). Teaching the Media. London: Comedia Publishing Group.

Masuda, Y. (1980). The Information Society and Post-Industrial Society. Washington: World Future Society.

Ministry of Education (Malaysia). (1997). Huraian Sukatan Pelajaran: Bahasa Inggeris. Kuala Lumpur: Dewan Bahasa & Pustaka.

Mission, R. (2004). Friends and Families and Other Funny Things. Australian Screen Education, Summer(37), 124-128.

Mitchell, W. J. (1995). City of Bits: Space, Place and the Infobahn. Cambridge MA: MIT Press.

Montessori, M. (1964 (1912)). The Montessori Method. New York: Schocken Books.

New London Group. (1996). A Pedagogy of Multiliteracies: Designing Social Futures. Harvard Educational Review, 66(1), 60-92.

Newmann, F. (1996). Authentic Achievement : Restructuring Schools for Intellectual Quality. San Francisco: Jossey-Bass.

Nofke, S., & Stephenson, R. (Eds.). (1995). Educational Action Research: Becoming Practically Critical. New York: Teachers College Press.

Ong, W. J. (1958). Ramus, Method and the Decay of Dialogue. Cambridge MA: Harvard University Press.

Ong, W. J. (1982). Orality and Literacy: The Technologizing of the Word. London: Methuen.

Papert, S. (1994). The Children's Machine: Rethinking School in the Age of the Computer. New York: Basic Books.

Polanyi, M. (1962). Personal Knowledge. Chicago: University of Chicago Press.

Professional Support and Curriculum Directorate. (2003). Count Me In Too Professional Development Package. Ryde, NSW: NSW Department of Education and Training.

Public Education Inquiry NSW. (2002). Inquiry into the Provision of Public Education in NSW. Sydney: New South Wales Department of Education and Training.

Queensland Government. (2001). Years 1-10 Curriculum Framework for Education in Queensland Schools. Brisbane: State of Queensland, Department of Education and The Arts.

Queensland Government. (2003). New Basics Project: Productive Pedagogies. Retrieved 13 October, 2003, from http://education.qld.gov.au/corporate/newbasics/html/pedagogies/pedagog.html

Rowe, K. J. (2003). The Importance of Teacher Quality as a Key Determinant of Students' Experiences of Schooling: A Context and Discussion Paper Prepared on Behalf of the Interim Committee for a NSW Institute of Teachers. Melbourne: ACER.

Rowe, K. J. (2004). The importance of teaching: Ensuring better schooling by building teacher capacities that maximise the quality of teaching and learning provision implications of findings from the international and Australian evidence-based research. Paper presented at the Making Schools Better: A Summit Conference on the Performance, Management and Funding of Australian Schools, University of Melbourne.

Scarbrough, H. (2001, July). From Knowledge Management to Knowledge Sharing. BHERT News, 18-20.

Schon, D. (1983). The Reflective Practitioner: How Professionals Think in Action. London: Temple Smith.

Scown, A. (2004). On-line Supplementation of Adult Education: A Change in Pedagogy and a Pedagogy of Change. In P. Kell, S. Shore & M. Singh (Eds.), Adult Education @ 21st Century (pp. 203-220). New York: Peter Lang.

Senge, P. M. (1990). The Fifth Discipline: The Art and Practice of the Learning Organization. New York: Doubleday Currency.

Shulman, L. (1987). Knowledge and Teaching: Foundations of the New Reform. Harvard Educational Review, 57(1), 1-22.

Singh, M., Kell, P., & Pandian, A. (2002). Appropriating English: Innovation in the Global Business of English Language Teaching. New York: Lang Publishers.

Snyder, I. (2002). Silicon Literacies: Communication, Innovation and Education in the Electronic Age. New York: Routledge.

Stewart, T. A. (1998). Intellectual Capital: The New Wealth of Organizations. New York: Bantam Books.

The Learning by Design Website. (2004-2005). from http://www.L-by-D.com

Thomson, P. (2002). Schooling the Rustbelt Kids. Crows Nest, NSW: Allen & Unwin.

Victorian Government. (2003). Curriculum in Government Schools: Blueprint for Education Directions Paper. Melbourne: Department of Education and Training.

Virilio, P. (1997). Open Sky. London: Verso.

Vygotsky, L. (1962). Thought and Language. Cambridge, MA: MIT Press.

Vygotsky, L. S. (1978). Mind in Society: The Development of Higher Psychological Processes. Cambridge, MA: Harvard University Press.

Wenger, E. (1999). Communities of Practice: Learning, Meaning and Identity. Cambridge: Cambridge University Press.

Wenger, E., McDermott, R., & Snyder, W. M. (2002). Cultivating Communities of Practice: A Guide to Managing Knowledge. Cambridge MA: Harvard Business School Press.

Windschitl, M., & Sahl, K. (2002). Tracing Teachers' Use of Technology in a Laptop Computer School: The Interplay of Teacher Beliefs, Social Dynamics, and Institutional Culture. American Educational Research Journal, 39(1), 165-205.

Yelland, N. (1998). Empowerment and Control with Technology for Young Children. Educational Theory and Practice, 20(2), 45-55.

Yelland, N. (1999). Reconceptualising Schooling with Technology for the 21st Century: Images and Reflections. In D. D. Shade (Ed.), Information Technology in Childhood Education Annual (pp. 39-59). Virginia: AACE.

www.ingramcontent.com/pod-product-compliance
Lightning Source LLC
Chambersburg PA
CBHW050858300426
44111CB00010B/1292